WEARING THE NIQAB

Dress cultures

Dress Cultures aims to foster innovative theoretical and methodological frameworks to understand how and why we dress, exploring the connections between clothing, commerce, and creativity in global contexts.

Reina Lewis: reina.lewis@fashion.arts.ac.uk
Elizabeth Wilson: elizabethwilson.auth@gmail.com

WEARING THE NIQAB

MUSLIM WOMEN IN THE UK AND THE US

by Anna Piela

BLOOMSBURY VISUAL ARTS
LONDON • NEW YORK • OXFORD • NEW DELHI • SYDNEY

BLOOMSBURY VISUAL ARTS
Bloomsbury Publishing Plc
50 Bedford Square, London, WC1B 3DP, UK
1385 Broadway, New York, NY 10018, USA
29 Earlsfort Terrace, Dublin 2, Ireland

BLOOMSBURY, BLOOMSBURY VISUAL ARTS and the Diana logo are trademarks of Bloomsbury
Publishing Plc

First published in Great Britain 2021
Paperback edition first published 2022

Series design by BRILL
Cover image © Hannah Habibi

A catalogue record for this book is available from the British Library.

Library of Congress Cataloging-in-Publication Data
Names: Piela, Anna, author.
Title: Wearing the niqab: Muslim women in the UK and US / by Anna Piela.
Description: London; New York: Bloomsbury Visual Arts, 2021. | Series: Dress cultures |
Includes bibliographical references and index.
Identifiers: LCCN 2020035667 (print) | LCCN 2020035668 (ebook) | ISBN 9781350166035
(hardback) | ISBN 9781350212657 (paperback) | ISBN 9781350166042 (pdf) |
ISBN 9781350166059 (epub)
Subjects: LCSH: Islamic clothing and dress. | Muslim women Clothing–Great Britain. |
Muslim women–Clothing–United States. | Masks–Religious aspects. | Islamophobia. | Racism.
Classification: LCC BP190.5.H44 P54 2021 (print) | LCC BP190.5.H44 (ebook) |
DDC 297.5/76–dc23
LC record available at https://lccn.loc.gov/2020035667
LC ebook record available at https://lccn.loc.gov/2020035668

ISBN: HB: 978-1-3501-6603-5
PB: 978-1-3502-1265-7
ePDF: 978-1-3501-6604-2
eBook: 978-1-3501-6605-9

Typeset by Deanta Global Publishing Services, Chennai, India

To find out more about our authors and books visit www.bloomsbury.com and sign up for our
newsletters.

To Zosia and Michael

CONTENTS

ILLUSTRATIONS

ACKNOWLEDGMENTS

I would like to thank the editors of the Dress Cultures series at Bloomsbury Visual Arts, Reina Lewis and Elizabeth Wilson, as well as the IB Taurus and Bloomsbury Visual Arts editors and editorial assistants: Philippa Brewster, Frances Arnold, Yvonne Thouroude, and Rebecca Hamilton, for their support. Also, I thank the two anonymous reviewers for their feedback that helped me improve the manuscript.

I am grateful to all the project participants who generously gave me their time and shared their life stories with me. This book would not have happened without them.

My thanks go to the Muslim Women's Council in the United Kingdom (especially Sofia Ashraf, Saadia Mushtaq, Bana Gora, and Nuzhat Ali) and the Islamic Cultural Center in Boston, MA, for their help. I am grateful to my friends who helped me with participant recruitment and cheered me on. I would also like to acknowledge the Scurrah Wainwright Foundation for funding a significant part of this project.

I benefited from institutional support during the writing of this book, including a sabbatical leave at Leeds Trinity University and a residential fellowship at Auburn Seminary in New York funded by the *Crosscurrents* journal, as well as two visiting scholarships: with the Women's, Gender, and Sexuality Studies Center at Northeastern University in Boston, MA, and with the Department of Religious Studies at Northwestern University in Evanston, IL.

I am indebted to Kecia Ali for her helpful feedback on the book proposal, Sandra Borland-Betts for her encouragement at the beginning of the project, and Joanna Krotofil for her extensive and constructive comments on the manuscript draft. I am thankful to Aisha Sadeemka and Asiyah Umm Ammar for our enlightening conversations.

Finally, thank you to my husband Michael C. W. Woolf for reading and commenting on my drafts, and being there for me during the arduous process of writing. You and our daughter Zosia always reminded me that there was a light at the end of this tunnel.

INTRODUCTION

This book brings to the fore the voices of women who wear the niqab in the United Kingdom and the United States. The Arabic word "niqab," transliterated as *niqāb* or *niqaab*, means a face covering worn by some Muslim women as part of their religious garment. The niqab is mislabeled in the popular imaginary as the "burka" or "burqa," a word usually used in the context of a "burka ban," but the burka, an all-enveloping piece of fabric with a grille covering up the eyes, common in Afghanistan and neighboring countries, is rarely seen in the West.[1] The Western obsession with the term "burka" may be explained by the fact that the Afghan-style burka touches the Western "cultural raw nerve" more than the eye-revealing niqab (Inglis 2017: 289). It is so because the burka obscures the eyes, rendering the wearer invisible, inscrutable, and therefore, uncontrollable. Its eye-concealing feature resonates unsettlingly with the medieval carnival mask, feared and detested by the Church, moralists, and authorities (Inglis 2017). Covering up one's eyes with a mask enabled anonymity and therefore, according to Christian moralists, a release from responsibility for one's actions. The symbolism of the burka was also central to the gendered and colonial logic that propped up the US-led invasion of Afghanistan. The burka itself was constructed as a "legitimate object of (in) security" (Kearns 2017: 492). Thus, the niqab is often discursively framed as the burka, a garment encapsulating deeply rooted Western fears. In this book, I use the word "niqab," taking my cue from the participants, but occasionally I use the word "burka" for clarity in my analyses of texts and political statements that explicitly refer to it.[2]

It is worth emphasizing that modest Islamic dress cannot be reduced simply to traditional garments such as the Iranian chador that first dominated the Western

---

[1]The terms "West" and "Western" used in this book are deployed with an awareness of the problematic and hierarchical vision of the world divided into "East" and "West," analyzed famously by Said in his now classic work *Orientalism* (1978). Listing countries or regions that are broadly considered to be a part of the West (most commonly Western Europe, the United States, Canada, and Australia) is not helpful without noting the problematic power dynamics of colonialism and neoliberalism. However, although much of contemporary social theory focuses on deconstructing "the topic, the authority, and the assumed primacy of 'the West'" (Young 1990: 19), it is difficult to disentangle oneself from the East/West dichotomy because it has infused public discourse globally, and this is reflected in participants' narratives. In fact, as Bonnett (2017) notes, postcolonial studies has inexplicably failed to sufficiently examine perspectives of groups commonly constructed as "non-Western" on the notion of the West. Therefore, I borrow here from Patel's disclaimer (2009: 292) stating that she uses the term "West" to denote "rich, industrialized, pre-dominantly white, Judeo-Christian countries that have hegemony in the global community and that exercise omnipresent colonial domination worldwide. However, I also understand the term to refer to a racialized, mythical construct defined in relation to 'the Rest'—that is, to nonwhite, often colonized nations." Hall (2007 [1997]: 56–60) offers a robust examination of the debates pertaining to the idea of "the West."
[2]For a comparison of regional variations of female Islamic dress, see Amer (2014).

imaginary during the Islamic Revolution in Iran in 1979 (Chan-Malik 2011). While black is a fairly popular option, Islam-conscious outfits come in many colors and shapes and can also be put together using "mainstream" clothes, provided that they conceal the figure of the wearer. Many women intentionally cover their faces with light-colored niqabs to avoid the negative associations that black Islamic clothing often invokes. Similarly, a long skirt, a loose tunic and a denim jacket, with a pashmina wrapped across the face (to cover up the nose and the mouth) is a common combination among young niqabi women in the United Kingdom and the United States (Lewis 2015).

With the modest fashion industry booming and with major brands finally beginning to recognize the fashion needs of pious consumers (Tarlo 2010; Tarlo and Moors 2013; Lewis 2013; Bucar 2017), women who wear the niqab are creatively putting together outfits using elements from various cultural contexts, communicating hybridization of identities through fashion. That said, Johnson (2017: 278) critiques the recent interest in the more contemporary, "hip" Muslim fashion by arguing that this focus negatively reinscribes the black abaya as still "too strange" to engage in a similar manner. Similarly, Islam (2018) argues that the Muslim celebrity culture which embraces designer outfits and full makeup opens the door to stigmatization of those women who prefer inconspicuous clothing and no makeup, and who may speak out against unethical practices in the fashion and beauty business.

Women who choose to wear the niqab often talk about the long and complex process of reflection and self-questioning prior to their adoption of the niqab. In this book, I focus on a particular aspect of their narrative arc—I analyze the ways in which they assert their agency by arguing that the wearing of the niqab is an Islamic practice that has a legitimate place in Western, secular societies.

The Background of the Project

When I first came up with the idea for this book in 2013, "niqab controversies,"[3] by which I mean events involving intense nationwide opinion-sharing about the niqab characterized by spikes in media coverage, had been flaring up regularly in Europe. These controversies created a platform, in the main part, for various advocates of a "burka ban." The French and the Belgian states had created a precedent for this demand, passing nationwide legislation that effectively banned Islamic face coverings, in 2010 and 2011, respectively. Despite the completely different relationship of the British state with religion—after all, the Queen heads the Church of England, which is in contrast to the French secularism—British politicians seeking to increase their currency with various

---

[3] I intentionally use the term "niqab controversies," to reflect the moral panic created by such reporting. I consider the alternative term "niqab debates" dishonest, as women who wear the niqab are not included in the conversation.

demographics, by no means only right-wing or conservative, courted them by pitching the idea of banning the Islamic face covering.

In the United Kingdom, the first large niqab controversy was sparked in 2006 by Jack Straw, at the time the Labour Party Member of Parliament (MP) for Blackburn, a post-industrial town in the north of England with a considerable British Asian Muslim population. Straw famously said that he preferred his constituents not to wear the niqab in his office (BBC News 2006a). This statement was followed by a barrage of op-eds which expressed resentment toward women who wear the niqab (Khiabany and Williamson 2008). In that period, British media tended to report on different groups' views of the niqab; however, voices of women who wear the niqab were ignored. Similarly, prior to the introduction of legislation banning the niqab from the public sphere in France in 2010, "the sidelining of the people at the heart of these debates has been a recurring motif" (Bouteldja 2014: 115). In addition to Jack Straw's comments, negative statements about the niqab were made by other members of the Labour Cabinet: Prime Minister Tony Blair called it a "mark of separation"; Culture Secretary Theresa Jowell described it as a "symbol of women's subjugation to men"; and Harriet Harman, a minister in the Department of Constitutional Affairs, said she would like to see an end to the niqab, which she called an "obstacle to full equality" (Kabir 2010: 146). In 2010, Philip Hollobone, a Conservative MP who tried to put through a private members' bill to introduce a niqab ban, was threatened with legal action for refusing to meet his niqab-wearing constituents (Pidd 2010).

Such statements are echoed by some journalists and academics. Yasmin Alibhai-Brown, a *Guardian* columnist wrote: "[the niqab] rejects human commonalities and even the membership of society itself. . . . It is hard to be a Muslim today. And it becomes harder still when some choose deliberately to act and dress as aliens" (in Meer, Dwyer, and Modood 2010: 96). A director of an MA program in investigative journalism at a London university wrote in her article in *The Independent: Education*:

> I was particularly disturbed by the sight of Muslim female students wearing the niqab, a dress statement I find offensive and threatening. Don't they value the rights and freedoms they enjoy in Britain? . . . I think the niqab should be banned at university.
>
> (Waterhouse 2010: np)

The "niqab controversies" had been framed from the beginning by questions of assimilation/integration of religious Muslim women but the discussion was framed in such a way that the women concerned were almost completely excluded from it. Even for an academic like me, armed with access to extensive scholarly databases of journals and newspaper archives, the search for work where women who wear the niqab were actually engaged in a robust conversation, returned only a handful of articles in the local press and a report commissioned by the Open Society Foundations (Bouteldja 2011) to gauge the views of niqab-wearing women in France. Otherwise, the academic literature tended to interrogate the niqab as an object of other people's suspicion and contempt (see O'Neill, Gidengil, Côté, and Young 2015; Shirazi and Mishra 2010), or a parameter of legal proceedings within the courtroom (see Kirk 2013; Laird 2014; Clerget 2011; Ogilvie 2013). National and regional legislative acts that prohibited the wearing of the niqab were also examined (Ferrari and Pastorelli 2013).

All that scholarly work is immensely helpful in understanding the position of the niqab in the sociocultural European milieu but, on the whole, women who chose to wear it are absent from these writings. Based on that absence, one could be excused for thinking that the niqab is a living object that walks and breathes on its own. For me, as a women's studies graduate, it was all the more surprising to find that there was hardly any feminist work on the topic, even though there was a body of research that explored it from legal and other theoretical perspectives. Although I initially expected to see plentiful analyses of divergent voices of niqab-wearing women, there were none. Compared with the richness of scholarship that examined the hijab, this was not only intriguing—it was alarming, given that choices of niqab-wearing women were being increasingly curtailed across Europe and globally.[4] Having discovered this glaring gap, I decided to find niqab-wearing women willing to speak to me, a non-Muslim, Eastern European women's studies scholar, about their lives, beliefs, and perspectives.

When I began this project, I lived in Leeds, a city in the north of England that neighbors Bradford, Dewsbury, and Huddersfield. Northern England is inhabited by a large population of British South Asian Muslims representing many Islamic traditions. I had the privilege of having many Muslim friends and colleagues. One of them was particularly helpful with the project, as she introduced me to a teacher at an Islamic girls' school in a neighboring town who agreed to act as a gatekeeper. The school was an excellent ethnographic site, but access to other spaces frequented by niqab wearers was difficult. How could they trust a stranger to not misinterpret their views? Because of stereotyped misrepresentations, they are a highly vulnerable population. The manner in which they are represented in most mainstream media suggests that their voices do not matter. They are pictured as a threat, an aberration in the ostensibly secular-liberal Britain. Even if their voices have been addressed in a balanced and fair way in academic literature, it is difficult and expensive to access.

Later, I was helped by another friend who was serving as a legal adviser on the board of the Muslim Women's Council (MWC), an organization representing the interests of Muslim women in West Yorkshire and beyond. As they sought to raise their profile nationally, they offered their support for my project, in particular to help with recruitment and funding applications. I became MWC's research consultant, which was an affiliation that helped me much more than my educational or institutional credentials. Between 2014 and 2016, often accompanied by another MWC staff member, I attended study

---

[4]As of 2020, seven European countries (Austria, Belgium, Bulgaria, Denmark, France, Latvia, and the Netherlands) and several regional governments have banned the niqab. In the Canadian province of Quebec, niqab wearers are prohibited from receiving or providing public services.

circles, fundraising events, conferences, and community meetings. I visited homes, schools, and women's gyms. I also identified some niqab-wearing women online who were high-profile niqab advocates; two of them agreed to be interviewed as well. In the second part of the project I also included niqab-wearing women who lived in the United States in the analysis. I began by interviewing niqab-wearing women in Boston face-to-face, but the approach that proved most efficient in the United States involved online recruitment through the project blog and internet-based female Muslim communities.

Subsequently, I came to a second realization. Women who wear the niqab rarely organize *as niqab wearers*. The women I sought did not attend any one particular mosque, and later I found that many did not attend mosque services at all. I was trying to study a "non-organized" Muslim minority (Jeldtoft 2011: 1134) whose practice of niqab-wearing is denounced by its critics as "un-Islamic" (Braasch 2010; Selby 2011). I was looking for a particular sample of women who shared a practice that was, to a degree, context-dependent, contingent, and shifting. This highly individualized aspect of niqab-wearing also meant it was impossible to conduct a traditional ethnographic study, for instance, one such as Inge (2016) has carried out with the Salafi community of women in London. Inge spent an extended period of time attending one mosque as an observer, which facilitated recruitment among the mosque members. There were many niqabis among her participants, but I did not intend to engage only Salafi women; I hoped to engage niqabis from different Islamic traditions.

There was no easy way to find and convince them to share their experiences and perspectives. This definitely accounts for the disproportionate paucity of literature on the subject; however, I expect the bias with which Muslim women, and niqab-wearing women in particular, are viewed, played a part here. The idea that they cannot speak for themselves, or that they are apparently suffering from a false consciousness excusing their oppression undoubtedly came into play as well. The result was a lack of input in the public "debate" from niqab-wearing women. But in reality, what silences these women (who can articulate their life choices really well) is the failure of the mainstream to listen to them. Banning the niqab is not about security, or British, European, Canadian, or American values, ease of communication, or protection of women's rights. It is about being offended that there are women who dare to make their own choices about their religious practices and bodies. Demonizing them offers political currency. In this sense, this was nothing new. But what did the women have to say about all this?

The Participants

Between 2013 and 2019 I interviewed forty participants—twenty-one British and nineteen American[5] women—who wear the niqab full-time or part-time, as well as one American woman who stopped wearing the niqab in 2017. In the course of the project, I also

---

[5] I use "American" in the sense of "US American."

interviewed one Canadian and one South African woman. The respondents' age range was twenty-one to fifty-six years. Among the British women, there were eleven British Pakistani women, four British Indian women, two British Bangladeshi women, and four converts (two Polish women living in the United Kingdom, one Scottish, and one Irish woman). In the British group, two women had completed their PhD degrees, five had master's degrees, while eight had completed or were about to complete their BA degrees. Five women had completed their secondary education (A-levels or overseas equivalent), and one had completed primary education. Two-thirds (fourteen) were in full-time or part-time employment, and their occupations included teaching, working as a driving instructor, an interpreter for the National Health Service, a radio presenter, business owner, and food vendor. The remaining one-third (seven) were homemakers. The majority of women were located in the West Yorkshire and West Midlands regions of England.

Among the American women, there were three Arab Americans, two Indian Americans, two Pakistani Americans, two Somali Americans (one of whom identified as African American), and eleven converts (six African American and five White[6] Caucasian, including one identifying as ethnically Jewish). Five women had completed master's degrees, six had completed or were studying for a BA, and five had completed secondary education. Twelve women were in full-time or part-time employment, and their occupations included working as an engineer, or as an online business owner, educator, health care professional, HR professional, fashion designer, hairstylist, call-center operative, and early education specialist. One was a retired member of the military who had been deployed on a mission to Iraq and had converted many years later. The remaining six identified as homemakers or stay-at-home mothers taking a break in their careers. The majority of American participants were based in the Midwest and the Northeast, but a significant cluster resided in Texas as well.

All interviews were conducted in English. Informed consent was obtained before the interview, and the participants signed a form containing a clause allowing them to withdraw at any point before publication. Interview transcripts have been anonymized so as to conceal information that could lead to identification of participants. I invited the participants to suggest their own pseudonyms, and many selected names they preferred to be used instead of their own.

The Choice of the British and American Contexts for Research

At the beginning of my research project, there was no literature directly engaging niqab wearers in the United Kingdom or the United States. As I note in the next section of this Introduction, some interview-based research focused on women's responses to niqab bans and Islamophobic harassment that had emerged in the United Kingdom,

---

[6]I follow a convention for capitalizing both "Black" and "White" racial identities suggested by Appiah (2020). Capitalization calls attention to their historical and social roots, and prevents them from being understood as a purely biological category. The point of capitalization, in particular in relation to Whiteness, writes Appiah, "isn't to elevate; it's to situate."

but the experiences of American niqab wearers are still largely undocumented in the scholarship. Thus, as the topic is still under-researched in sociological terms in both contexts (although more so in the context of the United States), especially in comparison to France and Canada, where, understandably, it has been in the research limelight as a practice regulated by policy, I think examining narratives of British and American women who wear the niqab provides an interesting counterpoint to the French and Canadian discussions. It takes into account not just British experiments that some diagnose as "failed multiculturalism" (McGhee 2008) and American racial struggles, but also the sharp turn to the right as demonstrated by the 2016 Brexit referendum in the United Kingdom and the presidential election in the United States, respectively.

The leading role of the United States and the United Kingdom in the coalition formed to engage in the "War on Terror" was bolstered by a shared distinction between the "bad" and "good" Islam proposed by President Bush and Prime Minister Blair (McGhee 2008). This distinction, introduced alongside anti-terrorism legislation (Anti-Terrorism, Crime and Security Act 2001 and the Prevention of Terrorism Act 2005 in the United Kingdom and the 2001 Patriot Act in the United States) allowed the curtailing of rights and freedoms domestically through increased powers of surveillance, racial profiling, stop-and-search policies, and detention without charge. McGhee (2008: 36) argues: "We are constantly told that 9/11 changed everything. The result is that the states of emergency that were introduced in the USA and in Britain have resulted in fundamental changes with regard to the respect for human, asylum, citizenship and residence rights as well as expanded surveillance and police powers. . . . The logic associated with this new common sense is that because terrorists use the USA and Britain's freedoms as a weapon against 'us', then in order to defend 'us' 'our' freedoms need to be limited." The accounts I present in this book demonstrate that niqab wearers have become one of the most obvious targets of freedom-curtailing policies in both countries, because their rights to religious expression may be taken away under the guise of championing their liberation.

Simultaneously, Mazrouki (2017) argues that anti-Muslim arguments on both sides of the Atlantic continuously converge; she has traced discursive flows between the US and French contexts, but as I demonstrate in Chapters 1 and 4, they exist between the United Kingdom and the United States as well. She asks:

[C]ould it be, then, that the Western disputes over Islam are not, as is commonly believed, the direct result of certain legal traditions and particular sociological characteristics? My hypothesis is that the public controversies over Islam are not simply the latest manifestations of the contradictions and internal breakdowns of each "tradition" or "model" (in the United States, the contradiction between open secularism and persistent racism; in France, the contradiction between an ideology of equality and an intransigent and exclusive *laïcité*).

(Mazrouki 2017: 6–7)

To a certain degree, this contextual convergence is mirrored by the convergence of participants' narratives, with the proviso that there are some particularities that are specific to their settings. First, these narratives are dialogical; they emerge in response to the contexts. As the contexts overlap, so do the women's responses to, and interpretations of, the contexts. Thus, some British participants were telling me about their difficult experiences in the United Kingdom post-9/11, rather than 7/7; some American women shared their anxieties related to the burqa ban wave as it took place in Europe.[7] Second, the specifically religious discourse mobilized by niqab wearers in both countries is brought into sharper focus by discursive flows within the Anglophone *ummah*. The online context is a useful example of that; in my previous work (2012) I indicated that many online discussion groups bring together women who share a widely defined Islamic affiliation and English language fluency regardless of national backgrounds. Such spaces inevitably facilitate not just an exchange of ideas, but also mutually constitutive projects of production of transnational religious selves. Mandaville (2010: 275) observes that this is not a new phenomenon, as "the movement of peoples and ideas across borders and territories has been an intrinsic part of Islamic history." Thus, the juxtaposition of niqab experiences in the United Kingdom and the United States highlights the convergence of global and local Islamic discourses, practices, affects, and affiliations.

This book relies on a theoretical and discursive framing of the niqab that links it to female agentic religious experiences that cannot be discounted as resistance against hegemonic discourses or any other reductive explanations which remain blind to motivations outside of liberal sensibilities. Women who choose to wear the niqab reject the notions of being powerless by narrating the long and complex process of reflection and self-questioning that precedes their adoption of the niqab. While many non-Muslims are against the niqab because they see it essentially as a symbol of "fundamentalist Islam," many Muslims, including scholars, argue that on the contrary, the niqab is not Islamic,[8] therefore the right to wear it should not be protected by legislation (see, for example, opinions issued by the Oxford imam Taj Hargey [Witworth 2018] or the Grand Imam of Cairo and the Al-Azhar University, Mohammed Sayed al-Tantawi [Rosemarine 2010]). The women I interviewed disagree with both these points of view. Refusing to fit into rigid political or theological categories, they reimagine religious authority by producing alternative religious discourses which then circulate across digital platforms, cultural contexts, and among individual women.

---

[7]Minority groups, including Muslims, demonstrate a high level of awareness of prejudice against them in different national contexts. This is not surprising, given the long history of ethnic and religious diasporas' intensive use of various communication networks predating the rise of the internet (Karim 1998 and 2002).

[8]Strictly speaking, three out of four juristic schools of thought (Hanafi, Shafi, and Maliki) consider the niqab as *mustahhab* (recommended), and only one, Hanbali, considers it *fard* (obligatory). It is unclear why the niqab would be considered un-Islamic altogether. Notably, just one participant, who identified as Salafi, said that she followed the Hanbali school. Others said they were "Sunni" or "Just Muslim." The latter label may be problematic, however, since in its most extreme version, the literalist interpretation of Islam lays claim to be the only authoritative, or truly Islamic one, dismissing those who follow all other Muslim traditions as heretics who embrace *bid'a* (innovation). This suggests that the category of "just Muslim" may operate variously in inclusive or exclusionary modalities, depending on context.

In recognition of this standpoint, I invoke the phenomenological conceptualization of religious actions which allows us to understand them on their own terms (Cox 2010). Unlike many social scientific or theological definitions of a religious act that "convey the presuppositions of the one doing the defining" (Cox 2010: 2–3), this approach helps the scholar to categorize certain actions as religious based on the religious individual's perception. Thus, it provides a nuanced perspective that recognizes that she is capable of interpreting her own social realities and executing action.

Scholarly Approaches to the Niqab

The topic of the niqab has been tackled in the past decade by authors situated in a wide range of disciplines, from law (Williams 2008; Bakht 2009, 2012, and 2015; Schwartzbaum 2011; Allen 2014) and political science (Tissot 2011), to cultural studies (Žižek 2010). There has been a steady stream of research examining individual and group responses to the niqab (Shirazi and Mishra 2010; Bakht 2012; Sarrasin 2016). This work provides a useful context for reflecting on the contentious role of the niqab in the West, but I argue that there is a striking imbalance between the attention to the context and, what seems to me the core consideration, the niqab wearers' own perspectives on the niqab.

There are a number of studies (see Tissot 2011; Ferrari and Pastorelli 2013) that provide a thorough historical and socio-legal analysis of the situation of European niqab wearers. However, some authors seem at a loss to explain the niqab's rising popularity among Muslim women in Europe. For example, Hill (2013: 80) suggests, without evidence to support his assertion, that, in the British context, it may be a result of trying to "emulate Saudis" or "be more orthodox than their parents." Such conjecture, frequently observed in discussions about the niqab, may lead to a situation where "the veil is completely separated from women wearing it" (Chakraborty and Zempi 2012: 276). Mahmood (2005: 16) points out to a further lacuna in this large body of literature: "while these studies have made important contributions, it is surprising that their authors have paid so little attention to Islamic virtues of female modesty or piety, especially given that many of the women who have taken up the veil frame their decision precisely in these terms." She critiques reductivism in the work of "analysts [who] often explain the motivations of veiled women in terms of standard models of sociological causality (such as social protest, economic necessity, anomie, or utilitarian strategy), while [dismissing] terms like morality, divinity, and virtue [as] . . . phantom imaginings of the hegemonized" (Mahmood 2005: 16). I suggest in Chapter 2 that niqab wearers recognize this reductivism and often adjust their explanatory narratives accordingly, omitting the religious aspect of the practice of niqab-wearing, which has problematic implications for their ability to enjoy legal protection of the freedom of religious expression in Europe.

Bosankić (2014) examined the psychosocial aspects of the practice of niqab-wearing in Bosnia, but she focused mainly on identity and the nation-state as the political context for it, and the women's religious agency aspect, the notion that spearheads my explorations, is not explored in her work. A large proportion of the literature on face covering and head-covering in the United Kingdom tackles the problem of Islamophobia, from its discursive emanations in the media (MacDonald 2006; Khiabany and Williamson 2008) and politics (Afshar 2008 and 2013) to the verbal and physical attacks on Muslim women (Zempi and Chakraborti 2014).

There are three important reports based on community research where niqab wearers were interviewed. Bouteldja carried out the French (2011) and the British (2015) case studies, and Clarke (2013) examined the Canadian context. A total of thirty-two women were interviewed for the French case study and 122 women were interviewed for the British study, while a multimethod approach was utilized in the Canadian study, where thirty-eight women filled in an online questionnaire, thirty-five participated in focus groups, and eight were interviewed. All three publications state that their aim was to address the public controversy around the niqab and blatant stereotyping in the media by presenting the voices of niqab wearers who were left out of the discussion. Clarke (2013: iii) wrote poignantly that it was important to "cast light on the existing agency" of Canadian niqab wearers, emphasizing that, contrary to public perceptions, they did not need to be empowered because they already possessed agency and voice; it was the lack of other people's knowledge of their actual circumstances that led to such misperceptions.

Findings from these three studies are broadly similar. All emphasized the spiritual significance the niqab held for the participants; motivations were expressed in a religious, not political, language. In all cases but one, the decision to wear the niqab was made freely and following a considerable period of religious reflection. Relatives appeared equally likely to support wearing the niqab or discourage it. Neither report indicated that niqab wearers were reclusive; in fact, the majority of the interviewed women had busy lives, working or studying, participating in local events, working for charities, and socializing. Women in all three settings experienced Islamophobic abuse in different forms. There were also some differences among them; the French women, despite possessing French citizenship, felt they had a fraught relationship with France due to being alienated from society by other people due to their religion, while the Canadian and British women were very positive about Canada and the United Kingdom and expressed patriotic attitudes. The key problem with reading the niqab as a sign of patriarchal oppression, as some secular feminists tend to do, is that, of all French and British women who wear the niqab interviewed by the Open Society Foundations (Bouteldja 2011 and 2015, respectively) and Canadian women interviewed for the Canadian Council of Muslim Women report (Clarke 2013), none said they were forced to wear it. Banning of the niqab by the state will not help advance feminism. Mahmood (2005: 36). warns that "if there is one lesson we have learned from the machinations of colonial feminism and the politics of 'global sisterhood,' it is that any social and political transformation is always a function of local, contingent, and emplaced struggles whose blueprint cannot be worked out or predicted in advance." Any external attempt to "save Muslim women," using Abu-Lughod's ironic paraphrasing (2013) of Spivak's famous statement,[9] is "typically a violent

---

[9]"White men are saving brown women from brown men" (Spivak 1988: 286).

imposition whose results are likely to be far worse than anything it seeks to displace" (Mahmood 2005: 36).

The literature that considers insider perspectives on the niqab in the West, produced after the French and Belgian "burka bans" were introduced in 2010 and 2011, often situates the analysis in one of two ways: the legal and sociopolitical contexts of the bans, or experiences of Islamophobia (Chakraborti and Zempi 2012; Zempi and Chakraborti 2014 and 2015; Zempi 2019). In other words, the bans and victimization, two types of power dynamic that disadvantage niqab wearers have become the key conceptual framework for interrogating them about their experiences (Brems et al. 2012; Moors 2014; Østergaard, Warburg, and Johansen 2014), even in national contexts where, as of 2019, no such bans have been introduced (see Zempi 2019). These critiques are extremely necessary and helpful in understanding the questionable legal and ethical reasoning that led to the burka bans in Europe (Bribosia and Rorive 2014) as well as the relationship between the bans and Islamophobic hate crimes on women who wear the niqab and other types of Islamic dress. However, I argue that these two frameworks alone do not enable a holistic understanding of the lives of niqab wearers. In other words, while the academic scholarship is slowly catching up with the feminist principle of centering women's voices, especially in analyses that concern these very women, in the case of face-veiled women, it has, so far, mostly been done on terms that privilege frameworks of cultural and political domination over them. This book, while recognizing the impact of these frameworks on niqab wearers' lives, centers these women's own agendas that often prioritize faith as part of everyday, mundane, and often joyful existence.

One of the limitations of the (otherwise very valuable) body of research is that in many cases, scholars do not step beyond the observation that women who wear the niqab unanimously say it is their choice. Yet, this simple and unambiguous statement made by many interviewed women, as well as women who use online platforms to talk about the niqab, begs the question: Why is their explanation not taken at face value? Why are they charged with false consciousness so as to deny the viability of such a decision? After all, the "machinations of colonial feminism" (Mahmood 2005: 36) have been exposed by multiple critics who have warned against forcing nations, social groups, and communities to be "free" against their will. We have become so embroiled in the dominant explanatory frameworks of burka bans, radicalization, and security risks that criminalization and dehumanization of an entire group of women because of what they choose to wear has become normalized. Is there a complementary explanation for this ethical negligence that approaches the issue from a perspective other than benefiting the often sexist and Islamophobic detractors of the niqab?

I argue that the way that Muslim women who wear the niqab talk about the practice of face covering is unintelligible to secular-liberal actors. The religious vocabulary and concepts they use have been negatively resignified, and so "piety," "submission," and "righteousness" have become, at best, ambivalent to the secular interlocutor (Robert 2005: 230), and at worst, are on their way to joining "jihad" and "Shari'a" as notions associated with the "clash of civilizations" imaginary (Bottici and Challand 2013). In this book, especially in Chapter 3, I show how niqab wearers recognize this process and address it by translating the discourse of faith into secular reasoning that non-Muslims are likely to comprehend.

Everyday Religious Practices in the Secular-Liberal Domain: From Marginalization to Recognition

These disputes point to a deeper issue that requires consideration in this context: What can be classified as religious practice? More to the point, what can be classified as religious practice in the exclusionary space of the liberal public domain which, as Asad (1999a) argues, is a space necessarily articulated by power and its asymmetry, where women, those without property, and religious minorities are excluded? The two instances of delegitimizing the niqab through scholarly and religious authority cited earlier illustrate that what counts in the public sphere is

> not merely the physical ability to speak but *to be heard. . . . To make others listen* even if they would prefer not to hear, to speak to some consequence so that something in the political world is affected, to come to a conclusion, to have the authority to make practical decisions on the basis of that conclusion—these are all presupposed in the idea of free public debate as a liberal virtue. But these performatives are not open equally to everyone because the domain of free speech is always shaped by preestablished limits.
>
> (Asad 1999a: 180)

Asad asks three questions based on this observation regarding the public sphere (1999a: 181). First, how have different conceptions and practices of religion conditioned those who would be the listeners of the new religious discourses? Second, is it possible that when the new religious subjects (such as, for example, the face-veiled women) enter the public debate about religion, its structure—logic, grammar, and key concepts, as well as argumentation styles and epistemological foundations—will remain intact or does it necessarily have to be altered? Third, why are the proponents of secularism feeling so threatened by religion guiding personal choices of adherents? These concerns inform the lived realities of niqab wearers who are finding themselves constricted by secular-liberal discourses on Islam and gender, common understandings of religion as a cultural category, as well as relationships between religion, politics, and law.

McGuire's discussion of embodied religious practices and their marginalization in the West (2006) offers some insights into these questions posed by Asad and, consequently, into the historical context of the current moral delegitimization of the niqab in the West. She argues that the definition of religion itself has been shaped by reform movements during the "long Reformation" period (from the thirteenth to the seventeenth century). A negative evaluation of people's everyday religious practices, in particular those that "involved their bodies and emotions" (2006: 189) was a result of these movements. Thus, belief became considered more important than religious practice, which disproportionately affected women. Embodied religious practices came to be considered marginal, impure, or dangerous. It is quite obvious that the wearing of the niqab, a practice aimed at covering the female body, is questioned partly due to this historically situated conception of what religion is. The lack of an unambiguous Qur'anic commandment to wear it constitutes grounds for its rejection within a doctrinally oriented institutional structure.

The continuation of such a structure relies on consistent control over interpretive authority related to doctrine. McGuire (2006) notes that embodied religious practices (which included diverse cultural elements that were selected, borrowed, adapted, and blended) have been historically seen as a challenge to established religious institutions. Thus, she argues, "embodied religious practice is often an important site of contested authority, dominance, and resistance" (2006: 189). It is particularly visible in the spiritual lives of those who go "beyond the boundaries of ordinary religiosity" (McGuire 2006: 191). In the context of modern secularism, the state continues to attempt to regulate these private religious lives of its citizens (Asad 2009b: 30–1). I argue that the niqab is a poignant example of an embodied practice which threatens the power status quo between the secular state and established religious authorities that aims to delimit, if not entirely remove from public view, radical religious practices and spiritual experiences which flow from them.

Notably, niqab-wearing women represent a category of Muslimness that tends to rankle both right-wing and left-wing, ostensibly progressive actors. To the former, they are the symbol of Islam's perceived barbarity; to the latter, they pose a problem, as their focus on piety and distinct looks hinders an easy incorporation into the "good," "patriotic" American or British Muslim narrative. As Islam (2018) notes, Muslims who center their faith are often treated instrumentally by non-Muslim allies and "cultural" Muslims who are at the helm of organizing against Islamophobia. Furthermore, campaigns against Islamophobia narratively prioritize the figure of the "Muslim who is just like you" (that is, a well-integrated Muslim), simultaneously disenfranchising those Muslims who may not be perceived as well-integrated. This latter group includes the too "religiously conservative," speakers of accented or broken English, low-income workers, and Muslims with a criminal record (Islam 2018). These Muslims are the most vulnerable to Islamophobia. Islam (2018: 280) comments that in many ostensibly liberal, progressive settings that orient themselves to social justice, "Islamophobia [is] the focus. Islam [is] an afterthought."

Recognizing the paradox of secular societies which claim to embrace diversity but remain uncomfortable with the increasing prominence of religion in the public sphere, sociologists of religion now advocate for the notion of the "postsecular turn"—an approach that defines scholarship where religion is not "bracketed out" but "into" the research design (Davie 2017). It creates a foundation for an expanded understanding of religion and religiosity, one that accommodates bodies, physical objects, and spaces. Furthermore, it acknowledges the ways in which religion may illuminate other dimensions of social lives, in particular gender, sexuality, ethnicity, race, class, ability, and health

(Doggett and Arat 2017). It also recognizes the imbrication of religion in other aspects of contemporary life such as commodification (Lewis 2015 and 2017), mediatization (Lövheim 2017), and the rise of populisms (Arato and Cohen 2018). Notably, Ammerman (2017) links this transition to women entering the discipline of sociology and the expansion of the disciplinary focus beyond the North Atlantic region. Divisions and boundaries between "religion" and "no religion" are increasingly blurred; the postsecular turn enabled the observation of religious dimensions of social life, symbolism, and logics in ritual practices conventionally situated outside of traditional religious formations such as nationalism, humanitarianism, as well as "no religion" humanistic movements (Lynch 2017), illustrating the need for making of symbolic meanings during the life course. Situated in this postsecular current of sociology of religion, I consider why the niqab disputes are still raging in the West, in spite of hundreds, if not thousands, of niqab-wearing women asserting that they simply wish to be given the opportunity to practice their faith without garnering attention or controversy.

The structure of the book is intended to introduce the reader to the background of the problem in Chapter 1. Here I demonstrate how niqab wearers' perspectives are silenced in the Western public sphere and how their agendas are rendered negligible, which paves the way to ideologically biased legal restrictions on niqab-wearing. In Chapter 2, I discuss niqab wearers' responses to negative media representations of the niqab and Islam more widely. I also trace their various modes of engagement on social media as an alternative platform of communication with the public. In Chapter 3, I focus on religious framing of the niqab offered by the participants. By prioritizing the religious aspects of the niqab, they offered a sophisticated critique of narratives examined in Chapter 1. Chapter 4 complements Chapter 3 in that it analyzes secular narratives defending the place of the niqab in the secular-liberal polity deployed by women who choose to wear the niqab. Together, they showcase a discursive versatility that characterizes the women's talk. Finally, Chapter 5 looks at various social outcomes of niqab-wearing, in particular, intersections of Islamophobia, racism, and sexism that often affect their interactions in the public sphere in the West. It also identifies coping strategies used by the women to mitigate these risks.

CHAPTER 1
ERASING NIQABI WOMEN'S VOICES
MAINSTREAM MEDIA REPRESENTATIONS

Media representations of women who wear the niqab were a direct trigger for this research project in 2013. Several incidents pertaining to the niqab between July and September 2013 in the United Kingdom (including a ban proposal, a judicial ruling in a court case, and a reversal of a niqab ban instituted by a college in Birmingham) prompted the usual flurry of news, op-eds, columns, and letters to the editor offering multiple views on the niqab and whether it has a place in modern-day Britain, how the writers understand the niqab, how it is used to oppress women in other countries, and what the feminist response to the niqab ought to be. A sober question posed by Kira Cochrane in an editorial in *The Guardian* (2013: np): "Is the veil the biggest issue we face in the UK?" went unheard. Everyone had a view, and it seemed that they were at pains to express it. What was missing from that echo chamber were the voices of women who wear the niqab.

Traditional mainstream broadcast and print media take a variety of positions on the niqab, but it appears that many outlets, especially the conservative ones, promote hard-line solutions to the "problem" of the niqab in British and American streets: they do give a considerable platform to individuals and groups (such as the UK Independence Party) who openly wish to control what Muslim women may or may not wear. Unfortunately, the principle of journalistic balance rarely applies in this case—few niqabi women over the years have been given space to present their views in mass media. Where their voices were included, it was usually in a TV studio setting where they had been invited to defend their choices in a hostile atmosphere whipped up by co-discussants (see Channel 4 2013). These interrogations seemed more like trials rather than debates. One of the American participants whom I interviewed and who had appeared in a few of those programs, said that she had to start turning such invitations down as she felt that her lifestyle choices were presented as deviant, and she had experienced psychological distress as a result of these engagements.

Having keenly observed media reporting and fueling these controversies in the United Kingdom, continental Europe, Canada, and the United States, I have noticed how the approach to the topic has changed during the last twelve years. While in the past, media content producers engaged niqabis' own accounts only rarely, these days there is more pretence of including them, but as I have shown earlier, this is not necessarily helpful for creating culturally sensitive representations of women who wear the niqab. Truly committed journalism on the topic is rare, but it exists. There are several media frames to discuss the niqab. It is this qualitative change in reporting rather than an exhaustive chronological record of "niqab controversies" that this chapter is structured around. That said, most opinion pieces about the niqab do appear in response to wider controversies, as it is when the interest in the topic spikes in the West.

My analysis in this chapter is informed by principles formulated by critical discourse analysis (CDA) theorists. Van Dijk (1993: 28) defines CDA as a "systematic discourse analysis of the genres or communicative events that play a role in the reproduction of racism, such as everyday conversations, novels, films, textbooks, lessons, laws . . . or any other discourse genre that may be about ethnic groups and ethnic relations." Further, "critical targets [of the analysis] are the power elites that enact, sustain, legitimate, condone or ignore social inequality and injustice" (Van Dijk 1993: 252). By identifying discontinuities and fissures in hegemonic discourse, CDA makes space for minority voices. Van Dijk(1993: 253) states that "if immigrants, refugees, and (other) minorities suffer from prejudice, discrimination, and racism, and if women continue to be subjected to male dominance, violence, or sexual harassment, it will be essential to examine and evaluate such events and their consequences essentially from their point of view. That is, such events will be called 'racist' or 'sexist' if knowledgeable Blacks or women say so, despite white or male denials." The CDA approach is then particularly fitting for the following discussion because while critiquing discursive reproduction of inequality, it compels scholars to privilege insiders' perspectives. These form the backbone of the last section of this chapter, where I consider niqab wearers' responses to media representations of the niqab, and, indeed, the rest of this book. For the purpose of this chapter, I thematically analyzed ninety-seven articles about the niqab/burka (news reports, "long reads," and opinion pieces), published in the British and American press across the political spectrum between January 1, 2010, and December 31, 2018. The articles discussed here through the CDA lens were chosen as particularly illustrative examples of discursive themes which emerged from the analysis. This selection is not offered as representative or typical of media portrayals of Muslims and Islam; rather, they encapsulate the mainstream discourses about the niqab.

Negative Framing of the Niqab

In order to provide context for the remainder of the book, I first focus on the negative framing of the niqab in mainstream media through three distinct yet intertwined hegemonic discourses about the niqab. These include a "values discourse" which casts the niqab as incompatible with a secular, undefined "national culture," a "paternalistic feminist" discourse which reinvents the old Orientalist argument that the niqab is a sign of patriarchal oppression, and the security discourse which portrays the niqab as an "Islamist" security threat.

Values/Identity Discourse

The niqab is by no means opposed only by non-Muslims. It has many opponents among Muslims, including Muslim women. Pieces by a handful of Muslim-identifying female journalists appear to be staple fare as far as opining on the niqab is concerned. The values/

identity discourse opposed to the niqab is ostensibly meant to produce an alternative "progressive Muslimness" palatable to the West, including its relative invisibility (but of course, "Muslimness" can rarely be entirely invisible, as it is routinely racialized in both the United Kingdom and the United States (Franks 2000; Moosavi 2015; Galonnier 2015; Selod 2015), a fixed idea of what is Islamic, and conflation of condemnation of political regimes that force Islamic clothing on women with the condemnation of women who wear the niqab by choice.

In this section, I analyze three articles, each of them mounting a slightly different critque of the niqab, but with the same implication—that there is no place for the niqab in the West. While all three pieces discursively overlap in that they agree that the niqab should not be worn, they differ in the severity of their preferred solution. Eltahawy opts for a nationwide legal ban; the two others recognize that a ban constitutes violence to women's bodies. I find that these articles are illustrative of arguments mobilized in this context, especially as they are all written by Muslim female journalists, each of whom proposes a particular vision of what constitutes an appropriate Muslim femininity in the West. All three media platforms where these articles were published—*The Guardian*, *The New York Times*, and *The HuffPost*—are generally considered left-wing-leaning and respectable as far as journalistic standards are concerned.

The Veil as a Rejection of Progressive Values

In her piece, titled "As a Muslim woman, I see the veil as a rejection of progressive values" Yasmin Alibhai-Brown (2015), a secular, liberal British Muslim feminist of Pakistani background (2011), lumps together women who wear the niqab with "new puritans." At the same time, she represents herself as a member of the silent Muslim majority who "tremble" watching their covered sisters. In just a few discursive strokes, she mobilizes the neat divide between the "liberals" and the "puritans," castigating the latter as unaware of the veil's darker symbolism, uneducated, and lacking in agency. Alibhai-Brown described an episode when she was sitting on a park bench while a face-veiled woman and her children walked past. There could be no conversation, because, as she complained, "Behind fabric, she was more unapproachable than a fort." Of course, while she blamed the other woman for her own perception, Alibhai-Brown appears to equate readiness for conversation with her specifically with progressive values at large. Following that logic, everyone with headphones or browsing through their phones could be denounced as anti-progressive, because they do not signal an interest in interaction with strangers. Alibhai-Brown seemed unable to recognize that the interaction was possibly hindered more by her own prejudice rather than the other woman's clothing. At the end of that paragraph, rather haphazardly, she demanded: "Whatever happened to sisterhood?", not noticing the obvious irony of the statement appearing in a column where she castigates other women for their choices. Sisterhood does not operate on terrain where some women claim the right to silence others.

"Debunking the Burqa"

Mona Eltahawy, an American Egyptian journalist ("a secular, radical feminist Muslim" [El Rashidi 2013: np]) wrote in a *New York Times* column (2009), "The best way to debunk the burqa as an expression of Muslim faith is to listen to Muslims who oppose it." While on the face of it, it is a commonsensical statement—if you wish to ignore a positive aspect of the burqa, listen to its opponents who will supply a negative narrative instead—its logic is faulty. The opponents cannot debunk its quality as *other people's expression of faith*—it is those other people's expression, and theirs alone. It is simply not in their sphere of experience to be able to question other people's beliefs and their expression. The fact that the journalist may nominally share the faith with the women who face-veil, but interprets its central texts differently, does not put her in a position that would allow her to exercise power over them.

Critics of the niqab and burka often argue in the media that they are not "Islamic" but, instead, "cultural," implying that they belong in the areas where they have been traditionally worn (and, at times, forced on women by political regimes and patriarchal cultures). However, the narrative casting the niqab as un-Islamic relies on a very fixed, doctrinal understanding of religion and religious practice that does not allow for personal religious agency. Both Alibhai-Brown (2015) and Eltahawy (2009) deploy such an understanding in their pieces. The former seemingly describes the veil as a metaphor offered by the Qur'an. In the same piece, she also quotes a scholar of Islam, Sahar Amer, who states that the Qur'an does not prescribe the covering of head or face, instead requiring believers of both genders to dress modestly.[1]

Simultaneously "Hating the Burqa" and Wearing One

Sabria Jawhar (2011) speaks from a different perspective in her Huffington Post article. Jawhar is a Saudi journalist and columnist who, by her own admission, wears the niqab when she is in Saudi Arabia, but not in the United Kingdom. She has a doctorate in applied linguistics from Newcastle University and her piece is a reflection on an incident involving a woman in a niqab in Newcastle that she witnessed and similar incidents elsewhere. She demonstrates a degree of compassion toward her fellow niqabi sisters and criticizes the argumentation used to advocate for a ban: "There is no argument that can

---

[1] This deployment of the discourse of Islamic scholarship calls for some theological contextualization. Alibhai-Brown mentions a verse where the wives of the Prophet (all highly revered in Islam) were told to cover their faces (Qur'an 33:5). This verse itself means that modern-day women who follow the practice (or, using a phrase common in Anglophone Islamic world, *emulate* the wives of the Prophet), follow Sunnah—the second, after the Qur'an, most important source of Islamic law. To follow Sunna is to try to live one's life according to the example of Prophet Muhammad and his family, considered in Islam to be role models for Muslim men and women (Lamptey 2018; see also Qur'an 68:4). It is important to note that the Prophet's wives chose to interpret prescriptions regarding hijab (understood both as modest comportment and as clothing) very differently— Sawda, on the one hand, adopted a strict understanding of the hijab, staying at home at all times, while on the other hand, Aisha moved around freely (Sayeed 2013). It follows then that, in fact, a wide range of choices women make in this respect are "Sunnah" (i.e., in accordance with the Sunnah) and by all means Islamic. Furthermore, the "Islam versus culture" distinction as deployed here by Alibhai-Brown as an argument against face-veiling is also wielded by young Muslim women who reason within their communities that the niqab is a more suitable expression of Islam than "ethnic clothing" (for example, *shalwar kameez* or sari) (Tarlo 2013). Therefore, as noted by Asad (2009a), it is, rather, a double-edged sword in terms of debates over the authenticity of Islam.

persuade me that laws designed to bully women into abandoning their cultural traditions because it makes people uncomfortable are essential in a free society. If a woman chooses to wear the niqab who are we to pass judgment? Lawmakers who argue that banning the burqa is a blow against extremism are naïve and lazy. Band-Aid approaches to fighting extremism are rarely successful" (Jawhar 2011: np). Elsewhere in her article, she refers to an attack on a niqabi in Glasgow where a man ripped a niqab off from a woman's face, and comments: "To her, the attack was an act of rape" (Jawhar 2011: np). And yet, as she explains her position signaled in the title of her article—*Why I hate the burqa, and yes, I wear one*—she simultaneously propagates a host of stereotypes about the niqab, for example, that many women wear it to pander to their husbands' jealousy ("I'm guessing that more than a few Saudi girls wear the niqab because their husbands insist on it."), or that women who wear the niqab must be foreign, and they should either "reconsider [their] religious and cultural values, or go home." The fact that many women who wear the niqab in the United Kingdom were born in that country[2] and they do not have another home to go to seems to escape her. She advises them that "it doesn't take much to compromise and adapt at some level to a new environment." It is necessary, because "non-Muslims will continue to fear Muslims wearing traditional clothing and hijabs because it represents beliefs alien to them."

Jawhar, even though she tries to empathize, ends up judging women who wear the niqab in the West through her specific Saudi experience of the niqab. This perspective stems from the cultural expectation and performance of modesty in that context as well as its state-regulated parameters, in particular the predominant interpretation of Islam (Hanbali school) and the religious police that target perceived infractions of morality. She refers to a ruling by a Saudi scholar who "issued a fatwa that Muslim women may show their faces in countries where the niqab is banned or when wearing the niqab may pose a danger to the woman" (Jawhar 2011: np). In citing such a fatwa, she again centers on the Saudi experience, instead of recognizing that British niqab wearers may have a different, individualized understanding of Islamic teachings about modesty and religious practice. In other words, UK Muslims may not care what Saudi scholars say. In effect, Jawhar turns them into outsiders and forever pilgrim members of society, as opposed to legitimate citizens who have a right to shape British national identity. In sum, imaging a global, univocal, homogenous community of niqab wearers does not work, because of diffused centers of authority and meaning-making structures that are in operation. The Saudi experience of the niqab cannot be used as a legitimation of representing UK niqab wearers which is demonstrated by this example—it simply falls flat.

It is equally problematic to assume the right to represent niqabis from a secular feminist Muslim position. As the examples of Alibhai-Brown and Eltahawy demonstrate, they are invested in a particular project of secular and assimilated Islam. While the objective of such a project is a legitimate one in a pluralistic society, the means through

---

[2]Over 80 per cent of UK-based respondents in this study were born in the United Kingdom.

which they are trying to achieve it—by denigrating the niqab wearers and delegitimizing their perspectives—is questionable.[3]

Paternalistic Feminist Discourse

Feminism and the "burqa" do not go together, argue some commentators who self-label as feminists, among them Julie Bindel (2013) and Tracy Murray (2013) in the United Kingdom, and Phyllis Chesler (2010) in the United States.[4] The platforms chosen by these writers to advocate their interpretations of feminism are often bias-propagating, right-wing outlets, such as the *Daily Mail*,[5] *Fox News*, or *Middle East Quarterly* that take pride in their prejudiced stance regarding Muslim women. While the *Daily Mail* and *Fox News* are known for their xenophobic political bias (Auestad 2015; Jardina 2019), which I also discuss later in this chapter, the *Middle East Quarterly* requires a brief introduction. It is produced by an anti-Muslim think-tank called the Middle East Forum. The latter was cited by Anders Breivik eighteen times in his manifesto published before he massacred sixty-nine Norwegian Labour Party youth camp members and eight other people in July 2011 (Center for American Progress 2011: 42). It perpetuates Islamophobia in "academic garb" (Yaqzan 2019: np), as it is styled after a scholarly journal, with professional-looking editing and typesetting. Its mission is to "promote American interests in the Middle East and protect Western values from Middle Eastern threats." (Middle Eastern Forum 2019). *MEQ* is active on campuses through the project Campus Watch (tracking what it sees as "intellectual roots of bias" in the teaching of Middle Eastern studies. Its other projects include Islamist Watch, Jihad-Intel, and The Israel Victory Project. Daniel Pipes, the editor of the *MEQ*, is one of the key individuals heading anti-Islamic think-tanks. He is notable for attacking President Obama for "enforcing Islamic law" in America (Center for American Progress 2011: 29).

---

[3]The prominence of the values/identity discourse is striking in particular because opinions voiced by Muslim women who defend others' right to wear the niqab, while not necessarily considering the practice Islamically mandatory or necessary, are hardly represented in mainstream media. Directors of Muslim women's organizations, such as Shaista Gohir, chair of Muslim Women's Network UK 2007–2011, tend to oppose burka bans. Gohir was quoted by the BBC News in 2010 as being against a ban, but that "There needs to be more research on why some women choose to wear the veil and how they think they are perceived. Muslim communities need to instigate, be proactive, rather than wait for politicians like Jack Straw to say something and respond" (Barford 2010: np). However, in articles claiming to represent balanced reporting, these comments are often buried toward the end and usually sought out during controversies. In the United States, three prominent women activists (Hadeer Soliman, vice president of the Muslim Student Union at UC Irvine; Edina Lekovic, director of policy and programming for the Muslim Public Affairs Council in Los Angeles; and Zahra Billoo, executive director of the San Francisco Bay Area chapter of the Council on American-Islamic Relations) were asked by the KPCC Radio in 2011 to share their views on the French burka ban, and they unanimously opposed it, regardless of their personal stance on face-veiling (Berenstein Rojas and Nouh 2011).
[4]Each of these contributors has a long history of anti-Muslim writings, and these particular articles have been chosen for analysis as the authors argue specifically for the "burka ban."
[5]One of the *Daily Mail*'s journalists, Melanie Philips, was cited by Anders Breivik in his manifesto (Auestad 2015).

Niqab as Patriarchal Oppression

Put succinctly, the argument advocating that feminists take a stance against the niqab is based on the following premises: the niqab is unequivocally a sign of patriarchy and oppression of women, therefore "real feminists" must oppose it. Chesler (2010: 34) writes in the *MEQ*: "full body and face cover is not a religious requirement in Islam but represents a minority tradition among a small Islamist minority; that it is not a matter of free choice but a highly forced choice and a visual Islamist symbol—one that is ostentatiously anti-secularist and misogynist." It is notable that she replaces the usual adjectives used in this context ("Muslim" and "Islamic") with the value-laden "Islamist," invoking negative connotations of "militant expressions of political Islam" (Martin and Barzegar 2010: vii) associated with niqab and burka wearers. Chesler's glaring oxymoron, "a highly forced choice," represents the classic argument that denies niqab and burka wearers agency by essentializing these garments as tools of oppression by the Taliban. The examples of violent and criminal acts against women in those contexts are used as a reason to ban the burqa in the West. This apparent blindness to the cultural context enables them somehow to justify exertion of secular control over niqabi women's bodies in the West by arguing that Islam is a patriarchal ideology and is used to oppress Muslim women in places like Afghanistan and Saudi Arabia. Further, Chesler dismisses the fact that niqab and burka wearers in the West write articles, appear in TV debates, and participate in public protests against "burka bans," communicating adamantly that what they do consider oppressive is the legislative attempts to prevent them from practicing their religion through modest dress. Chesler discards all those activities, suggesting that the notion of choice, when the choice is not aligned with her sensibilities, is a result of brainwashing:

> Many children who are brought up within fundamentalist religions or in cults are trained, by a system of reward and punishment, to obey their parents, teachers, and religious leaders. As adults, if they wish to remain within the community . . . they must continue to conform to its norms. Most are already socialized to do so and thus, some Muslim women will say that they do not feel that anyone is forcing them to wear the headscarf; many will, in a private conversation, denounce the face veil, the burqa, the chador, and the Saudi abaya.

> (2010: 41)

Here, she derationalizes these women's voices because their choices are not to her liking through equating their religious belief with cultism, and pictures their reasoning as insincere, by suggesting that their views expressed in private are different to those in public. Effectively, she renders them mute, because any argument in defense of the niqab or burka made by the wearers is dismissed as irrational. There is nothing they can say that is of rhetorical value in this framing. Chesler (2010) does not provide any examples that would suggest that this is the prevailing situation in the West, such as interviews or reports. In Chapter 2 of this book, I deal with such manipulations by applying the feminist methodological principle of centering on women's voices in my analysis with full attention given to their reasoning, sensibilities, and concerns.

De-Veiling, Feminism, and Imperialism

It is not just the niqab and burka wearers who are under fire from these commentators. In unison, they challenge those who refuse to issue a blanket criticism of the niqab such as theirs. Such "fair weather feminists" (Murray 2013: np), "cultural relativists," are shown up as cowards fearing being called racist or Islamophobic if they dared to criticize patriarchal practices among Muslims (Murray 2013 and Bindel 2013). They are either "female Muslim academics who work and publish from comfortable posts in prominent universities in the United States or Europe, who do not live under the constraints of Sharia law" (Murray 2013: np), "unwitting sympathizers [of Islamists] in the West" (Chesler 2010: 38), or "white do-gooders" (Bindel 2013: np). The implication is that benevolent accommodation of Islam (and the niqab) mistakenly trumps "real" concerns over the apparent oppression of women in Islam. Mazrouki (2017: 5) traces the origins of this discourse denouncing "alleged collusion between leftist intellectuals and Islamists" to French public debates but observes that it has crossed over to the United States. This chapter indicates that it is also prominent in the United Kingdom.

Invoking feminism in order to condemn, occupy, and colonize entire nations is nothing new. Lila Abu-Lughod (2013) has traced this unholy alliance between proponents of "women's liberation" from the time of the British colonial occupation of Egypt until the American invasion in Afghanistan. The fact that the Taliban regime oppressed women— which was usually conveyed by portraying Afghan women as forced into burkas—was molded into the rationale of the invasion. Similarly, Chan-Malik (2011: 112, emphasis mine) in her analysis of the representation of the Islamic veil in the American press after the Islamic revolution in Iran has argued that "discourses of second-wave feminism, a post-civil rights rhetoric of racial and cultural pluralism, and late-Cold War logics of secularism and liberal democracy intersected to create a racial-orientalist discourse of the veil, which would subsequently be deployed to justify US military aggression in the Middle East *while perpetuating state violence against women, immigrants, and people of color* throughout the 1980s and into the post-9/11 era." Khiabany and Williamson (2011) have offered an excellent critique of British and American hegemonic discourses expressing false concerns for Afghan women which were used as one of the key justifications for the occupation of Afghanistan. In their article, they quote Laura Bush's 2001 speech that weaved together her delight about the impending end to "the brutality against women and children by the al-Qaida terrorist network and the regime it supports in Afghanistan, the Taliban" with joy about American military gains in Afghanistan (2011: 174). Similar sentiments were expressed by Cherie Blair and two female members of the Labour government in Britain. This association was necessary to create the impression that the war in Afghanistan was not simply an exercise in "brute force or raw plunder . . . but in the name of a noble idea" (Said 2001: 574). The lack of resources allocated to women's education and health in subsequent years underscores the fact that the "noble idea" remained in the sphere of fantasy (Khiabany and Williamson 2011). However, it gave rise to thousands of articles in the British and American press about the plight of women in Afghanistan, with the burka, unsurprisingly, becoming the visual "synecdoche for fundamentalism" (Sreberny in Khiabany and Williamson 2011: 174).

The 2001 article by Polly Toynbee in *The Guardian* was identified by Khiabany and Williamson as one of the first ones that symbolically ripped the burka apart as a symbol of women's oppression; yet, what is telling here is the timing of this article and the thousands that followed. Between 1996 and 2000 there was hardly any media coverage of the hardships that Afghan women suffered under the Taliban; at the time, it did not have political value as a justification for war.

It seems then that the case of the niqab also highlights the rift between paternalistic feminism (labeled more poignantly by Eddo-Lodge (2017, passim) as "white feminism"), still embroiled in the project of colonizing the "Third World woman" experiences by White Western women, and indigenous feminism which avoids universalizing the experience of patriarchy. Apparently, not only White men but also White women are trying to save brown women from brown men, if we were to paraphrase Spivak's famous statement (1988). Therefore, when Bindel writes elsewhere that "disrespect for religion, including Islam, should be at the heart of feminism" (2018: np), she negates the experiences and achievements of women who oppose patriarchy by working within a religious framework. Her experience as a White, secular British woman is forced on women who choose to wear the niqab and are vocal about their right to do so. Crosby (2014) argues that such sentiments, and their legal emanations in the form of bans, form what she calls "faux feminism"—an appropriation of feminist sentiment for the purpose of propagating Orientalist ideas and policies.

Islamophobia Networks and the National Security Discourse

Dovetailing with the paternalistic feminist discourse on the burka and niqab is the security discourse, prominent in both the United States and the United Kingdom. Within this discourse, the niqab is constructed as a symptom (and cause) of Islamist radicalization that should be erased along with terrorist networks. Women who wear the niqab are made out to be feared as female counterparts of male jihadists. The origins of this discourse are to be found in the changing political context pertaining to the "war on terror"; Khiabany and Williamson (2011) note that "the meanings of the veil in phase two of the 'War on Terror' have moved from an external image of victimhood and a justification for military intervention to an internal sign of fundamentalism and a visible threat at home." Representative of this discourse are Pearson's piece titled "For the sake of national security, we must ban the burka" in *The Daily Telegraph*, a British right-leaning (All Sides 2019) broadsheet daily newspaper and Geller's piece (2016) titled "Yes, ban the burqa, it is a national security necessity" in *The Hill*, a Washington D.C.-based American newspaper rated as centrist (All Sides 2019). Both Pearson and Geller are leading voices in the "anti-Muslim chorus" (Isaacs 2018: np) in the United Kingdom and the United States, respectively, having attacked not only British and American Muslim communities, but journalists who defended those communities as well (see Pearson 2011, 2014, 2018; Barnard and Feuer 2010). Pearson is a prolific anti-Muslim column writer for the right-wing British press. Geller, a contributor to the far-right Breitbart News outlet, has been named "the anti-Muslim movement's most visible and flamboyant figurehead" by the

Southern Poverty Law Center who say that she works "with extremists on both sides of the Atlantic" such as the English Defense League (Southern Poverty Law Center 2019: np). Geller is considered one of the figures in the extensive and well-funded network of individuals and organizations that successfully spread anti-Muslim myths (Center for American Progress 2011).

United States of America: The Niqab as an Equivalent of the Ku Klux Klan Mask

In her piece, Geller relied largely on a Washington Post article (Bever 2016) detailing the circumstances of submission and withdrawal of House Bill 3, by State Rep. Jason Spencer in the Georgia House of Representatives. The bill was intended to widen the scope of original anti-masking laws aimed at curbing the Ku Klux Klan's terrorist activity, to include women (the original wording referred only to men) and rules regulating driving license photos and driving in the state. Geller reproduced the inconsistency in Rep. Spencer's justifications for the bill; although he said at one point that "there is no intention of targeting a specific group," he also mentioned that the bill was proposed "in response to constituents that do have concerns of the rise of Islamic terrorism" (Bever 2016: np). The claim to it being ideologically neutral was necessary to position the bill as non-prejudiced and constitutionally legal; the claim to address Islamic terrorism garnered support of commentators like Geller; the real impact of the extended bill would have been felt only by Muslim women who wear the niqab. To date, the only terrorist attacks that happened in Georgia were organized and carried out by right-wing, anti-abortion, and anti-government groups (State of Georgia 2015).

Geller (2016) incorporated Rep. Spencer's logical inconsistency in her own piece, removing some facts and adding conspiracy theories. She ascribed protests against the proposed bill to the operation of the "Islamophobia victimhood industry" (Geller 2016: np), omitting to mention the legitimate concerns over the sharp rise of Islamophobic hate crimes (257 in 2015, up by 67 percent compared to 2014) cited in the *Washington Post* article (Bever 2016) and dismissing the impact of such hate crimes by adopting a phrase that suggests ill-intentioned manufacturing of victimhood. Further, she undermined the legitimacy of the claim that the bill proposed by Rep. Spencer targeted Muslims made by the Council of American Muslim Relations (CAIR) by promoting the debunked (Isaacs 2018) conspiracy theory that CAIR was a jihadist organization (Geller 2016). By attempting to link CAIR to jihadism, she symbolically put the right to wear the niqab on the undefined, imagined terrorist agenda.

Trying to associate the niqab with extremist organizations and acts, Geller (2016: np) directly compared it to Ku-Klux-Klan (KKK) face coverings: "Indeed, from a security standpoint, what's the difference between KKK face coverings and the niqab and burqa?" Answering this allusion disguised as a rhetorical question, firstly, the KKK throughout its existence has been a violent, secretive organization whose members hid their identity because they did not want to be recognized as Klansmen. In day-to-day life they appeared ordinary and adopted their costumes only during gatherings. Niqab wearers wear the face veil openly, to identify as Muslim, and the vast majority of them comply with legitimate requests to show their faces; those who refuse to lift the niqab in the presence of men, do so if the official is female. Both the KKK mask and the niqab cover up the face, but so do surgical and ski masks, and motorcycle helmets. Of all those, only the KKK mask was designed with the distinct aim of putting terror in the hearts of the public. Wade (1998: 33) wrote in his historical account of the KKK: "every stage in the development of the Klan was made to enhance or 'harmonize with' the members' idea of themselves as spooks. Elaborate and menacing costumes were adopted. . . . Tall conical witches' hats of white cloth over cardboard completely concealed their heads; eyeholes were punched out for vision. These headpieces exaggerated the height of the wearer, adding anywhere from eighteen inches to two feet to his stature. Imagination was encouraged in costume design." Such comparisons as Geller's (2016), while ironic (equating minority religious dress to a costume of an extremist organization that sought to restore White supremacy in the South by terrorizing Black people, religious minorities, and immigrants), is meant to introduce false equivalence to the public understanding of the niqab.

The highly emotive language of war that Geller (2016: np) employed in sections that appear to be her own reflection further implies that the women who wear the niqab, as well as their advocates, are the enemies of America. "We are at war, despite the fog of misinformation, disinformation and apologetics that keeps people from understanding the nature and magnitude of the war we are in." Leaving the question "who are we at war with?" open, she attempts to maintain a veneer of neutrality to bolster the claim that House Bill 3 was not intended as anti-Muslim. Yet, the nature of conspiracy theories involving CAIR she advocates, as well as the entirety of her writings, especially the book titled *Stop the Islamization of America: A Practical Guide to the Resistance* (2016), contradicts this. Geller's point is evocative of McGhee's (2008: 35) observation that the absence in the "war on terror" of a tangible opponent wielding traditional weapons leads to the emergence of a war mentality that compulsively seeks out enemies:

> It is increasingly difficult to work out in the post-9/11 world just who "we" are supposed to be at "war" with: a network (Al-Qaeda), an individual (Osama Bin Laden), a State (Afghanistan) or States (the "axis of evil"), a tyrant (the late Saddam Hussein), or are we at war with "terror" in general? . . . As a result of this, according to Žižek, the "war on terrorism" has introduced a new era of paranoiac warfare in which the greatest task will be to identify the enemy and his weapons.
>
> (2002: 109)

Further, Geller (2016: np) evoked the archetypal light-dark metaphor to describe the proposed ban: "The tangential benefit of such a ban is that it would constitute support for liberalism against darkness." Heavily value-laden, distinctions between representatives of Light and Dark unambiguously identify the enemy. Osborn (1967: 117) argues that "darkness [brings] fear of the unknown . . . because of their strong positive and negative associations with survival and development motives, such metaphors express intense value judgements and may thus be expected to elicit significant value responses from an audience. When light and dark images are used together in a speech, they indicate and perpetuate the simplistic, two-valued, black-white attitudes." Geller's article illustrates how fact is mixed with fiction, omission, and logical inconsistencies in the echo chamber of alternative facts and misinformation.

Distracting From the Role of the Domestic White Supremacist Terrorism

There seems to be a reason for this kind of manipulation in which the niqab is misused as a prop. The constant focus on "Islamic terrorism" maintained by these writings attempts to divert attention from the fact that since 9/11, no foreign terrorist group has managed to successfully conduct an attack on US soil. In fact, many political commentators argue that the main terrorist threat facing America at the moment of writing is domestic terrorism propelled by right-wing, White-supremacist, and misogynistic "incel" ideologies (Bergen and Sterman 2018). After the El-Paso mass shooting, the number of deaths caused by White supremacist terrorists (107) has overtaken the number of deaths that resulted from radical Islam-inspired attacks (104) since 9/11 (Byman 2019). Furthermore, "far-right extremists have been responsible for almost three times as many attacks on U.S. soil as Islamic terrorists, the government reported. From 2009 through 2018, the far right has been responsible for 73 percent of domestic extremist-related fatalities, according to a 2019 study by the Anti-Defamation League (ADL)" (Bergengruen and Hennigan 2019: np). And yet, only 20 percent of FBI agents are working on domestic terrorism cases today (Bergegruen and Hennigan 2019). This disparity in the assignment of resources to combating Islam-inspired and domestic terrorism has a long tradition: when in 2009, an intelligence briefing warning of the impending rise of right-wing extremism in the United States was sent to American law enforcement agencies, the public outrage was so strong that the team that prepared the briefing was disbanded and reassigned to work on Islam-inspired terrorism instead (Beckett 2019). Aaronson (2019) wrote that "268 right-wing extremists prosecuted in federal courts since 9/11 were allegedly involved in crimes that appear to meet the legal definition of domestic terrorism. Yet the Justice Department applied anti-terrorism laws against only 34 of them, compared to more than 500 alleged international terrorists." The failure of the Justice Department to brand right-wing crimes as domestic terrorism which reifies them as individual, non-ideological acts contributes to the relative scarcity of resources and programs to address them. This is reinforced by the disproportionate media attention on Islam-inspired terrorist attacks, which, according to a University of Alabama study (Kearns, Betus, and Lemieux 2019) receive 357 percent more coverage in American media than right-wing terrorist attacks. This creates a feedback loop where the public, upon discovering that a crime perpetrator was Muslim, interpret the crime as terrorism. Marzouki (2017), citing a quantitative study of influence strategies of 120 organizations that participate in the debate on Islam, notes that it is the fringe right-wing organizations' financial resources and their ability to attract mainstream media's attention that shift the conversation and perceptions rightward. Articles such as Geller's (2016), especially those published in ostensibly mainstream media, legitimize such a status quo in the eyes of the public. They mask the emergence of a serious terrorist threat posed by right-wing supremacy, a threat that is difficult for many Americans to conceive as such, and "manufacture and naturalize hate speech and hateful feelings" (Marzouki 2017: 17).

United Kingdom: The Niqab as a Sign of Radicalization and ISIS Advocacy

Pearson's piece (2017) which I selected for close analysis here came on the back of a comment by Paul Nuttall, the United Kingdom Independence Party (UKIP) chairman, who proposed banning the face veil on national security grounds. It illustrates quite well the haphazard manner in which the niqab is embroiled in national security incidents, as if it was the piece of clothing itself that was responsible for terrorist plots or acts. Once Pearson listed an incident in which the niqab appeared to be worn by suspects, she referred to another series of arrests of "Muslim women" in connection with a suspected terrorist plot: "It's not known if the suspects were wearing burkas, but it would be pretty surprising if they weren't" (Pearson 2017: np, emphasis mine). In other words, an assumption is used here as evidence to make a point. Pearson seems to be under the illusion that radicalization can be automatically triggered by the niqab—after all, it would be surprising if terror suspects did not wear it, and, following her argument, banning the "burka" would automatically diminish the risk of terrorism. She blames the clothing for a "multitude of sins," including allowing terrorists to hide under it. Other than citing two examples where that was the case, she provides no viable statistics to show that the Islamic face veil facilitates terrorist acts. When Channel 4's Fact Check (2017) requested such statistics from Scotland Yard, the response was that no such statistics existed. So, concluded Fact Check, "there appears to be no statistical evidence that burqas hamper the effectiveness of CCTV any more so than hoodies, big hats, balaclavas, masks or anything else. . . . Paul Nuttall said the issue was of particular concern because of the 'heightened terror'; [yet], women who wear the burqa only make up a tiny proportion of terrorism-related offences. The overwhelming majority of people arrested for terror offences are male" (2017: np).

To make up for that inconsistency, Pearson then talked about British Muslim women who joined the so-called Islamic State in Syria and declared that "most of us" were concerned about those that are "allowed to come back." While this has, indeed, been an intensely debated issue in the British media, Pearson failed to make a logical connection between it and her support for the burka ban. Therefore, while on the face of it, it is unclear how this paragraph supports her point, we can only assume that she was loosely trying to refocus the fear of radicalized IS supporters to niqab wearers living in the United Kingdom without even bothering to construct an argument for this connection.

Pearson's piece is clearly meant to fuel the anti-Muslim moral panic by the use of highly emotive language ("it's utterly horrifying"; "hateful message it [the burka] sends"; "misogynist brutes"). The reference to radicalized women returning from Syria in the context of the case made for a burka ban is likely to facilitate the perception that the ban can potentially prevent, expose, or neutralize religious radicalization. This, of course, is a "Band-Aid approach to extremism," so aptly labeled by Jawhar earlier on (2011: np), that tackles none of the broader reasons for radicalization, such as socioeconomic deprivation, political marginalization, and an identity crisis (Al-Lami 2009), or, importantly, resentment against Western military involvement in wars where millions of civilians are dying (Kundnani 2009).

One of Pearson's qualifications to write about the "burka ban" is having driven through Tower Hamlets, the London borough with the highest rate of poverty, child poverty, unemployment, and pay inequality of any London borough (Trust for London 2019). It also has one of the highest Muslim populations in the United Kingdom. Pearson briefly summarized her impression of Tower Hamlets thus: "I drove through Tower Hamlets at the weekend and, in sartorial terms, the female population might as well be living in Saudi Arabia" (Pearson 2017: np). Leaving aside the question of the validity of such observations made from within a car, this description of a fact-finding mission insincerely suggests that Tower Hamlets, an ethnically diverse area, is too dangerous to engage with the inhabitants of this part of London face to face. Further, the deployment of an image of a borough dominated by niqab-clad women functions not only as a highlight of the sheer number of niqab wearers in London; it also aims to suggest that the ideological enemy has already crossed our gates. A fixed boundary has been drawn. Such talk of Muslim "no-go zones" in major European cities, brought up frequently by Donald Trump and his officials (Brown 2017; Kuruvilla 2018) further bolsters these false claims. As Kundnani (2009) argues, this focus on Western Muslim populations is a new development in the never-ending war on terror, originally meant to target faraway lands. Their otherness and implied susceptibility to radicalization, it is argued, requires heightened surveillance and control; these, in turn, help refocus the attention from the atrocities against civilians happening in the war zones of Iraq, Afghanistan, Syria, Yemen, and other countries.

Similarly to Geller (2016), Pearson closed off her piece by issuing moral judgment of the burka with a clichéd metaphor of the contrast between darkness and light: "Some of the worst crimes are committed under the cover of darkness. The burka allows the cover of darkness to operate in broad daylight. It has no place in a modern, equal, free society." (2017: np). The discursive association of the burka, criminality, and (moral) darkness casts all women who cover as evil; the burka is pictured here as enabling darkness in a place of light, or, in a more down-to-earth language, as an accessory to crime. This fits in very well with the clear-cut vision of the non-Western, and in particular, "Muslim" world and all its actions as un-modern, un-equal, and un-free, in contrast to the West.

Both Geller and Pearson paint a "spectacle of the burka" through a web of endlessly rehearsed negative associations, metaphors, oppositions, and silences. Importantly, the public, mentioned in Rep. Spencer's justification for his ban proposal, are now actively engaged in this spectacle of fear. Proponents of the security discourse no longer pity the veiled Muslim women. As the earlier frames of the veil are transferred into this new context of national security and resignified in a dramatic way, women who wear the niqab are increasingly seen as the fifth column, only to be feared. In this context, it is particularly important to read the last section of this chapter in which the women I interviewed narrated how these perceptions impact on their and their families' lives.

Fake Representations Discourse — "Niqab for a Day"

The niqab is a radical experience in the sense that it inevitably singles out the wearer in the West. The women who wear it often talk about the challenges they experience as a result of wearing one, most commonly the stigma that is attached to it. This involves a host of negative assumptions and reactions, from interlocutors' surprise that the wearer can speak English (which suggests that they do not expect niqabi women to come from their own cultural background, which the latter often do) to verbal and physical abuse. The fact that the women still decide to cover their faces demonstrates that they perceive the spiritual benefits that they derive from the practice to outweigh the challenges, as I demonstrate in Chapter 4. This experience puts them in a very unique position. And yet, a new journalistic genre has evolved that attempts to throw light on the "niqab experience" based on putting on a niqab for a day and then reporting on it.

The "Blackface Logic" of Niqab-for-a-Day Performances

In a day and age where performing blackface by White people has been widely denounced as racist, it appears acceptable for non-niqab wearers to "perform niqab" in order to provoke or share individual insights. John Howard Griffin, a White American writer who impersonated an African American man in the 1950s in the American South and later described his experience in a controversial book *Black Like Me* (1961), only belatedly recognized that his experiment had ultimately failed; as a White man dressed up as Black he simply never could fully comprehend the experience of African Americans living under segregation. Further, by assuming the position of a Black man, he silenced those who had a genuine experience of racism.

Greil Marcus (2013: xi) in his Foreword to Lott's *Love and Theft: Blackface Minstrelsy and the American Working Class* wrote of those who performed blackface in pre-war America thus: "White men stole the songs, speech, and gestures of American slaves or free African Americans, as they profited by turning black people into infantilized monsters of stupidity . . . some of them, like Tom Rice, trying to speak with wit and dignity not only for but as African Americans, while others, less conscious or less noble, were caught up in an always shifting drama of attraction." I argue that the "niqab-for-a day" genre could be interpreted as a modern-day cultural practice rooted in performing blackface, regardless of how well intended the articles in question are. Ultimately, they do not shift the dominant discourse about the niqab; they do, however, benefit from the "drama of attraction" at particular points in time. By taking up the voice of women who wear the niqab, and performing bogus representations, they cultivate Islamophobic attitudes in sociopolitical contexts where Islamophobia is still socially acceptable in many contexts (Grosfoguel and Mielants 2006; Nadal et al. 2012). Perhaps in order to avoid accusations of Islamophobia, outlets that publish such stories often recruit Muslim female journalists to dress up in a niqab for a day. The assumption here is that a Muslim woman is better equipped to write about other Muslim women, even if she chooses to use her own performance to represent their experiences.

Reenacting "the Oppressed"

One example of this genre is the article by Zaiba Malik in *The Guardian* (2006), published two weeks after the 2006 Jack Straw niqab controversy. The title of the piece, strangely evocative of the sensationalist style of British tabloids, is: "Zaiba Malik Wears a Niqab for a Day and Is Shocked by the Reaction of Strangers." In her piece, the author is open about her lack of familiarity with the garment itself ("I would have thought that one size fits all but it turns out I'm a size 54."). She writes:

> I look at myself in my full-length mirror. I'm horrified. I have disappeared and somebody I don't recognise is looking back at me. I cannot tell how old she is, how much she weighs, whether she has a kind or a sad face, whether she has long or short hair, whether she has any distinctive facial features at all. I've seen this person in black on the television and in newspapers, in the mountains of Afghanistan and the cities of Saudi Arabia, but she doesn't look right here, in my bedroom in a terraced house in west London.

Malik distances herself emotionally from women who wear the niqab by consigning their position to objects of televised coverage. She contrasts the familiarity and safety of her home with the otherness of faraway places, where, in her view, the niqab belongs. This is rather strange, considering that many of them live in London (Iqbal 2010), quite possibly even in her West London neighborhood.[6]

Another writer with a Muslim background, Pakistani-Canadian artist Mariam Magsi, performed a similar experiment, arguing that her "experience with performing arts and expression" qualified her to do it (Magsi 2012: np). Her narrative of her niqab experience was similar to that of Malik's, recounting one unpleasant encounter after another. Disappointingly, neither writer reflected on the fundamental difference between their and real niqab wearers' experience—eventually, they simply cast off the garment, and together with it, the stigma. While they were able to easily return to their usual privileged identities, for most niqabi women, this is not a viable option. Neither writer attempted to engage any women who wear niqab full-time, and the interactions of both during these performances were limited to their own social circles. It would be far more informative on their part to conduct an interview with a niqab wearer and share their communication privilege with those who are denied it.

The Niqab as Disappearance

The idea of "disappearing" due to the wearing of the niqab is also mobilized by Liz Jones, the author of "My Week Wearing a Burka: Just a Few Yards of Black Fabric, But It Felt Like a Prison" (2009) in the *Daily Mail*: "I caught sight of myself in a Knightsbridge store window. Instead of me staring back, I saw a dark, depressed alien. A smudge. A nothing." What is palpable in these accounts is the fear of becoming that which they only "intend to symbolize," to paraphrase Ellison who wrote about blackface performers (in Lott 2013: 25). There is a dissociation between the image these journalists saw in the mirror (with

---

[6]The mention of the author's living quarters in West London is also likely to be meaningful because the West–East divide in London, as well as in many other British cities, serves to mark out the traditionally deprived, industrial areas in the eastern sections. While recently the London East End began to gentrify in some areas, partly due to the effect of the 2012 London Olympic Games, it is East London boroughs, such as Tower Hamlets, that are still affected by poverty, unemployment, low housing quality, and high levels of crime (Benedictus 2017).

all its connotations) and their self-perception. That starting premise, the sense of horror, disgust, and disappearing inevitably shapes their subsequent accounts. The references to Saudi Arabia and Afghanistan in Malik's piece, and Somalia in Jones's, all of them political regimes where women have been forced to cover their faces are usually made to throw doubt on the idea that women in the West might independently choose to wear the face covering. In these accounts, the niqab (or "burka") is always associated with oppression.

While these pieces are created to investigate the "experience," they frame women who wear the niqab as alien. While the authors recount some instances of sexual and racist/Islamophobic harassment during their performances, they do not provide a counterpoint examining the motivations of women who choose to wear the niqab full-time despite regularly having these traumatizing experiences. Malik (2006: np) reveals the extent to which her experiment was unsuccessful in illuminating the lives of niqabis in the following paragraph: "The women I have met who have taken to wearing the niqab tell me that it gives them confidence. I find that it saps mine. Nobody has forced me to wear it but I feel like I have oppressed and isolated myself." This also suggests that she could have produced a more informative piece, as she admits she had talked to niqab wearers. Instead, the reader is likely to be confused, as the only explanation for wearing the niqab suggested in the article is signaled by the references to political regimes that oppress women who live there.

Visiting the Empire State Building in "Islamic garb"

Anette Lamothe-Ramos, a journalist writing for *Vice*, wrote: "After watching 74 YouTube videos and parsing 108 Google search pages, I couldn't find one article or video explaining if burqas were comfortable or how Americans reacted to seeing someone resembling the Grim Reaper float by them in line at Starbucks. I figured that the only way I'd really know what life was like for women who have been consigned to wear the least-revealing piece of clothing of all time was to dress up as one of them" (2012: np). Although, as stated in the title of the piece, she was not Muslim, she nevertheless suggested what a "proper burqa" was, at the same time misappropriating the term burqa: "Saudi burqas consist of five pieces and seemed much more in line with my idea of a 'proper' burqa than the Afghan version with bedazzled 'fashion sleeves.'" The photographs illustrating Lamothe-Ramos's jaunt through Manhattan, indeed, show her wearing an all-black niqab which is easier to present stereotypically than a "decorated burqa" which is vaguely evocative of regional and ethnic, but not necessarily Islamic, dress traditions (TRC Leiden, nd). Another passage in this piece references the terrorist stereotype: "So we went to [the Empire State Building]. I didn't realize the significance of visiting one of the tallest buildings in New York dressed in Islamic garb until we reached the entrance. I felt like a jerk" (2012: np). This embarrassment was quickly revealed as tongue in-cheek when she confessed what the real aim of the performance was: "When scaring tourists got boring, we decided to walk further uptown to Central Park in an attempt to bother some locals."

Some readers criticized Lamothe-Ramos for being insensitive. They complained in the comments section of the article that it promoted ignorance about Islam and Orientalist essentialism. One of them compared the provocation to a situation whereby an able-bodied person writes about wheelchair users' experiences after just one day in a wheelchair. In response, the editor of *Vice* defended the journalist's performance as an ideologically neutral act:

> She is not Muslim, and if you read the article carefully you will notice that there is hardly a mention of religion. The point was to treat these articles of clothing as any other— completely secular and devoid of higher meaning. In our view, she accomplished this.
>
> (*Vice* 2012: np)

Lamothe-Ramos clarified:

> I was in no way making any kind of statement about Muslim women or Islam. I was writing about a bunch of fabric that was sewn together to make clothing.
>
> (Lamothe-Ramos in *Vice* 2012: np)

The dubiousness of the claim that the article did not target Islam and Muslim women is suggested by the use of the term "Islamic garb" and references to Saudi Arabia and Afghanistan, both Muslim-majority countries. Furthermore, even if Islam were not explicitly mentioned, one may not simply dispose of the context in which the religious, cultural, and social act of niqab-wearing is enacted, as both Lamothe-Ramos and the *Vice* editor claim. Clothing is not neutral, as it constitutes a performance saturated with meanings and interpretations (McRobbie 2004). Any particular type of dress is no more just a "bunch of fabric that was sewn together" than a sentence is simply just a string of letters.

In these and many other similar pieces, it is surmised that the niqab-wearing experience has to be translated from a genuine into a mock one in order to be intelligible and valid. The central, religious aspect of niqab-wearing is removed from the accounts. Its obturation reduces the niqab to a stage costume: something that fits in with the perceptive limits and discursive repertoire possessed by these journalists, that is, an exotic adventure, a personal nuisance, a fancy dress, or an impediment to the full expression of the self. The articles discussed here claim to be authoritative and educational for the wider public, when in fact, only niqab wearers are in position to speak about this experience. Such work is different than, for example, the once-famous NiqaBitch performers who could not really be presumed to be Muslim (as they wore niqabs coupled with hot pants) and who later commented that by raising a controversy, their performance was meant to critique the French ban (Moors 2011).

Visual Media Representations of the Niqab

Photographs of women who wear the niqab used in journalism are an important consideration. I have argued elsewhere (Piela 2013) that women who wear the niqab are visually represented in ways that engender fear and disjointedness. This is achieved by overusing either close-up portraits (Image 1) or depressing backgrounds (Image 2). While niqabs are often black, the lack of background (which normally constitutes the social context of journalistic photography) in close-up portraits has the effect of disconnection of the subject from the surrounding world. Such striking imagery is also often used without credits or captions which increases the disembodied quality of these portrayals.

In a *Daily Mail Online* article by Bindel (2013), three portraits of women in niqab, unduly focused on their eyes and with a strange hypnotic effect, are used to illustrate her provocative argument that British feminists should speak out against the niqab (and by association, women who wear it). Another article in the *Daily Telegraph*, proclaiming that girls in British Muslim schools are forced to wear the niqab (a charge which was later debunked), is headed by a similar image (see in Barett 2010). Such close-up portraits can also be found in balanced, factual pieces such as Picheta's article (2018) reporting that the United Nations Human Rights Committee issued a statement that the French niqab ban violates human rights. The photograph shows two women wearing niqabs, but the caption clarifies who one of them is: Kenza Drider, a high-profile staunch critic of France's policy on niqab who refuses to remove her niqab.

The use of photographs where the background is visible, but bleak, has a similar effect. Sometimes the location used for the photo is dreary, as in the case of a photograph of a woman used in a piece in which Sahar Al-Faifi lays out her views on the niqab and her right to wear it (Al-Faifi 2013). While the article itself is a welcome change from the usual style of reporting and commenting, the photograph presents the woman and a distressed young child walking up a dark, flooded side street, with debris and rotten vegetables strewn around. Such a disheartening image does not illustrate Al-Faifi's point—that, essentially, she is very happy to wear the niqab. This dissonance is an example of mixed-messaging—whoever selected the photograph for the article, likely undermined her argument via visual means, regardless of their intention.

Another example, equally striking, is seen in Iqbal (2010), where the subject, Fatima Barktulla, poses with her two young sons who are wearing their school uniforms. The

Image 1 Jasmin Merdan, *Arabian Woman with Nikab and Blue Eyes*. Bosnia and Herzegovina. © Jasmin Merdan/Getty Images.

Image 2 Ozgur Donmaz, *Muslim Women in Burka*. Istanbul, Turkey. © Ozgur Donmaz/Getty Images.

Image 3 Dan Kitwood, *Eid-al-Fitr Celebrated in London*. London, United Kingdom, 2013. © Dan Kitwood/Getty Images.

sky behind them is dark, and the flashbulb used to light them provides an otherworldly light. The mother has her arms wrapped around her children protectively; they all look like apparitions. While it appears this effect was unintended, the photograph is rather menacing. None of the three individuals looks comfortable or happy, although in the article Barktulla is described as "cheery" (Iqbal 2010: np).

At the other end of the continuum, and certainly a minority of cases, are photographs where care was taken to present the women in a way that humanizes them: showing them in a variety of mundane settings, undertaking mundane tasks, and interacting with a variety of people (Images 3 to 11). These photographs, by including everyday objects, emotional states, places, and actions establish a type of temporary intimacy with the

Image 4 Riana Ambarsari Photography, *Muslim Woman in Hijab and Veil Holding Qur'an in Her Face*. Jakarta, Indonesia. © Riana Ambarsari Photography/Getty Images.

Image 5 Vince Talotta, *Zunera Ishaq*. © Vince Talotta/Getty Images.

audiences/readers who can identify themselves with these elements (Piela 2013). An example of a different presentation of a niqabi mother with her children can be found in the *New Statesman* accompanying my article (Piela 2018). This photograph demonstrates the editorial team's sensitivity to the impact of visual representations. It shows a woman in a niqab looking dotingly at her young daughter who is gazing back at her while eating candy floss (Image 3). They are relaxed and contented, sitting on a grassy bank in a park on a sunny day. There is a pink balloon with Arabic writing on it. The key elements of the photograph are similar to the one in Iqbal (2010)—niqab-wearing mother, children, outdoors—but there is a striking qualitative difference between them. The one used by the *New Statesman* is uplifting because it is mundane and relatable.

Image 6 Alexander Shcherbak, *Femininity*. Doha, Qatar. 2019. © Alexander Shcherbak/Getty Images.

Image 7 Jasmin Merdan, *Arabic Muslim Woman with Veil and Scarf Driving Car*. Riyadh, Saudi Arabia. © Jasmin Merdan/Getty Images.

In 2017, Getty Images recognized the problem of misrepresentations of Muslim women online and addressed it by setting up a partnership with *MuslimGirl.com* that resulted in the production of several stock images of Muslim women "that authentically represent Muslim women in a fresh and contemporary light" (Getty Images 2017). The problem with a diverse and positive visual representation of women who wear the niqab is symptomatic of the wider lack of diversity in stock photography databases. Platforms such as Getty have only recently turned to broadening their offerings, including collections of images of people representing different genders (including transgender people), sexualities, sizes, abilities, and skin tones (Taylor 2019 Stylus). Minority groups are also developing their own stock photography collections, creating self-representations on their own terms (Carter 2018 Forbes)

Amani Al-Khatahtbeh, founder and editor in chief of *MuslimGirl.com*, said she had feedback from journalists who said "having more image options than just 'veiled women with dark cloth' would make their jobs [writing about Muslim women] easier" (Bonazzo 2017: np). It is worth considering that veiled women "with dark cloth" also deserve a fairer, more varied representation, which is possible, as examples discussed here demonstrate. However,

Image 8 David Grossman, *United American Muslim Day Parade on Madison Avenue in New York City. Religious Traditional Bangladeshi Immigrant Women March in the Parade.* New York, 2016. © David Grossman/Getty Images.

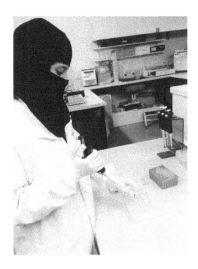

Image 9 Sahar Al-Faifi, *Sahar Al-Faifi in a Lab.* © Sahar Al-Faifi.

a search for "niqab" on the Getty Images website (2019) does not return a satisfactory variety of representations. Only a handful of photographs show them in everyday situations, with the social context around them. Perhaps there is space for another partnership? Another option is to procure photographs from Flickr.com where niqab wearers sometimes upload their self-portraits (Piela 2013). This would be a respectful way of acknowledging these women's preferences as to how they wish to be portrayed visually.

Image 10 Sahar Al-Faifi, *Sahar Al-Faifi After a Skydive*. © Sahar Al-Faifi.

Image 11 Nacho Calonge, *Demonstration Against Law Banning Use of The Niqab*. The Hague, The Netherlands, 2020. © Nacho Calonge/Getty Images.

Concluding Remarks

In this chapter, I have outlined the role played by the media in constructing, mobilizing, reproducing, and silencing of certain ideas about what the niqab means to different groups in Western societies. This introduction to the landscape of dominant frames used to make sense of the niqab has set the stage for the subsequent arguments I lay out in this book. It is important to understand the benefits that different groups of critics of the niqab derive from taking this position. The argument that the niqab is incompatible with "Western (British, American, European) culture" formulated by female politicians and commentators of Muslim heritage enables them to position themselves as "good Muslims," and/or "good immigrants," who comply with the demands of the secular state. The argument that the niqab constitutes "patriarchal oppression" formulated by secular feminists (also referred to as "governance feminists" by Halley [2006: 20–2]) bolsters their questionable claim that the West offers ultimate equality for women who are willing to reject the chains of religion. This kind of feminism wields power that ought to be contended with, writes Halley (2006: 22): "It has convinced lots of men that the 'new man' must defer to feminism on questions relating to women's welfare in sex and reproduction." Governance feminists do not only wish to represent other women on "women's issues"; as the example of the niqab ban promotion illustrates, they want to govern other women's choices by virtue of being women in positions of power, and many are convinced by this stance. Finally, the advocates of the "countering extremism" family of arguments strive to create an impression that they are effectively dealing with security threats related to religious radicalization, when in reality, they are struggling to understand the reasons for radicalization that could be operationalized into effective prevention measures. I have demonstrated the convergence of the values of paternalistic feminist and security discourses on both sides of the Atlantic in the United Kingdom and the United States. This significant overlap has "real social and political consequences," as anti-Muslim discourse circulates between national contexts, having been previously contained "behind closed doors within distinct national territories" (Marzouki 2017: 5); Marzouki demonstrates this by showing linkages between terrorist attacks in France and knee-jerk anti-Muslim acts in the United States. Similarly, Chakraborti and Zempi (2012) found that the institution of the French niqab ban was followed by a wave of attacks on veiled women in the United Kingdom.

In line with critical discourse analysis, I have highlighted the ways in which operation of various discourses about the niqab reproduces and challenges dominance, defined here as "the exercise of social power by elites, institutions or groups, that results in social inequality, including political, cultural, class, ethnic, racial and gender inequality" (Van Dijk 1993: 249–50). In my discussions of textual and visual representations of the niqab I have illuminated the operation of a particular aesthetic that works to reduce women who wear the niqab to the niqab itself, dehumanizing them as a result.

This tactic is chiefly enabled by exclusion of these women from the segment of the society allowed to speak and be heard on the experience and meaning of the niqab.

Constructed as devoid of agency and disembodied, they are prevented from narrating their own lives in public; instead, this task is undertaken by impersonators who portray their "niqab experiences" as a legitimate, representative narrative when, in fact, their accounts, wittingly or unwittingly, propagate Islamophobia. Thus, I have demonstrated how much the assumption underpinning critical discourse analysis—that "one of the social resources on which power and dominance are based is the privileged access to discourse and communication" (Van Dijk 1993: 256)—plays out in the lives of women who wear the niqab.

The analysis offered in this chapter strongly indicates that the existence of women who wear the niqab demarcates the extent of tolerance, equality, and freedom the secular-liberal polity is willing to bestow on the Other. Regardless of what they might say about their motivations and inclinations, women who adopt the religious dress, and in particular the niqab, are catapulted from the category of a "good Muslim," "liberated woman," and a "complying citizen" to that of a "bad Muslim," "oppressed woman," and a "security threat." Razack (2018: 176) aptly put this in her diagnosis of the pan-European push to ban the niqab: "The niqab is the sight we cannot bear if we are to be who we say we are." It is not surprising that most mainstream media lack subtlety in their coverage of the practice of wearing the niqab. Religious practices perceived as radical, in particular those outside of normative Christianity, and those enacted by women, rarely receive generous portrayals. "Social violence toward women is . . . enacted not only through visible social practices, but also through structures that are unconsciously incorporated into gendered historical and current social imagery, such as language." Witch-hunting manuals that decried spiritual healing practices among rural and indigenous communities, writes Yakushko (2018), were a prime example of demonization of non-Christian women's practices in the past. Representation of niqabi women in most mainstream media is a fitting modern-day example of such stigmatization.

Although Munnik (2017) argues that in the recent years, Muslim sources in news reporting have become diversified and plentiful, these developments do not apply, as yet, to Muslim women who wear the niqab. Journalists, on the whole, seem curiously unable or uninterested in seeking out niqab wearers as sources for stories about the niqab. Few such women fit in the categories of privileged "authorized knowers" or even "new entrants" who, in Munnik's study (2017), had organizational structures (although with insufficient social capital to control the news cycle) at their disposal. In addition to discussing the rare instances of niqabi women being authorized to speak out on mainstream media, Chapter 2 focuses on alternative ways of niqabi women taking control over representation on social media. It also considers responses of niqab wearers to media representations of Islam and niqab and identifies their strategies of coping with the ubiquity of Islamophobic content.

CHAPTER 2
RECLAIMING NIQABI VOICES
REFLECTIVE ENGAGEMENT WITH THE MEDIA

Positive representations of Muslims and Islam in Western mainstream media are few and far between (Imtoual 2011; Guimond 2017). Those that do exist are overshadowed by negative representations and may still be problematic. In television and cinematography, they tend to involve "good Muslims" as those aligned with particular ideals, loyalties, and beliefs; these characters are usually inserted to balance the negative character of a terrorist (Alsultany 2012). This leads to the construction of acceptable Muslim identities that cause the least discomfort to the majority population. Needless to say, women who choose to wear the niqab in the West are unlikely to be deployed in such a capacity. These projections of "feel good" Muslimness create an illusion of a post-race society and cover up institutionalized racism and Islamophobia (Alsultany 2012). This is a particularly insidious process as this new form of racism "projects antiracism and multiculturalism on the surface but simultaneously produces the logics and affects necessary to legitimize racist policies and practices" (Alsultany 2012: 16). Thus, what is intended as positive representations is transformed into "sympathetic representations" that ultimately reproduce marginalization and injustice through stereotyping.

This chapter draws from a bricolage of niqabi voices inhabiting online spaces as well as those occasionally represented in the mainstream press. It also considers participants' critical assessments of what they saw as typical niqab representations in mainstream media. In the last section of this chapter, I identify different strategies of engagement with mainstream media that the participants developed in an attempt to make sense of the prejudice directed at them. It is my intention to position this chapter as a counterbalance to the dominant exclusionary modes of writing about the niqab critiqued in Chapter 1.[1]

---

[1]More alternative cultural texts such as graphic novels also struggle with the creation of realistic, complex Muslim characters. This challenge may be observed in the character development of Dust, one of the mutants in *X-Men*, who was introduced to the universe of Marvel comics less than a year after 9/11. Dust's real name is Sooraya Qadir; she is a sixteen-year-old refugee from Afghanistan who attends the Mutant school. Dust is arguably one of the rare positive and powerful portrayals of Muslim women who wear the niqab in American popular culture (Davis and Westerfelhaus 2013), but criticisms were directed at sexualized versions of her clothing (she wore a niqab, but her dress was often shown as form-fitting and shape-revealing) (Pierpoint 2018), and questionable storylines (Dar 2008). Many young Muslim women appreciate Dust's powerful performance, even if her costume does not always reflect Islamic modesty norms embraced by more conservative believers; a young Muslim artist from Boston was so invested in Dust's representation that she designed some new, street-fashion inspired clothes for her that were less revealing (Pierpoint 2018). Ostensibly, even a sci-fi genre cannot accommodate a female character whose body is entirely concealed, as would be the case if Dust's "niqab-style" mutant costume was more in line with Islamic modesty norms.

Niqabi-inclusive Framing in Mainstream Media

This section focuses on five pieces in the mainstream British and American press either written by niqab-wearing women or engaging them as sources. I examine both the subject matter of these writings as well as their stylistic and rhetorical aspects, identifying to what extent their agendas, as presented in the pieces, are shaped by current affairs, structural challenges, as well as their personal experiences and beliefs. The examined content reflects many principles of "inclusive journalism" (Rupar 2017: 419). Such an approach allows journalists to respond to social inequalities; the objective of inclusive journalism is to "develop inclusive communicative competence to enable reflective thinking, experience of social, political and cultural pluralism, and recognition of otherness and critical stand towards the process of constructing identities" (Rupar 2017: 419). In other words, inclusive journalism shows that there are different communities, groups, and individuals who may have their own perspectives on issues that we thought were common sense and obvious. It also puts into practice the phrase "nothing about us without us," adopted by many marginalized groups, for example, Roma communities in Europe (Ryder, Rostas, and Taba 2014) and disability rights advocates in North America (Scotch 2009).

Niqabi Women as Story Sources

Hendrix (2011) wrote in the *Washington Post* about four niqabi women, but one of them, Safiyyah Abdullah, is central in the article. She is described as a social science researcher living in Washington D.C., a convert who embraced Islam in the seventies. Inevitably, as the story unfolds, it reveals the often-challenging reality of living in the United States while fully veiled. Hendrix reports that for Safiyyah Abdullah, "daily outings have been a mix of harassment and compassion, comfort and alienation." Two typically "risky spaces" are mentioned, a subway line and the airport. Abdullah is also described as a "stereotype buster," but little personal information about her is shared here, other than that she has blue eyes and a Chicago accent, writes poetry, likes Thai food, and enjoys going to Cheesecake Factory. The reference to this popular chain restaurant is poignant; Abdullah's Otherness is mitigated in the article by her consumption habits that emphasize her American identity, long ritualized through food (McGovern 2006). Other women who are mentioned are a jewelry designer and a nurse; the former explained that she had adopted the niqab in order to better manage interactions with men, while the latter said she had had to transition from a hospital-based job to being a Muslim-run homeless shelter manager due to being face-veiled. Both are converts, like Abdullah.

Interestingly, religion as a practice or belief does not appear to be mentioned much in the article in relation to the women described in the article. It is invoked, however, in the last paragraph, where Asra Nomani, a non-niqab-wearer and a Muslim activist, is quoted. "You'd be hard-pressed to find many native-born Muslims who wear niqab," said Nomani, who would support a ban on religious face coverings here. "It's been mostly accepted within Islam that women are not required to wear the veil. Even these women who adopt the veil voluntarily are promoting a hard-line ideology" (in Hendrix 2011: np).

This article is certainly unusual as it attempts to construct a normalized subject who wears the niqab, but the quote at the closing of the article presents three problems. First, it changes the tone of this largely factual article to negative based on someone's personal opinion about the niqab (it is also mentioned in the article that Nomani would support a face-veil ban in the United States). While the author may have sought an opinion like hers to make the article more balanced, this quote would require more commentary to situate it. As it is, it gives off the impression of being the "final word." Furthermore, it introduces a rift between converts and born Muslims, implying that converts are somehow less discerning in embracing some practices that, like the niqab, are seen as conservative. The niqab is constructed as something less authentic that born Muslims do not practice. Finally, it pigeonholes niqabi women ideologically, even though none of the three women mentioned in this section appear to be "hard-liners," and as this book demonstrates, the niqab usually reflects just one of its wearers' many identities.

Another article in the American press about a woman who wears the niqab that uses inclusive framing is by Lorraine Ali (2010). It was published in *The New York Times*. The central character of the story, Hebah Ahmed, is a born Muslim (belying Asra Nomani's statement cited earlier), an American-born daughter of immigrants from Egypt. Similar to women in the other article, she is described as a confident, outspoken, and educated woman who made the choice to wear the niqab, independently. The article goes into some depth to describe the challenges she experienced, in terms of both harassment and practicalities of life in a niqab. Being born and raised in the United States suddenly paled into insignificance for non-Muslim people around her after 9/11, and she described having to face suspicion and resentment especially after she adopted religious dress. She is portrayed as having a good sense of humor, and, at times, as being quite emotional. The author of the article goes into more depth unpacking Ahmed's and other interviewees' motivations behind the adoption of the niqab. There were some "secular" considerations, namely sexual harassment in the workplace, but Hebah Ahmed said that the main reason for wearing the niqab was religious. She described this practice as a test which she willingly took.

In the United Kingdom, Nosheen Iqbal (2010) interviewed several niqabis for her article about the practice of face covering becoming apparently more commonplace in London. The article, published in the *London Evening Standard*, a free daily title evaluated as representing centre-right bias (Media Bias Fact Check, nd), quoted Fatima Barktulla and Amoola Ismail who wear the niqab. Barktulla, similar to Ahmed, underscores the effect of wearing the niqab which makes her feel close to God. It is not, contrary to stereotypes, a rejection of society or a political statement. Iqbal situated her article more locally, linking it to controversies related to the niqab which emerged in London at the time—here specifically, she touched on the uproar caused by Muslim secondary school students who wore the niqab to and from school in three Islamic educational institutions. This was later spun by right-wing media as a policy of obligatory niqab at school (see Barrett 2010).

Both Barktulla and Ismail emphasized that they wore the niqab of their own accord, mindful that the charge leveled against niqab wearers in the West is that they are forced into it. Ismail is quoted as saying, "The irony is that when people get hot and bothered about Islam and criticise it for oppressing women and forcing them to cover up, they forget that removing any woman's individual right to choose makes them oppressors too" (in Iqbal 2010: np). Barktulla also responded to a charge she hears often that she should move back to an Islamic country, pinpointing the racism undergirding such comments: "It doesn't contradict my being British either. I love this country—it's my home. Mine and my husband's parents come from India but it's alien to us. People ask whether we wouldn't be better off living in an Islamic country, but it's only because we're brown-skinned and not part of the indigenous population. What would you say to the White English convert whose family has been here for centuries? Where would they go?"

These examples demonstrate that it is possible to discuss the practice of face-veiling with empathy, in a manner that does not dehumanize the subject. Instead, by engaging with them as knowledgeable subjects who can expertly and eloquently comment on their experiences, these articles reframe their representation. It is fundamentally important that in future news cycles that involve the niqab, more content of this kind balances out work that excludes niqab-wearing women from mainstream media platforms.

Women Who Wear the Niqab as Mainstream Media Content Authors

Sahar Al-Faifi, as of 2020, is a molecular geneticist, a Plaid Cymru[2] member and a regional manager for the Muslim-lobbying organization MEND. A high-profile anti-Islamophobia activist, she presented her views in a piece titled "I wear the niqab, let me speak on my own behalf" (Al-Faifi 2013) in *The Independent*, a liberal British broadsheet. She is a rare example of a niqab wearer who gained access to a mainstream media outlet to write, rather than just commenting as a source. In her article, she made three points regarding the niqab: that niqab wearers' voices were missing from the debate about the niqab, that the topic is given much more attention than is necessary, and that she was an educated, independent person who made her own decisions about her attire. She positioned herself as a responsible Welsh and British citizen who is an active community organizer, and is therefore able to see that niqab controversies are used by those in power to divert attention

---

[2]Plaid Cymru is a social-democratic and democratic socialist political party in Wales advocating Welsh independence from the United Kingdom. Al-Faifi has launched her bid to run for Plaid Cymru in the 2021 Welsh Assembly elections. If she is successful, she will be not only the first niqabi, but also the first Muslim woman Welsh Assembly Member (Gu 2020).

from the real problems plaguing Britain: "institutional racism, unemployment, affordable housing and growing inequality" (2013: np). Al-Faifi's piece is clearly structured to address the usual charges aimed at the niqab. She tried to balance the main thrust of her narrative, framed in religious terms, with secular reasoning. In the following extract, she connected the niqab to practicing Islam, but she mentioned the fact, perhaps not known to many non-Muslims, that Islam recognized prophets of Judaism and Christianity, and venerated Jesus as a prophet. Further, she connected Islamic beliefs to modern-day concerns, such as protection of the natural environment, again, an unusual association in the common imaginary of Islam. Thus, she attempted to "domesticate" the aspects of Islam which are seen as controversial, such as radical modesty:

I wear the niqab as a personal act of worship, and I deeply believe that it brings me closer to God, the Creator. . . . To understand the niqab it helps to understand the religion behind it. Islam has three simple messages—liberation from worshipping anything but the one God, following in the way of His Prophets including Moses, Jesus and Muhammad, and servitude to the whole of humanity. Islam's practical acts of liberation are many—from the duty of environmentalism (protecting "the Creation" from the "excessiveness" of humankind) to the imperative of modesty for women and men—one part of which is the face-veil.

(Al-Faifi 2013: np)

In the following extract of her piece, she mobilizes two rhetorical devices: the discourse of rights and freedoms understood as central to the organization of the civic society, and, grammatically, the plural first person ("we," "our"). As a result, she indicates that she is part of the British society and is entitled to enjoy these rights along with everyone else:

In Britain, public freedom is a part of the fabric of our society. Those public freedoms extend to religious freedoms that give us the right to practice and articulate our religious freedoms and rights. We cannot take this public freedom for granted for the sake of social scares, deep-seated psychological fears, ignorance and fear of the unknown.

(Al-Faifi 2013: np)

This blending of discourses reflects an understanding that successful reasoning entails building a degree of commonality with the audience. Further, Al-Faifi recognizes that by the virtue of speaking up, she may establish her position as a "knowing subject" (Foucault 1981) who produces "counter-knowledges" (Foucault 1980). She writes: "Indeed, Muslim women too must raise their heads, speak on behalf of themselves and platforms should be given to them" (Al-Faifi 2013: np).

Another rare piece written by a niqabi appeared in *The Guardian* series "What I'm really thinking," where people anonymously share their reflections about their unusual circumstances (The Guardian 2011). The niqabi sets the stage for her reflection by briefly mentioning that she decided to wear the niqab to "express her faith," without delving into theological issues. Her piece is, rather, meant to address common assumptions about the niqab and Islam. She challenges the positive perception of British people as universally polite, commenting how British good manners don't extend to her in public: "thank you's are rare, and being ignored when waiting to be served in a shop is common, too" (The Guardian 2011: np). It is her faith that prevents her from retaliating to the hostility she experiences in public, she writes; her introducing the notion of Islamically motivated techniques of self-control challenges the stereotype of this religion as barbaric and aggressive. Next, she undermines the belief that niqabi women are forced by their husbands to cover; she asserts her independence by noting that on the contrary, her husband sometimes asks her to discard the niqab, and that she ignores this request. Finishing on a lighter note, she jokes that covering her face protects her from premature aging. This is a rhetorical device that signals "I'm really not unlike you," as it highlights an ostensibly shared concern with other women who engage in skin care regimes to maintain their youthful looks. While inconsistent with the discourse that promotes the niqab as a tool that helps refocus the wearer from outer to inner beauty, this register switch could be read as an attempt to rationalize the choice to wear the niqab for secular audiences.

It is notable that four of the five pieces discussed here were written in 2010 and 2011, briefly preceding or following the introduction of the first two "burka bans" in Europe (in Belgium and France) that prompted a wave of interest in the niqab. Al-Faifi's article is from September 2013, during another niqab controversy. Certainly, the controversies have not disappeared, but mainstream media are still not a space where inclusive and positive representations of niqab wearers can be easily found. Access of niqab-wearing women to traditional media platforms continues to be restricted, therefore they can usually only influence narratives produced in print and broadcast media in limited ways that fit in with the dominant frames prescribed for them. They are conditionally included during niqab controversies and subsequently often drowned out by niqab detractors.

Inclusion of niqabi women as sources in stories framed by niqab controversies is the necessary first step to improve the disappointing track record of reporting on this topic. However, in order to represent niqabi women fairly, news and feature writing should go beyond the niqab controversy framing (inherent in the timing of coverage and forcing dominant agendas on stories and their subjects) and incorporate frames that portray niqab-wearing women as women who perform a variety of extraordinary or ordinary roles and happen to wear a niqab, which could potentially generate interest beyond a single news cycle of a niqab controversy.

Niqabi Voices and Agendas on Social Media

Hashtag Activism

Niqab wearers are active on all social media platforms. They produce various kinds of content, both religious and non-religious in character. Twitter in particular is lauded for its capacity to support organizing around causes, famously during the Arab Spring (Newsom and Lengel 2012), and, more recently, during the #mosquemetoo (denouncing sexual violence in religious institutions, founded by Mona Eltantawy; Eltantawy 2018), and #MuslimWomensDay campaigns (Pennington 2018). The important feature of such hashtag activism is related to the ability to talk back to those in authority.

To illustrate this affordance in a relevant context, here I refer to one such moment when a hashtag campaign (#DressCodePM) challenged the then Canadian prime minister Stephen Harper's statement that "the niqab is rooted in a culture that is anti-women." This comment, made on March 12, 2015, fueled the controversy sparked earlier by Zunera Ishaq's legal challenge to a ban on niqab during Canadian citizenship ceremonies (Thamin 2016: 79). Harper also attributed the opposition to the niqab to all Canadians, including "moderate Muslims" (Thamin 2016: 80–1). These remarks understandably caused an uproar across Canada. #DressCodePM was started by a *Globe and Mail* journalist Thabatha Southey who mockingly asked Harper for approval of her choice of clothing that day, adding the hashtag. The hashtag became wildly popular in Canada, trending over the next two days in 17,000 tweets and reaching 1.5 million Twitter users (Thamin 2016). Importantly, the hashtag was picked up by the main Canadian media outlets which have large followings, thus popularizing the issue among a wide section of the Canadian society. To examine the potential impact of the hashtag on mainstream reporting, Thamin (2016) analyzed differences in reporting on the controversy between news reports and other pieces that did not mention #DressCodePM and those that did. She contextualized her findings by conducting additional archival research of 136 articles about the niqab with a connection to Canada which appeared in one of the largest Canadian daily newspapers *The Globe and Mail* between 1977 and 2015. She found that a total of two (!) articles quoted a woman who wore the niqab (Thamin 2016).

Having examined *The Globe and Mail* stories that followed Harper's statement, Thamin (2016) found that the stories without a reference to the hashtag overwhelmingly quoted White male politicians (only one, non-niqabi Muslim woman was quoted by stories in this data corpus). This is reminiscent of scientific, political, and media "manels" (all-male, usually White panels) discussing a wide range of women's issues and often ridiculed by feminists (Chcruiyot 2019; Särmä 2019; Rubin 2019). The stories that framed the story with the #DressCodePM Twitter reactions mainly quoted "ordinary" non-Muslim people, but tweets from Muslim women were the main sources for stories by *Maclean's* (a general interest news magazine) and the Canadian Broadcasting Corporation (CBC). Disappointingly, however, the only Canadian niqabi woman who retweeted the hashtag was featured in a news story in the United States, but not Canada. While the absence of niqabi sources was still an issue in that corpus, the hashtag seems to have opened up the stories for ordinary Canadians, including Muslim women, for comment. The niqabi voices were eventually included: a few days later, another newspaper, the *Toronto Star*, published a story that brought into focus a report commissioned by the Canadian Council of Muslim Women titled "Women in Niqab Speak" (Clarke 2013) which surveyed Canadian women who wear the niqab (Thamin 2016). Then, the *Toronto Star* published an opinion piece by Zunera Ishaq titled "Why I Intend to Wear a Niqab at

My Citizenship Ceremony"; three niqabi women were interviewed by the CBC radio and another one wrote a piece for an online magazine. Using the terminology of the gatekeeping theory (Shoemaker 1991), the power dynamics between the gatekeepers (the mainstream media) and the gated (the ordinary stakeholders in the stories, especially Muslim women) significantly shifted. Thamin (2016: 101) quoted a media executive whose reaction to these new perspectives in the mainstream was one of amazement: "these glimpses [of niqabi voices] are revelatory. They destroy every single assumption I made, in my ignorance, about niqabis." It is certainly disappointing that it took a Twitter hashtag intervention to balance the field by inviting niqabi women to comment on stories in which they were central stakeholders as those affected by legislation and disrespectful remarks. Thamin (2016) suggests that up until the hashtag trended, showing a large amount of public support for women's right to wear the niqab, journalists may have considered niqabi voices as "deviant," hence not qualified to be represented. As soon as media users defied the boundaries set for this questionable debate, more ordinary users became legitimate discussants.

Thamin's analysis of this fairly discrete media event in Canada throws some light on the logic of niqab representation that operates in the United Kingdom, and in the United States as well. Arguably, it was possible to include niqabi voices in mainstream media only after their cause was taken up by non-Muslim Canadians through the circulation of the hashtag; niqabi women were allowed to speak only after seemingly everyone else had had their share of the media attention pie, in this case after the hashtag stopped trending. Despite these problematic aspects of the entire process, a quick look through *The Globe and Mail* stories published around the time of passing legislation restricting the wearing of niqab[3] in the Canadian province of Quebec in 2017 and 2019 suggests that women who wear the niqab enjoy a more pronounced role as sources than before #DressCodePM. For example, in a first-person account titled "What it's like to wear the niqab in (not so tolerant) Canada," Riza Khamal (2019) talks about her experience of wearing the niqab. In another story (published on December 21, 2019), Fatima Ahmad, a student at McGill University who was part of the successful legal challenge to Bill 62, comments, "I feel like a second-class citizen with limited rights. I feel increasingly un-Canadian," in response to the passing of Bill 21 (in Youssef 2019). A video presenting the story of Aima Warriach, a feminist niqabi, was published on *The Globe and Mail* website on October 27, 2017, ten days after the passing of Bill 62 (*The Globe and Mail 2019*).

All this suggests that while there is a lot of resistance to widening the "circle of legitimate debate" (Thamin 2016: 132), social media users are able to effect change through a concerted effort at "talking back" to those in power. The Canadian example shows that while inviting niqabis to be sources in stories where they are the central subject is a necessary first step, there is still scope for improvement. Paradoxically, in order to

---

[3]Bill 62 which banned the wearing of face coverings while using public services, passed on October 18, 2017, and Bill 21 which banned the wearing of religious symbols including the niqab and hijab by public servants, passed on June 16, 2019.

achieve a degree of fair reporting about this group, the reactive "niqab framing," that is, reporting on niqabis only in response to niqab controversies caused by racist legislation or politicians' remarks, must be replaced with other frames that recognize and celebrate other aspects of niqabi women's identities: as citizens and residents who give back to their communities through charity work; as teachers, nurses, writers, entrepreneurs, and mothers,[4] and as women who are not constantly involved in tussles with legislators about their freedoms. This would require the recognition that women who wear the niqab may be of interest to audiences for reasons other than their niqab. Given the media's critical role in creating a discursive public sphere, truly positive representations should tell stories about multidimensional individuals whose trajectories are informed by complex backgrounds, talents, personalities, contexts, and relationships.

Niqabi Self-Representations on Social Media

This section examines ways in which niqab-wearing women engage with, respond to, and challenge hegemonic representations of niqab wearers on photo-sharing sites, text-based discussion forums, blogs, and other online spaces. The existing literature has not, so far, amply addressed niqab-wearing women's efforts aimed at situating their pious lifestyles online, although some of them are active on social media, commenting on a wide range of social and political issues. Instead, academic study of niqabi women's voices on social media is focused on non-organized women who are not involved in prominent activism. For instance, Nisa (2013) has looked at the use of the internet among local niqab-wearing, mostly Salafi, Indonesian women and found that they create and maintain digital subcultures of piety and run online businesses, which enables them to engage in "pious projects of self-shaping and learning" (2013: 251). My earlier work (Piela 2015 and 2018) detailed the role of Islamic online communities of learning for converts who are preparing to adopt the niqab, and the discussions about niqab wearers' self-portraits that demystify the niqab and its implications on secular digital forums.

As noted in Chapter 1, typical journalistic representations of niqab-wearing women involve a particular composition, most notably a focus on the eyes, with a simultaneous loss of a silhouette achieved through the merging of the subject's body with others (when representing a group) or the background. The result is frequently a photograph of a dehumanized entity that signifies niqabis as a "silent mass." This is further compounded by the color scheme of these photographs which often relies on the color black, with the frame dominated by a black niqab worn by the subject. She is often shown in poses that suggest aggression or invoke alarming associations (Caetano 2006). The lighting of the scene has an alarming quality, while the background, where applicable, involves settings

---

[4]See, for example, professional websites of three women who wear the niqab: two Young Adult Fiction writers, Na'ima Robert (Robert, nd) and Hafsah Faizal (Faizal, nd), as well as the activist and geneticist Sahar Al-Faifi (Al-Faifi, nd), who strike a delicate balance between mobilizing their religious identity in their brands, while focusing chiefly on their creative work.

that mobilize associations with poverty, terrorism, and foreign lands. Such images may engender fear and resentment in the viewer, and it is telling that in my examination of the niqabosphere I never encountered any instances of the use of such images by actual niqab-wearing women, for example, as profile pictures. Zainab bint Younous, a niqabi known on social media as the "Salafi Feminist," criticized the use of stock photographs of niqabi women for decontextualizing them and not showing them interacting with others, which causes an impression of alienation and one-dimensionality (Peterson 2016).

The photostreams which I analyzed in my previous work (Piela 2013) included images of niqab wearers which could be construed as an all-encompassing challenge to this style of representation. Although silhouettes of the photographers in these self-portraits did not accentuate feminine body traits (for example, the waist), they never left any doubt that they were human, female silhouettes. Most self-portraits included entire silhouettes, as one of the women commented, to show that she was "correctly covered." The outfits presented in the photographs demonstrated varied styles and colors, for example, one of the women created 167 self-portraits, each of them using a different set of garments, over the four years of her account's operation. The colors she favored were beige, green, and brown. The poses communicated relaxation and openness. The subjects were often shown sitting back in an armchair or studying their reflection in a mirror. This was compounded by muted light, which helped create serene, almost lyrical scenes. Finally, the background of the self-portraits involved bedrooms, hallways, and kitchens. Such private, household settings allow for a different type of photograph representing niqabis—mainstream journalistic imaging almost without exception shows women in public, urban settings, or, indeed, as completely decontextualized. The simplicity of these domestic backdrops in the analyzed photostreams kept the attention on the subjects, but simultaneously communicated intimacy and authenticity. As Petersen (2016) argues, famous Muslim YouTube personalities Amenakin and Dina Tokio also achieve an aura of authenticity by using domestic backgrounds in their Islamic lifestyle videos. Overall, the self-portraits I analyzed (2013) demystify the niqab's aesthetic styles while remaining firmly within the Islamic parameters of modesty adopted by the authors. Notably, the features of these styles—composure, intimacy, and attention to artistic aspects of the work—so different from the alarming and alienating associations evoked by mainstream photographic representations of niqab-wearing women, attract diverse audiences and facilitate a form of dialogue between the photographers and the viewers (Piela 2018).

Interactions with Social Media Publics

Other social media facilitate dialogue with niqabis even more effectively: one such example is the r/IAmA subreddit, a space where individuals can be asked questions by other Reddit users. The r/IAmA tagline reads: "I Am A, where the mundane becomes fascinating and the outrageous suddenly seems normal" (Reddit 2011). In August 2011, user "niqabi" (an American Caucasian convert in her twenties living on the West Coast) participated in a lengthy thread where over a 100 other users asked her about her life as a niqabi, sometimes in a respectful manner, at other times confrontationally. For example, user Ronoh posted: "Very interesting and unusual AMA, thanks for sharing your views! These are some of my questions . . ." Even the less friendly interactions were, generally, somewhat civil: "Can you explain why you think that the best way to show that a woman can focus people's attention on her intelligence and integrity is by covering up her face? To be totally honest with you I think it is a stretched justification for something that is a pretty backwards practice. Sorry if that offends you" (user Turkmenitron). Most questions pertained to her religious beliefs and practices, relationships, sexual life, career aspirations, mechanics of wearing the niqab, and her perceptions of non-Muslims, LGBTQ people, and terrorism. She patiently explained the basics of Islam to those unfamiliar with it, and engaged in advanced theological discussions with others. Some users mentioned that the thread inspired them to read more about Islam elsewhere. In other cases, the thread became multidirectional, as other users cleared up misconceptions about Islam present in some questions; when a (now deleted) user asked, "How do you feel that there have been thousands of prophets and gods, how do you know your doctrine is right and that all of those thousands of other people are wrong?", user exiledsnake explained how Islam venerates prophets mentioned in the Bible as well as Jesus.

These examples demonstrate that social media spaces may facilitate resistance to dominant discourses about the niqab and Islam and construction of women's own expressions of religiosity. Furthermore, they act as "educators in diversity" who educate members of the public about their understandings of Islam. As the Reddit thread shows, sometimes they act in collaboration with others in spaces that, contrary to closed Facebook groups, are more volatile and unpredictable, but with larger audiences that may be unfamiliar with Islam. Consequently, these actions disrupt the normalized associations of the niqab with passivity, hostility, and otherness.

It would be problematic, however, to assume that the ostensible freedom of expression online creates a natural setting for non-mainstream religious identities. Sometimes, it may be unclear what constitutes non-mainstream narratives anyway—it depends on where we locate the notion of "mainstream." In the case of the women who wear the niqab, non-mainstream narratives could focus on piety-motivated niqab adoption that contradicts mainstream Western perceptions of the "oppressed" niqabi; women's religious authority that contests mainstream views of hierarchically structured religion in which male perspectives continue to be the authorized ones; non-typical concerns and alliances; and finally, the formulation of religious practice, which brings together theologies commonly perceived as incompatible—another emanation of non-mainstreaming. Some narratives combine all these elements and underpin the production of hybrid identities.

Hybrid Identities

Peterson (2016) examined the profile of Zainab bint Younous, a Canadian niqabi who is known as the "Salafi Feminist." This label catches the eye as it juxtaposes two identities not usually considered together. Zainab and other like-minded niqabis[5] "use these labels and their hybrid aesthetic styles to create what Zainab calls a 'visual shock' that works against stereotypes and assumptions. Through creative projects that circulate in digital spaces, these women confrontationally present their identities as Muslim women who are proud of their religious and cultural backgrounds but who also hold interests in popular culture and styles outside of their religion." The Salafi Feminist is a member of a discernible online community of niqabi women who elude reductions to their religion or dress by shifting the self-representation focus to their other interests and activities that often (but not always) become professional enterprises. They curate them in a manner that enables the reading of their profiles as those of writers, poets, educators, activists, fabric artists, and entrepreneurs, who, paraphrasing Myriam François-Cerrah, are good at what they do *and* happen to be Muslim niqabi women, which informs their views in a really interesting way (Ahmed 2019: 94). Although this seems to be a commonsensical observation, it is revolutionary in the context of how Muslim women are reduced to their gender and religious identities,[6] with other aspects of their selfhood erased (Peterson 2016 and 2020). Peterson (2016: 175) considers the Salafi Feminist and her peers through the prism of queer theory (Ahmed 2014) and assemblage theory (Puar 2007), concluding that these bodies of knowledge speak to Salafi Feminist's "refusal to be boxed into categories" and becoming a "willful subject." In her case, creating her alternative spaces, such as interconnected social media locations, is evocative of queer reorientations from normative spaces to new paths and dwellings (Ahmed in Peterson 2016). This is also evident in Salafi Feminists' breaking down or queering of simplistic dichotomies involving the face veil. In an interview with Peterson (2016: 184), she said:

I don't feel compelled to fit anyone's idea of who I should be. And I've actually gotten flack for that from fellow Muslims. Like they'll say, "A good Muslim woman, especially one with a niqab, should be conducting themselves with modesty." But I'm like, "What about me isn't modest?" They say, "Well, you're loud, or you laugh too much, or you talk too loudly, or you're too aggressive." I write a lot in my Facebook posts about the double standards in our community. They say, "Well, if you were really a modest woman, you wouldn't speak like this. You would be soft-spoken and demure." Like, "Are you kidding? Have you even met me?! Because, no that's not who I am."

The Salafi Feminist is aware that this positioning may prevent alliances with people who are comfortable in normative categories. Commenting on the perceived disconnect between Salafism and feminism, she said: "[S]ome Salafists would say this is really bad.

---

[5]For a discussion of an online profile of an American woman who wears the niqab, see Piela (forthcoming).
[6]To capture this phenomeneon, cooke (2008) coined the term "Muslimwoman," which draws from the term "blackwoman" (Martin 1993). Both are based on the ubiquitous conflation of gender and religious or racial identities.

And a feminist would be like, oh my God, how can you be an orthodox Muslim woman? Your entire religion is about oppressing women." However, she appears to relish the controversy as demonstrated by one of her blog post that reads "[I'm] someone who just likes to see everyone get their knickers in a knot when they see the words 'Salafi' and 'feminist' put together" (Peterson 2016: 185–6).

Examining a multiplatform self-presentation of another niqabi, Rivka Sajida (Piela, forthcoming), I identified similar narratives that deconstructed binaries based on presumably incompatible identities. Here, Rivka Sajida openly stated that she literally identified as a queer, feminist, Salafi-Sufi Muslim. Her identity and theological bricolage, as illustrated below in an extract from her blog, implies that traditional theological boundaries may not always apply:

I consider myself a Queer, Feminist Theologian with major Orthodox leanings. My Islamic theology looks to be a mix of Salafism and Sufism, and my ideas are out-of-the-box when it comes to Queer application of theology within Islam and Abrahamic religions as a whole.

(Rivka Sajida 2016)

Even though such a combination of identities is likely to be exceedingly rare, this deconstruction of boundaries, and consequently of academic typologies of progressive versus conservative Muslims has been noted by Zebiri (2008) in her study of British converts to Islam. Zebiri wrote about an "idiosyncratic mosaic" (2008: 252) of converts' views where depending on the issue, one person's opinions could be simultaneously conservative and progressive. This may also be bolstered by the fact that converts do not have their parents' religious communities to contend with, and are free to simultaneously draw from, or even adhere to, different theological traditions. I observed the same phenomenon in my earlier work (Piela 2012) on theological positions that emerged from interpretive discussions of Muslim women in online groups. Rivka Sajida's example demonstrates that the intensity of religious practice, often ascribed to converts as "the zeal of the converted" (Zebiri 2008: 39) does not necessarily have to be directed through orthodoxy. The intensity may translate into a radical project of self-discovery, with Islam functioning as a language for it, and hypermediated religious spaces (Evolvi 2018), characterized by a high degree of liminality where alternative discourses engage the mainstream ones, operating as a safe space to experiment with it.

Rivka Sajida's non-mainstream narratives manifest themselves in her content as she orients to various axes that shape her life (Piela, forthcoming). She cultivates her identity as a scholar of Islam through introducing herself as an alumna of a BA in comparative studies program and student on an MSc in Islamic theology program. Through this, she emphasizes her religious authority which she then deploys in the Deen Talk! video series on her YouTube channel. Secondly, her experience of disability and religious expertise situate her as a powerful advocate for other Muslims living with disabilities. Comments under her videos indicate that she successfully manages to raise awareness related to disability. Simultaneously, Rivka Sajida's other videos—reviews of Islamic clothing and halal cosmetics, also embedded on her blog—are performing a different role, one that shows that she responds to the needs and interests of her target audiences (Khamis et al. 2016: 6). While none of her videos speak specifically to her experiences as a Jewish convert to Islam, she makes references to her Jewishness in passing in her content to highlight that there is no conflict between her ethnic background and faith. By juxtaposing her wide array of identities across different platforms she constructs a complex personal brand; the appeal of her profile is based on a multilayered "public identity which is responsive to the needs and interests of her target audiences" (Khamis et al. 2016: 191). What is striking about her narrative is that very rarely does she address the niqab as a discrete topic. It is almost always present in her content, but positioned dialogically with other aspects of her identity, for example, related to disability, ethnic background, or feminism. Whether that is intended or not, it has a "humanizing" effect on the niqab she wears; it is demystified by Rivka Sajida's ordinary concerns and mechanics of everyday life.

Responding to Current Affairs

Social media provide ample space for criticism of political decision-making that affects Muslim women (Evolvi 2019). During the 2020 coronavirus pandemic discourses that were mobilized on "Muslim Twitter,"[7] and a variety of other Islam-oriented social media spaces focused on notions of modesty, covering, protection, purity (ritual and symbolic), patriarchy, Islamophobia, and health. Niqabi women created, distributed, and commented on memes in their online groups and on their profiles. Some of those (anonymous) memes and taglines were humorous, referencing the niqab along with the ritual washing and prayer prostrations: "Wait a minute! Coronavirus has people covering ther [sic] faces like a niqab, washing ther [sic] bodies like wudu, what next—doing 5 light exercises a day? LOL." Such memes could be interpreted as jocular advocacy of the religious Muslim lifestyle whose emphasis on purity and cleanliness resonated strongly with the public health recommendations such as frequent and thorough hand washing.

Inevitably, many tweets sent in that period drew parallels between the niqab and the protective equipment (PPE), both of which cover the nose and mouth. Some argued that the mass adoption of protective masks highlighted the hypocrisy of the arguments that the niqab was offensive to secular sensibilities or posed a security threat by hiding the identity of the wearer (both of which are analyzed in Chapter 1). Islam (2020) tweeted: "And here I was told that covering your face was objectively offensive and a security threat," with a reposting of a BBC News headline "Paris Fashion Week: Facemasks on show amid coronavirus concern" (BBC News 2020). This disjuncture was also noted by other, non-Muslim Twitter users. A Canadian user tweeted, addressing people who police others' mask adoption practices: "If you're gonna fight with others about masks

---

[7]Paraphrasing Meredith Clark's definition of "Black Twitter" (in Reid 2018: nd), I consider "Muslim Twitter" to be a network of culturally connected communicators using the platform to draw attention to issues of concern among Muslim communities. Black and Muslim Twitters often overlap in terms of shared content, hashtags, and active posters.

and face coverings in Canada, please situate it in context. We're a country that outlawed face coverings at protests and is constantly targeting Muslim women who wear hijab or niqab" (Lalonde 2020).

As the pandemic progressed and more and more cities across the United States locally enforced a form of face covering, niqabis worldwide retweeted these announcements with their own comments. Quoting a tweet by a Reuters reporter Brad Heath about face covering becoming obligatory in Laredo, TX (Heath 2020), @BikerNiqabi commented on April 2: "Did they . . . just make niqab *fardh* [obligatory]?" (Biker Niqabi 2020). Memes presenting niqab- and PPE-clad women side by side became a discrete meme category. They came with taglines that mobilized very different discourses. Some simply expressed a need for respecting women who cover their faces and who are targets of abuse. One such meme read: "People suddenly looking at niqabi sisters with a new sense of respect" (Allah. is.the.most.merciful1 2020). However, the normativity implicit in some juxtapositions of niqabis and female health workers in PPE gear was criticized. Reposting such an image tagged with a statement: "Mercy of Allah: Islam—Lifetime protection vs Wrath of Allah: Emergency protection," a Twitter user (presumably a niqabi, as her profile photo suggests) wrote: "This is a typical message from patriarchal Muslim men. That somehow #hijab and #niqab protect us. If that's the case, then why do fully covered women still get sexually assaulted? Why does this happen even on #Hajj?" (Sapphire 2020). This tweet is reminiscent of the iconic photograph portraying an Arab Spring protester known as the #bluebragirl being disrobed and beaten up by Egyptian military; the abaya she was wearing did not protect her from violence either (Amaria 2011). Such a critique challenges the men using a public health emergency to promote the niqab; it is consistent with notions of niqab as a personal choice based on reflection and individual circumstances, rather than external pressure, embraced by the participants in this research.

This is an example of deep engagement with current affairs and placing them in a wider cultural context. Here niqab wearers active on social media draw attention to the fluidity of meaning of face covering, as it was organically transformed from an object of derision and fear into a life-saving artifact which was suddenly encouraged and sometimes enforced (Piela 2020) in public spaces. Demonstrating a healthy dose of humor, they critique the prejudice inherent in negative attitudes to religious face covering displayed by individuals and authorities.[8]

Niqabi Women's Responses to Mainstream Media Representations

In contrast to the large volume of research regarding media representations of Muslims and Islam in the context of current events, the number of studies examining Muslims' responses

---

[8] At the moment of writing, some mainstream media have begun unpicking the problematic nature of mandated face covering for other minorities. An article in The Washington Post (Jan 2020) exposed the risks of mask wearing for African Americans who are routinely racially profiled in the United States.

to such media representations is small. Ahmad (2006) investigated British Muslims' perceptions of media coverage of 9/11, and her conclusions speak strongly to my findings in this section. She argues that the coverage of Islam post-9/11 was delivered in a climate of moral panic, in the form of easily digestible sound bites that failed to appropriately analyze political events in a wider context. A new, vilified subject of the Other came into view and under never-ending scrutiny. As a participant in Perry's study (2015: 4) remarked: "All of a sudden, there [were] Muslims." This emergence of a new subject position marks the catapulting of Muslims into abnormality since that which is considered normal remains "unmarked, unnoticed, unthematized, untheorized" (Brighenti 2007: 26).

In a more recent study, Ahmed (2019) interviewed five female British Muslim journalists who were able to provide insider perspectives on representations of Muslims, in particular Muslim women, in the British media. They agreed that while, on the whole, such representations continued to be problematic, there was improvement in some areas; for example, they felt that print media and radio enabled more new conversations and diverse views than television; that the BBC now engaged with more female Muslim voices than before; and that there were instances of cross-fertilization between online media where female Muslim voices are more prominent, and mainstream media. Reminiscent of the Canadian #DressCodePM campaign, Muslim women's scathing criticism of the then prime minister David Cameron's patronizing articulation of the role of the Muslim woman was organized around the #traditionallysubmissive hashtag and subsequently picked up by the BBC (BBC News 2016). However, the interviewed journalists observed that as Muslim women, they were still being asked to "talk about issues that placed them within a narrow set of frameworks" (Ahmed 2019: 93). In other words, they were only asked to comment only through their subjectivity of faith and gender which resulted in an "overdetermined religious identity" (Morris 2018: 411). Myriam François-Cerrah commented in an interview with Ahmed (2019: 94) that

> [your gender and religion are] necessarily a part of how you look at the world, but that should not be the reason that you are being called for a commission, you should be called for a commission because you are a [good] writer who happens to be a Muslim woman which informs your views in a really interesting way.

Consequently, Ahmed argues that this essentialist practice can be tackled only by diversifying the media professions, including editing and production which would streamline Muslim concerns in a more natural manner.

Linking Negative Representations to People's Reactions to the Niqab

The women I interviewed were well aware of the reductive, one-dimensional manner in which they were represented in the media. Further, they believed that these representations had a negative impact on their lives, reiterating observations of Ahmad's participants (2006). Since for many non-Muslims, media reporting is the sole source of information about Islam, and Muslim women's veiling, it is the women who wear the niqab who have to deal with the misconceptions and manipulations spread by some media outlets. Aisha (24, British Pakistani) observed that "there's certain areas, where I think they just haven't been in contact or spoken to Muslims before . . . they're just not used to that. So when they see someone who is covered all in black and they can't see their face, all they can see are two eyes, they kind of feel like maybe there's something to be afraid of." While she is able to shift perspectives to recognize the media-driven logic of anti-Muslim prejudice ("You can't blame them 'cos you have to look at it from their point of view as well. It's just the way Islam is being portrayed to them."), she indicates that this mechanism leads further to stigmatization. ("Obviously with all the bad publicity, Islam gets on the news and everything . . . people become more wary of us.")

Soraya (52, Scottish convert) noted that the visual trope of the "all-black niqab" lent itself to terrifying exaggerations: "They said people are terrified of niqabis and it was like: yeah because they use that forty-foot picture of women with the black niqab like that, all you can see. . . . It's scary! You know what I mean, eh? You see people are scared of niqabis—you see, I would be scared—there's the newsreader and behind there's a forty-foot picture of *that!* [emphasis added]." Indeed, stories told by several participants strongly suggest that women who wear the niqab are often feared by members of the public. Nabila recounted an incident during which her teenage daughter, also a niqab wearer, was met with the plea, "Please don't hurt me!" whispered by a terrified elderly woman at a service station. Ryan and Vacchelli (2013: 104) quoted a niqab-wearing participant who had been begged by another woman not to attack her baby as they were all boarding a crowded bus. Such experiences are traumatic for all involved and, as Nabila suggested, likely to be fueled by the media.

This feature of reporting on niqabis has also been noted by extant literature on media representations of Muslims. Certain aspects of photography—framing, dominating color, background, and composition—may reinforce some features of the photographed person while downplaying others (Caetano 2006). Poole (2002: 111) found that journalistic photographs of niqabis are dominated by black which obscures individual people in group photos and dehumanizes them, showing them as a "silent mass."[9] Menacing visual representations become tied to issues of national security, terrorism, and integration, all of which claim to engage the Muslim community, while shaping the "debates" in such a way that Muslim voices are ultimately dismissed and excluded (Poole 2011: 2). Nabila talked at length about her fear that she would be perceived as a terrorist in public after she saw some TV coverage from ISIS-controlled territories that showed both men and women with covered faces:

It didn't help that you had you know pictures of that Jihadi John wearing this black balaclava it looked very much like a face veil you know. Why did he have to wear a black balaclava? I personally felt my heart sink when I saw those pictures of him on the news. I thought, "Oh, fantastic. That looks like a niqab, you know, now

---

[9]Niqabis' photographic self-representations published online contrast with such imagery by emphasizing the mundane and the intimate (Piela 2013).

we're going to get it in the neck." And then obviously you got the jihadi bride photos you know those abayas that they're wearing the one pieces from head to toe and the face veils, I'll tell you what, they look exactly like what Salafi women wear, so all you need to do is cut the rifle out of their picture. And that's what we look like.

It was Nabila's view that such media messaging, without any explanation of motivations for adoption of the niqab, implied that there was a link between face coverings and religious militancy. Muslim women are increasingly portrayed as no longer in need of saving—they constitute a feminized and sexualized extension of the Muslim masculine terror (Zarabadi and Ringrose 2018). These transformed perceptions, documented both in the United Kingdom (Khiabany and Williamson 2008) and the United States (Aziz 2012), have serious consequences for women who wear the niqab, as they increasingly become the target of harassment and violence in public (Chakraborti and Zempi 2012; Zempi and Chakraborti 2014; Perry 2015). Simultaneously, Muslim women resist these ambiguous, stigmatizing narratives on social media (Evolvi 2019).

Several women expressed frustration with not just the quality, but also the quantity of stories involving Islam and Muslims in mainstream media. Sadiyah (37, British Pakistani) wholeheartedly embraced the popular saying that "no news is good news":

Why are they thinking about it so much? They're saying bad things about it, but if you look in the media there's like niqab stories all the time. I don't know whether I pick those up because I'm a Muslim or whether they are appearing a lot . . . it's going to make people think. Why do they do it? You know whether, the whole 9/11 . . . it made people aware of Islam. So even that, you know when they say, oh, what is it, all publicity is good. You know you get income, business that way, I kind of think . . . it's too much.

Bowe, Fahmy, and Wante (2013) note that there is a strong positive relationship between the frequency of coverage of substantive attributes of objects and the salience these attributes have for audiences, in line with the agenda-setting theory (McCombs and Shaw 1972). Further, it appears that negative information has a greater agenda-setting effect than positive information. The interplay between both the first and second level agenda-setting—frequency of coverage and relative negativity of coverage—is a powerful combination of factors guiding people how to think about issues (McCombs 1997). Recognizing this risk for niqabis, Sadiyah expresses a yearning for less coverage of the niqab which, for her, would facilitate reclaiming normality (Ryan 2011), and rejection of stigmatization.

Coping Strategies Related to Stigmatizing Media Representations

Individuals may respond to collective stigmatization by displaying complex and varied reactions which seek to "unsettle, challenge and potentially transform the representations and practices that stigmatize" (Howarth 2006: 445). In the Open Society Foundations report (Bouteldja, 2014) for which 122 niqabi women in the United Kingdom were asked to comment, an overwhelming majority agreed that negative portrayals of Islam led many individuals to double down on their efforts to learn about the religion and intensify religious practice. However, they also believed there was a distinct link between negative representations of Muslims and the abuse they experienced in public. In my research, I found that there were four pronounced ways in which the women I interviewed coped with negative reporting about Islam and news stories about the niqab, in particular: self-regulation, disengagement from the mainstream media, consumption of right-wing media, and focusing on positive, if rare, instances of niqab framing by the national media and political actors. A small group felt the need to "fly under the radar" and self-regulate their behaviour in public in order to avoid unnecessary attention because they knew they would be bearing the brunt of unfavorable media stories otherwise. Soraya appeared to be particularly anxious about not creating news headlines involving the niqab. She reflected on her experience of passing through Heathrow Airport and quickly obliging when asked to show her face: "If I'd delayed the flight, I may have scared the other passengers . . . and I could have caused more delay, caused more hassle, because I wear the niqab. And that could have been misconstrued, twisted, somebody'd say something to a newspaper, 'Flights delayed because of niqabis refusing to show their faces to security.' Stories are twisted, they use these incidents against us, and add and twist." Taking off the niqab allowed her to remain unmarked and safe. Soraya's concern is not unfounded; it has been evidenced that proliferation of alarming news stories that mention Muslims—for example, in the context of niqab bans (Razack 2018), terrorist attacks by people with a Muslim background (Hanes and Machin 2014) or history of ISIS activity (Van Gilder and Massey 2016), directly contribute to violence against Muslims marked out by religious dress, especially women.

A second, larger group of women told me that they disengaged from mainstream media, as they found that mainstream reporting about Islam and Muslims was usually hostile or biased.[10] Halima said that the tone of such reporting was so negative as to cause her a lot of anxiety and, eventually, depression:

> I don't follow the news at all . . . because I am such an intense person. And things affect me so easily that I was becoming so depressed. And so [following the news] turned me off from leaving my house or from even talking to another person, because the news convinces you that like, everybody is against you, and everybody is just waiting to attack you. And everybody hates you . . . And so I was like, you know, this isn't healthy for me. And, yeah, it's nice to know what's happening in the world. But can I really change that, you know, what I can change is within my community, what's happening with my neighbors, what's happening with the

---

[10]This strongly resonates with the findings of a University of Virginia report titled "The Vanishing Center of the American Democracy" (Hunter and Bowman 2016) which found that 74 percent of Americans distrusted the mainstream media.

people at the grocery store, but while I keep watching the news, I will be too scared to do any of those things. So I need to have hope. And I need to just deal with the people around me based on how they're reacting to me and treating me instead of creating, letting this fear factor basically debilitate me.

(Halima, 44, Arab American)

Halima contrasted global events, those which she has no influence on, with local ones, where it is possible to have impact. Further, she explained that anxiety caused by being too emotionally involved in global events affected her ability to build relationships locally. The disaffection and disconnection she describes here as intentional resonates strongly with Vidali's observation (2010: 376) that for some individuals "news filtering and avoidance is experienced as a strategy that makes their moral and emotional worlds manageable." Adopting such a coping strategy of avoidance may be reasonable, based on research by Ben-Zur, Gil, and Shamshins (2012) who found that exposure to coverage of traumatic events increases the likelihood of distress and secondary traumatization. "Niqab stories" have been mentioned by some participants as distressing, since they proliferate in moments of national debates focused on bans, court trials, and hostile remarks made by high-ranking politicians, for example, those made in a *Daily Telegraph* column by Boris Johnson, then the foreign secretary and currently the prime minister (Johnson 2018). The women I interviewed assessed the majority of news stories related to the niqab as inherently biased and preferred to avoid them at all cost. For example, Sadiyah said she did not engage in discussing "niqab stories" that appeared in the media:

I take the media with a pinch of salt now. Do not believe the things that they say. And erm, we have like you know in the family, we have the what's app group with all our cousins, and every time a niqab story comes up, erm, there's loads of us, it will be the non-niqabis that discuss the whole story. "What's your take on this, what's your take on that?" Whereas I won't, I don't see the point of discussing this story, and *it is not important for us to be discussing* [emphasis added].

(Sadiyah, 37, British Pakistani)

All these reactions—avoiding media attention, avoidance, and distrust of mainstream media—stem from the participants' belief that media organizations in the United Kingdom and the United States toe the government line in regard to home and foreign policy that affected Muslims, promoted stereotypes, and sought sensation, in line with Ahmad's findings (2006) from her interviews with British Muslim journalists and professionals. Many British niqabi women interviewed for the Open Society Foundations report (Bouteldja 2015) expressed a preference for global Islamic media, including Islamic satellite channels such as Islam Channel or Iqraa TV. However, some women in this research were adamant that they felt they needed to be on top of current news and obtained information from a broad range of sources. In the United Kingdom, the BBC, BBC Radio 4, and Al-Jazeera as well as local news outlets were mentioned most often, while American participants preferred ABC, NBC, and CNBC, as well as Al-Jazeera. In both countries, the majority of women obtained their information from the online platforms of these networks.

Aisha (24, British Pakistani) told me she and her friends watched both British and American news channels. She confessed, with some hilarity, that she sometimes watched Fox News, a network catering to conservative Republican viewers and considered as biased "to the right" (Zúñiga, Correa, and Valenzuela 2012): "I watch it so I can make an informed judgement so I sometimes watch Fox News and other right-wing channels [laughter]. This is going to sound crazy. But if you don't know the other side—you don't know what the other side is doing—then you can't make an informed decision or an informed comment about it." In contrast to Halima who chose to live a "media disconnected" life, Aisha consciously steps out of the bubble of her own beliefs and political leanings. This allows her to form opinions without relying entirely on her preferred media. Sometimes media consumption habits may be dangerous to disclose, as they may come with pejorative labels. Perceiving this clearly, Sadiyah (37, British Pakistani) mentioned that she sometimes read the *Daily Mail Online*, an online tabloid known for celebrity gossip and a strong anti-immigration and anti-Muslim stance, "for a joke." Simultaneously, these comments suggest that it may be difficult to fully disengage from racist, xenophobic media content which saturates everyday reality even for those who are targeted by it.

Sofia (39, British Pakistani) discerned that the situation of niqabi women in the United Kingdom was comparatively better than that in France where the niqab ban was in operation. Demonstrating an awareness of previous niqab controversies and their main actors, she took comfort in Theresa May's[11] defense of the women's right to wear the niqab:

I guess the media sensationalises, it stereotypes, it scapegoats people and groups and I guess that's what it's done to veiled women. Erm and as we've seen examples in the European area, in France, there's the biggest example of a secular society . . . what approach has been taken there. Whereas in Britain we've always known it to be a multicultural state, a multi faith society and it's very tolerant of all faiths, backgrounds and dress codes. And I think, was it one of our . . . I think was it the Home Secretary erm, Theresa May. Yeah, Theresa May, and she said I think her quote was something along the lines of everyone deserves to be dressed according to what they, you know, what they'd, what they are, and we shouldn't interfere as politicians in what they should or should not wear. And I think that was very erm, it was quite nice to hear that from a politician but who was a female and not

---

[11]At the time of the interview, Theresa May was home secretary (one of the most high-profile roles in British politics) and became prime minister in 2016. In 2019, she was replaced in this role by Boris Johnson who, shortly before he took office, made disparaging comments about women who wear the niqab (Piela 2018).

a Muslim. And yet she's quite dignified, yeah she's quite dignified to people who are veiling.

(Sofia, 39, British Pakistani)

Theresa May's remarks made in an interview with Sky News (Grierson 2013) were a rare example of a high-profile politician publicly expressing support for niqab-wearing. Her emphasis on May's gender may arguably indicate frustration with the domination of male politicians' perspectives on the niqab since 2006 when, she said, "Jack Straw voiced his view." Sofia also mentioned the then British deputy prime minister John Prescott who challenged Jack Straw in 2006 and openly declared his support for women's right to wear the niqab (BBC News 2006b).[12] This indicates a coping strategy that is very different from that of Halima and Sadiyah. Sofia's recollection (in a 2015 interview) of the key actors in the 2006 British niqab controversy points to her deep engagement with current affairs relevant to her. In spite of her assessment of the mainstream media as biased, she seems to derive comfort from being able to construct Britain as "tolerant," especially in contrast with France and other European countries where restrictions on the niqab are in place.

Concluding Remarks

In this chapter I examined how niqabi voices shape some mainstream and social media landscapes. Although only a handful (6) of articles and other pieces about the niqab published in the mainstream media in my data corpus could pass the "niqabi inclusivity test," there are signs that the mainstream media gradually reorients to incorporating more niqabis' voices, and occasionally it is possible to read a piece written by a woman who covers her face, usually in the "progressive" press. The optimism should be guarded, however, as these instances are usually in reaction to a political controversy, and the women who are given a platform are usually "on-duty" high-profile niqabis, such as Zunera Ishaq in Canada, Kenza Drider in France (who ran in the French presidential elections after she was fined for wearing the niqab), or Sahar Al-Faifi in the United Kingdom. Low-profile niqabi women are much less likely to be invited by mainstream media to share their views. Instead, many become active on social media where they can engage with current affairs.

The decreasing levels of trust in the mainstream media and the shift to social media in the quest for information and content result in a higher likelihood of incidental news exposure (Goyanes 2019). Furthermore, people incidentally exposed to news are more likely to hold diverse viewpoints than people who seek out information intentionally

---

[12]Globally, May's position, indeed, stood in stark contrast to the widely publicized critical comments about the niqab made in the same year by the French interior minister Manuel Valls (Reuters 2013), and the Canadian prime minister Stephen Harper in 2015 (Thamin 2016).

(Goyanes 2019). Therefore, it is possible that more nuanced and inclusive online-based constructions of the niqab will be more consequential than the limited mainstream media portrayals. However, as self-selection, echo chambers, and filter bubbles strongly shape online media landscapes (Goyanes 2019), this effect may not be very pronounced. Furthermore, the effect of convergence of traditional and online media, with all influential traditional outlets creating a powerful online presence, may mean that the gatekeeping practices that prevent minorities, including niqabis, from exerting influence over content production will continue to shape the representations of these groups.

Hashtags in particular have the potential to adjust the framing of the niqab to become more inclusive. Toledo Bastos, Galdini Raimundo, and Travitzki (2013: 260) found in their statistical analysis of top trending political hashtags that "intense activity of individuals with relatively few connections is capable of generating highly replicated messages that contribute to Trending Topics without relying on the activity of user hubs." This means that "prevailing majority opinion in a population can be rapidly reversed by a small fraction of randomly distributed committed agents" (Toledo Bastos, Galdini Raimundo, and Travitzki 2013: 260). Thus, niqabi Twitter users do not necessarily have to rely on powerful gatekeepers to make their perspectives known; this freedom also means that they are able to shape their messages visually, stylistically, and rhetorically. Hashtags that mobilize users around the issues of the niqab and Muslim women more widely often involve mockery and satire that expose bias and prejudice in comments made by high-profile political actors. Satire, argues Losh (2014: 16), is "an important way to effect political change." Certainly, scathing public criticisms of prime ministers' comments, such as those mobilized around the #DressCodePM and #traditionallysubmissive hashtags, would not have been possible on this scale before the advent of social media.

Women's responses to the media reporting on Islam and Muslims indicate that they are by no means passive recipients of media content; they engage with it critically and develop various coping strategies that help them retain their sense of self in a media-saturated society. Simultaneously, social media platforms offer the ability to critically respond to relevant issues, as demonstrated in the discussion of the Twitter debate on masking practices and "burka bans" during the coronavirus pandemic in 2020, in which niqab-wearing women took a strong stand. While mainstream media did not show interest in the fluid symbolism of the face mask, widely adopted during the pandemic, but perceived it with hostility when worn as part of Islamic practice, the niqabi community firmly assessed this discrepancy in attitudes.

Social media platforms are the spaces where niqabi women engage with audiences in an informative manner. They also engage in identity work, as they are able to exercise their agency by stating "I exist" on their own terms rather than in the narrow confines of the mainstream media, which not only represent them in stereotypical ways, but exclude their voices even from discussions central to these women's own lives, which I demonstrated in Chapter 1. By establishing non-threatening contexts, intimacy, and authenticity as part of their aesthetic style, they disrupt the normalized associations of the niqab with passivity, otherness, and violence. Evolvi (2019: 482) asserts that "the Internet is an embodied space where the materiality of the veil is displayed, mediated, and negotiated. The Internet both embeds forms of religious materiality and helps define the meanings beyond such materiality. By choosing the images and narratives they wish to make public, Muslim women take control of their hyper-visibility and challenge the idea that wearing a veil makes them invisible subjects."

This chapter builds on Chapter 1 which demonstrated how the voices of niqabi women were mostly excluded from news reporting pertaining to the niqab. Chapter 2 acknowledges that many niqab wearers are undeterred by this silencing. It examines the ways in which they carve out other spaces in both mainstream and social media where they are able to exercise more control over their representations and set their own agendas. It demonstrates that they are able and willing to communicate with their audiences on a variety of topics, including those well beyond the stereotypical narratives of religion and gender. This attention to agency, voice, and representation culminates in the final part of this chapter, based on the interviews with niqab-wearing women that form the core of this book. It thus sets the stage for Chapters 3, 4, and 5, which analyze these women's reflections about the niqab's religious, social, and political aspects.

CHAPTER 3
RELIGIOUS FRAMING OF THE NIQAB

This chapter is about how women who chose to wear the niqab in the West use religious argumentation to explain their decision to veil. Their religious argumentation reflects the wider debates of what religion is, what its boundaries are, how religious practices are defined, and what their role in the liberal, secular state is. The women often juxtapose the concepts of faith, Islamic doctrine, religious experience, and spirituality. In the narratives, these concepts are often intertwined and where I separate them in discussion, it is for analytical purposes only. First, I turn to the problem of religious framing of the niqab in the secular-liberal public spheres of the United Kingdom and the United States, flagged by Halima, who lives in the United States, and Sofia, who lives in the United Kingdom.

When I talked to Muslims and non-Muslims about the subject matter of this book, I often heard the opinion that "the niqab is not a religious thing, it's cultural." I was somewhat surprised that so many people had such a definitive view about it, and especially that few of them actually could formulate a definition of "a religious thing," and hardly any of my interlocutors had ever talked to a woman who *chose* to wear it. I then realized that this view was part and parcel of the hegemonic discourse which attempts to delegitimize the niqab. The discourse was mobilized by ostensibly disparate groups: "well-meaning liberals" who felt it was an oppressive, patriarchal practice; progressive, Western Muslims who did not wish to be associated with what it was commonly understood to represent; and those who argued that it should be legally prohibited because it heralded and enabled the rise of "extremist," "radical," or "fundamentalist" Islam.

This discourse is further driven by those scholars of Islam and the Islamic clergy who support legal niqab bans; in 2017, a Swiss-Yemeni professor of Sharia law, Elham Manea, commented in an article for the Australian ABC Network News (Hegarty 2017, np) that "it was naïve—and even racist—to regard wearing of a burka as a sincere act of faith." The article was published shortly after a political stunt by the far-right Australian politician Pauline Hanson who appeared in the Australian Parliament wearing a burka and calling for a ban on it. Manea linked the wearing of the burka to the culture of the Najd region of Saudi Arabia, as well as the "Wahhabi ideology" exported by Saudis globally, to finally state that the burka is not a religious requirement. She stated that "conversations around the validity and religiosity [*sic*] of the burka are essential" (Hegarty 2017, np). In 2009, one of the highest-ranking clerics in Sunni Islam, now deceased Grand Imam of Cairo and the Al-Azhar University, Mohammed Sayed al-Tantawi, ruled that the niqab was not religiously permissible in Islam and banned it from all Al-Azhar schools (Rosemarine 2010). Such controversies and the ensuing public debates suggest that the niqab is a focal point for various, sometimes disparate, political interests and power relations which fuel the process of legally banning it across Europe, Africa, and Asia.[1]

As argued earlier, dismissals of the niqab as un-Islamic rely on the common dichotomy of "religion versus culture," a framework defined by Bolognani as "a revivalist discourse that tends to refer to the idea of an orthodox Islam in opposition to its mediation through any cultural capital alien to the 'original' Arab matrix; as an analytical framework that uses 'culture' with an automatic negative connotation and, as an ethos, is based more on reputation and family ties than on 'genuine' religious principles" (in Bolognani and Mellor 2012: 213). What is striking here is that this dichotomy is used by both detractors of the niqab, who reduce it to Arab ethnic dress without significance for Islamic practice, and its advocates who, on the basis of various Hadith, identify it as one of the outfit styles worn during the lifetime of the Prophet (and therefore rooted in Islamic history), preferable over "ethnic" dress which may be insufficiently modest. In both cases, actors discursively construct somewhat different notions of "authentic" Islam, free from cultural contamination of either Arab or non-Arab culture. In contrast to North America and Europe, where this tension frames many discussions about the niqab, Omani women interviewed by Ahmed and Roche (2017) viewed the niqab as one of many veiling options available to them. They saw veiling as required by Islam *and* mediated by customs and social expectations. Both these motivations were considered complementary and, indeed, different stages of the same process, whereby they were inculcated with the notion of head-covering by their female relatives at first, later maturing intellectually and emotionally to embrace the practice internally (Ahmed and Roche 2017). The religion versus culture framework, so pervasive in the West, is absent from their interpretation of veiling.

The Challenge of Talking about the Niqab as a Religious Practice in the Secular-Liberal Public Sphere

Halima self-described as a former "100% American Western feminist," daughter of Egyptian immigrants based in the Southeastern United States and a graduate engineer. In the beginning of our conversations, she explained that a focus on faith is seen as problematic in the secular-liberal discursive framework; therefore, niqab wearers, when interrogated, focused on pragmatic reasons for wearing the niqab, when in fact, faith was central to the practice:

> We're so used to using the practical, pragmatic reasons for things and it's almost like taboo for us to say, I do this because I believe it is pleasing to God, and that's

---

[1] At the time of the writing of this book, the niqab was banned in fifteen countries: Tunisia, Austria, Denmark, France, Belgium, Tajikistan, Latvia, Bulgaria, Cameroon, Chad, Congo-Brazzaville, Gabon, Netherlands, China, Morocco, and Sri Lanka.

enough for me, but we always have to justify, justify, right? . . . in the West, when we're talking to non-Muslims, we try to use secular or societal or reasons to try to justify the niqab. But that's not that's not why we wear the niqab. It's a by-product of [trying to please God].

(Halima, 44, Arab American)

Halima recognizes that in the West, the discourse of piety, especially non-Christian piety, is a foreign language to many social actors and she accepts that she may be unable to convey that disposition using religious notions. Her reluctance to talk about religious beliefs was also, at least partly, due to having had to continuously challenge stereotypes linking Islam to terrorism. Having developed a need for a renewed commitment to Islam post-9/11, when American Muslims were beginning to experience the rise of Islamophobic hate crime, she initially adopted a headscarf. She said that when she first came to work wearing it, she was told by a co-worker: "Halima, what you need to do you need to just wrap a big ol' American flag around the head and then you can be covered but then nobody will worry about where your loyalties are." Others questioned her motives, implying that she supported the terrorists, to which she responded emphatically: "No, I'm trying to say that I'm with Islam." By coming out as a pious Muslim through the adoption of a visual signifier of Islam, Halima had her social citizenship symbolically revoked; her status as an American citizen (as well as her loyalties) was contested because as a Muslim, she was immediately cast as a threat to Western cultural values (Selod 2015). This phenomenon was widely described in research literature on Muslim experiences in post-9/11 America (Esposito 2010; Cesari 2013; Kundnani 2014). Halima's subsequent attempts to decouple Islam from stereotypes which, more often than not, frame non-Muslims' understandings of this religion often failed; she concluded that the religious argumentation that she utilized was simply unintelligible to most of her interlocutors.

Halima's point was echoed by Sofia, a British Pakistani Muslim whom I interviewed at her home in West Yorkshire. She talked a great deal about her experience of wearing the niqab as a driving instructor, and about her interactions with students, other drivers, pedestrians, and staff at the driving examination center where her students were tested. Her narrative, recounted below, illustrates how some women may deal with the issue of justifying the niqab to others. Her "pragmatic justification" was ostensibly framed by humor:

I'd say it myself, make a joke out of it, so I said to the examiner once, I don't get sunburnt, I don't get a chill on my nose, my nose doesn't get cold on frosty days, my face is nice and warm, on the hot, sunny days I'm not getting sunburnt or anything. So I'm all covered, I'm all protected throughout all the weather. Yeah [laughs]. So I make a joke out of it in a way, so they, you know, accept it.

(Sofia, 39, British Pakistani)

This interview extract illustrates the difficult situation in which Sofia found herself—having to discuss her religious beliefs not just with strangers, but strangers in a position of power (as a driving instructor, she had to maintain good professional relationships with examiners who controlled her students' results and therefore, Sofia's livelihood). Faced with the need to formulate a narrative that facilitates that goal in an intelligible (commonsensical, pragmatist) and *acceptable* manner in a professional context, she made use of flippant humor. The use of humor has been widely described as a stigma management strategy that compensates for the power imbalance between the stigmatized and their interlocutors (Marvasti 2005; Valenti 2011). It is also aligned with the concept of linguistic habitus, described by Bourdieu (1991: 82) as "the degree of constraint which a given field will bring to bear on the production of discourse, imposing silence or hyper-controlled language on some people while allowing others the liberties of a language that is securely established." Sofia "carefully managed the multicultural intimacies" (Hopkins 2014: 1577). By adopting a strategy of humor and deflection, she also protected her religious identity from being picked apart by strangers who felt they had the right to interrogate her on the subject. Goffman (1963) observed that individuals who deviate from the "ordinary morality" of the group lose the privilege of social distance; they can be approached at will by other members of the group. Goffman specified that in this case, "deviance" is a label often attached to those who "fail to use available opportunity for advancement in the various approved runways of society" including "the ethnic assimilation backsliders who are reared in the two worlds of the parent society and the society of their parents, and resolutely turn away from the conventional routes of mobility open to them, overlaying their public school socialization with what many normals [*sic*] will see as a grotesque costume of religious orthodoxy" (1963: 170). However, humor as a stigma management strategy may be a double-edged sword. While it sometimes relieves social tensions, it can equally contribute to a perception of the stigmatized individual as flippant, lacking self-respect, or unharmed by stereotyping (suggesting that all others affected by the stereotyping ought to laugh in response, lest they are seen as overreacting) (Marvasti 2005: 543).

Unlike Sofia, who had to negotiate the need for intelligibility and social acceptance in a professional setting in her justification, Shariqa, refused to disclose her reasons to strangers in a public context, here, when she was interviewed by a TV presenter hosting a debate on the niqab in Britain:

> [W]hen I was doing all my interviews, I would decline answering the question why do you cover your face, because I said this debate is not about why I cover my face, it's about the fact that you are impinging on somebody's religious freedom, you know, and someone's right to wear as much as they want to. . . . Just as we allow people to wear as little, but I refused to answer the question. But I couldn't answer the question because I knew that I can't give you something that's taken me years to come to an understanding and you want it in a couple of sentences, or a couple of minutes?
>
> (Shariqa, 37, British Pakistani)

By refusing to bare her soul to the public, she achieved two goals. First, she shifted the terms of the conversation—she questioned why the niqab debate was happening at all, given that other sartorial choices (such as wearing skimpy clothing) rarely garner sustained media debate. She firmly framed the choice to wear the niqab as religious and personal freedom, utilizing secular-liberal language, presumably intelligible (and acceptable) to the studio and TV audience. Just as importantly, she stopped there. She refused to play the game in which she was forced to defend her choices before staunch critics of the niqab. By putting up this boundary, Shariqa delineated the choice to wear the niqab as a private matter that stems from complex personal circumstances and reflections which may simply be inaccessible to her interlocutors. Thus, similarly to Reni Eddo-Lodge (2017) who announced that she would no longer talk to White people about race because they would not listen, Shariqa refused to bear moral responsibility for trying to change the negative affect toward the niqab. This is understandable, considering the toll exacted on individuals by the emotional labor of everyday explaining, noted in a study of young Australian Muslims (Harris and Hussein 2018). The authors of the study argue that in a social context characterized by an unequal distribution of power, the responsibility for social change is placed with the individual. The success of such explaining is never guaranteed or complete, and such ceaseless work may have a negative effect on the individual's well-being, including emotional and physical exhaustion (Harris and Hussein 2018). Several of the participants in this project talked about their achieved or intended withdrawal from the public sphere (especially media appearances) following a sense of burnout. Shariqa, by admitting that she is unable to provide a full justification to others, becomes, in Magnus's words (2006: 93), an "unaccountable" subject, a position which obliges one to relinquish similar expectations toward others, and be modest, generous, patient, tolerant, and forgiving (Butler 2003: 54–6) —virtues that are opposed to "ethical violence" and, strikingly, ones that are found by the interviewed women in the ethical framework of Islam.

There are two frames that dominate secular imaginaries of the veil, and restrict thinking that could lead to more helpful questions that could be asked about it. One mobilizes the veil as a symbol of submission, and in another the veil operates as a symbol of resistance (Bilge 2010). In the former, the women are perceived to have no agency whatsoever; they are cast in opposition to rational, free-willed, choosing agents. This framework, argues Bilge, defined the political discussions prior to the introduction of the "burka ban" in France; eminent French feminist scholars and activists, supported by women who took on the role of "accredited cultural insiders," able to translate the ostensibly patriarchal Islamic cultures to Western audiences, rejected the testimonies of women who chose to veil. Put simply, veiled women were dismissed as suffering from false consciousness that blinded them to their oppression (Bilge 2010: 15). This argument, constructing the figures of "bad Muslims," that is, veiled women and their patriarchal menfolk, played straight into the hands of the French government who realized that it was easier to introduce the "burka ban" and be seen as effectively addressing problems faced by French Muslims in the *banlieues* than to create and implement successful (and expensive) policies that would tackle the socioeconomic basis of violence and segregation affecting that population (Bilge 2010). This alliance illustrates what Halley (2006: 20) calls "governance feminism": in an apparent paradox, depictions of veiled women have branched out in the past decade to include messaging related to security threats and terrorism (Khabiany and Williamson 2008). Thus, in the "framework of subordination and false consciousness" (Bilge 2010: 15), veiled women are seen as individuals who either have relinquished their agency or are misusing it to threaten the West.

The latter frame of reference, termed variously "subversion and resistance" (Bilge 2010: 18) or "strategic compliance" (Avishai 2008: 412), challenges the racist and sexist assumptions of the former. It insists that gender inequalities in colonized societies are intimately connected to colonial politics of nation and race, and they have to be addressed as a matrix. It is embraced by postcolonial feminism which connects the act of veiling to agentic resistance against colonial domination. However, while it plays a significant role in "decolonising gender relations associated with Muslims" (Bilge 2010: 18), it neglects to acknowledge those types of agency that do not hinge on resistance or subversion, such as those analyzed by Mahmood (2005). The argument that reinforces the association between veiling and political resistance as somehow central is often produced by researchers who project their own affinities on their participants (Bilge, 2010) and thus contribute to this erasure of religious frameworks from women's narratives.

As mentioned earlier, these frameworks of reference are undergirded by formulation of opposition between religious choice/autonomy and constraint/authority. This supports the notion of Muslim subjects simply automatically acting out their roles through "readable gestures" in the dramaturgical interpretation of Islam offered by prominent anthropologists such as Gellner and Geertz (Asad 2009c: 12). In contrast, Asad (2009c) advocates for approaching Islamic actors as *thinking* individuals able to think critically, debate, and apply both religious and secular reasoning to their daily ethical conduct. Responding to that call, in Chapter 4 I turn to niqab wearers' secular narratives pertaining to their rights, while in the next section of the current chapter, I focus on women's reasoning pertaining to the centrality of faith in the practice of niqab-wearing.

The Practice of Niqab-Wearing as Flowing From Faith and Submission to God

An observation made by Bilge (2010) was helpful in organizing my thinking about the data; she notes that the subversion and resistance framework is characterized by confusion of motivations for and outcomes of veiling. She calls this phenomenon "instrumentalist reductionism" (2010: 20). Instrumentalist reductionism involves reducing the veil to its social, pragmatic functions. As demonstrated earlier in this chapter by Halima's point ("in the West, when we're talking to non-Muslims, we try to use secular or societal or reasons to try to justify the niqab. But that's not that's not why we wear the niqab. It's a by-product of it"), the dominance of instrumentalist reductionism narrows down the discursive repertoire veiled women may use in their interactions with non-Muslims; they feel that only reductive justifications for the veil will be legible and acceptable by this audience, thus being forced to obscure the religious reasoning even more. Examples of such a reductive approach to the veil include the interpretation of the veil as a symbol of "anti-imperialist movement" (Afshar in Bilge 2010), "identity rooted in their own tradition" (El-Hamel in Bilge 2010), "a political choice" contesting social exclusion and Islamophobic prejudice (Afshar, Aitken, and Franks in Bilge 2010), a vehicle for "emancipatory ends" such as access to schooling and employment (Bartkowski and Ghazal-Read in Bilge 2010), and finally, a tool for managing gender relations (Hoodfar in Bilge 2010). While these outcomes may be a part of many veiled women's experience, Bilge emphasizes that religious agency, often absent from analysis, is central to their motivation to adopt it.

As the accounts of the majority of the participants and the literature discussed here work in unison in advocating this shared goal, I also place it at the center of the discussion of *motivations* for veiling. This chapter is therefore organized around how women who wear the niqab in the United Kingdom and the United States enact their agency which, I argue, following Mahmood (2005: 188), operates in various modalities and within a "grammar of concepts in which its particular affect, meaning, and form resides." Meanwhile, socioreligious *outcomes* of niqab-wearing (which are necessarily social and religious, as they organize participants' social lives according to a particular religio-ethical framework), are addressed in Chapter 5.

Religious and spiritual experiences seem to have eluded feminist and liberal analyses based on particular assumptions about the autonomous subject (Bilge 2010). In particular, women's choice to participate in religious practices seen as conservative and endorsing female modesty, such as niqab-wearing, cause consternation. As Hollywood aptly put it (2004: 524), "the dilemma—how to take seriously the agency of the other, when the other seems intent on ascribing her agency to God . . . ?—remains unresolved." The solution to this contradiction may be offered by poststructuralist critiques of "subjecthood and agency as coterminous with acting against the system" (Bilge 2010: 22); here, power is understood as simultaneously constraining and productive, "constitutive of subjectivities." Limitations (such as those dictated by religious regimes of power) may be constitutive of one's subjecthood and agency, as per Butler's (1997: 16) "enabling constraints." Avishai (2008: 412) argued that the Butlerian notion of agency resides "in the work one does on oneself to become a willing subject of a particular discourse." She proposes a new notion of agency based on a combination of a poststructuralist deconstruction of the humanist subject; it is less sensitive to autonomy than a subjectivity powered by a "prior act of personal surrender" (Mack, 2003: 439), and intersectionality, which "anchors the formation of subjectivities and agency within a nexus of social relations and structures of race, class, gender, that work together to (re)produce power and privilege" (Bilge 2010: 23). Such a combination offers a useful avenue for examining "specific contexts and articulated social formations from which different forms of agency and subject positions arise" (Bilge 2010: 23). Mack (2003: 441) asserted that "however imperfect our understanding of a religious sensibility may be, we can understand it better by reference to everyday experience than by reference to a hypothetical and largely fictional free subject." Resonating with Mack's apt observation, I henceforth examine narratives of faith, paying particular attention to affect, meaning, and form that together comprise a particular "grammar of concepts" (Mahmood 2005: 188) used by participants to communicate their experience.

This approach may better illuminate the operation of agency in the following appellation to God's assistance with spiritual and daily struggles faced by Sidrah. I met her at a farmers' market where many British Asians shopped for groceries. She was one of the few women I approached at the market who agreed to be interviewed. At that time, Sidrah told me she was in a difficult personal situation, because she was living in the United Kingdom as an asylum seeker with her young son. An Ahmadiyya Muslim, Sidrah left Pakistan due to religious discrimination[2] and feared for the safety of her husband who remained there. Subjected to humiliating requirements of having to report weekly at a Home Office unit, unable to work and forced to subsist on very modest government benefits, stressed by the lack of certainty as to whether her asylum application would be accepted, she was able to find support in a community of local Ahmadiyya Muslims. When we met a few weeks later for the interview, she surprised me by taking the lead in telling me about political and religious challenges of the Ahmadiyya Muslims in Pakistan and sharing some printed materials containing further information. She said she wanted to use this opportunity to raise awareness of the issue in the United Kingdom, thus acting as an ambassador for her community. The following extract indicates that faith was crucial to her formation of her subjectivity, in that she insisted that she ceded her autonomy to God. This "personal surrender" to God imbued her with a sense of strength and resilience necessary to wear the niqab, and her exceptionally difficult circumstances only put this relationship in a sharper focus:

I keep wearing the niqab because God has given me this strength, no one can do this on their own. *I am not doing this just as me,* that *I, I am* something and *I am doing* [something], no. I believe that God has given me the strength to face all this.

(Sidrah, 27, Pakistani living in the UK, emphasis added)

Unsurprisingly, faith (in its particular, Islamic modality) emerged as a central religious sensibility in the practice of wearing the niqab in the participants' narratives. Here, Halima highlighted the importance of submission[3] as part of her everyday religious practice, and linked submission to the divine to the practice of covering; her statement quoted below highlights the logic of action concerning the adoption of the niqab: first comes belief, then submission ("I hear and I obey"), and finally, the understanding of what is expected from a believer. Based on these elements, she is able to enact a religious identity as a believing woman who can be known as such.

[O]nce you believe in Islam, once you believe that the message of Islam comes from the Creator, *then* whatever the Creator tells you to do, you would do because you

---

[2] Ahmadiyya Muslims are a persecuted religious minority in Pakistan. A 1984 amendment to the Constitution of Pakistan effectively put them outside the fold of Islam; they are not to call themselves Muslims, under threat of imprisonment.
[3] Based on the root of the Arabic world "Islam" (S-L-M), its religious meaning is "voluntary submission to God."

believe that he's your Creator. And so everything we do is to say, you know, it says in the Qur'an say, I have heard and I obey, whenever you, you learn something, and you hear, say, I hear and I obey. *And then* you can understand *the reasons why . . .* And it's the reasons that Allah gives in the Qur'an. And it says, where, you know, cover yourself so that *you can be known as a believing woman.*

(Halima, 44, Arab American, emphasis added)

This primacy of belief and submission over individual understanding of the "why" of specific commandments was also present in the narrative of Sadiqa. The daughter of immigrants from Somalia who lives on the East Coast of the United States, and like Halima, is an engineering graduate, said:

I'm doing this [wearing the niqab] because I feel like, ultimately, what He told us to do, and what we're doing is best for us, even though we don't sometimes know it or understand it. That's the whole concept of faith is sometimes you don't really understand or know everything, but you don't need to understand or know everything, because, you know, this kind of defeats the purpose. It's realizing, you know, in spite of understanding, you know, we, we have to believe that, you know, *God knows better than us*, that he's more wiser [*sic*]. So, that's why we do it. And that's why we follow him.

(Sadiqa, 25, Somali American, emphasis added)

Mirroring the famous Kantian statement of his having to deny knowledge in order to make room for faith (Stevenson 2003), Sadiqa reasoned that knowing everything would defeat the purpose of faith. However, some types of knowledge, especially the knowledge of religion itself is important (Asad 2009c), as correct observance is a necessary and challenging task, especially for those who turned to Islam later in life and had not routinely practiced it (and so, had not developed an ethical disposition early on in their practice). Participants tended to usually refer to their learning experience in some capacity as part of their religious formation. Some of them studied Islam individually, usually with the help of printed and online materials; others preferred collective, usually informal, learning environments such as study groups. Rafeeqah (23, British Pakistani) emphasized that women in her community enjoyed practicing Islam collectively through study; she specifically connected such Islamic learning practices to "having a voice": "we might seem not to have a lot of voice, but there's lots, there's lots of segregated gatherings are always going on around here, there is always, like you know women, they give talks, they erm, they pray some *nasheeds* [religious chants], they erm, they read Koran and it's like, something, a get together for women. They have fun days and it's, it's not like erm, it's not like we don't have a voice at all in the community."

Notably, the concept of submission is understood by the interviewees unambiguously as submission to God, in contrast to wifely submission, a notion that characterizes Christian evangelical movements which hold that submission to the Lord and submission to the husband are one and the same (Bartkowski and Read 2003). Highlighting the significance of early Muslim women's practice, Zahra, a niqab-wearer from Canada, understood the niqab to be a result of their interpretation of the "hijab verse." Zahra wants to emulate their example by taking a personal responsibility for her interpretation of the verse, while rejecting the notion of submission to the husband, held even by one as eminent as the Prophet Muhammad:

> [I]t grew into something more while I did the research around you know, why do women wear the niqab, what is the textual evidence for it when the first verse on hijab was revealed you know, the Prophet didn't come to the women and say ok now you have to cover your faces and cover this and cover that, *the women themselves heard the verse and they understood it to mean to cover themselves a certain way* and they chose to cover their faces because they wanted to fulfil the meaning of that verse and commenced to cover in the most complete way and you know the wife of the Prophet SAW Aisha, praised them, for doing so because, you know, *they didn't need a man to tell them, oh, you go do this* . . . and that's what was so admirable is a reflection of their spirituality, you know, *it was their initiative to take that on*, and I want to be that kind of person, I want to be the kind of person who hears God's words and this like, I'm going to do my best to fulfil this and *I don't need somebody else police me or comandeer me: "Oh, do this or do that."* I want to be the person who hears God's commands and obey to the best of my ability.
>
> (Zahra, 41, Canadian Muslim, emphasis added)

Here, Zahra used religious reasoning to refute interpretations framed by the "submission and false consciousness" argument that represents the veil as a practice forced on women by their menfolk. To achieve this, she referred throughout the interview to the two most important sources of Islamic law: the Qur'an, believed by Muslims to be the Divine Revelation sent down to Prophet Muhammad, and Hadith, a vast collection of sayings and actions of the Prophet, elaborating on the Qur'anic verses, first transmitted by his companions and later by respected scholars. Zahra's narrative suggests she attached higher spiritual value to early Muslim women's independent and generous application of the "hijab verse" (i.e., Qur'an 24:31, elaborated in the narration by the Prophet's wife A'isha (in Al-Bukhari 4,481 and Abu Dawood 4,102), who mentioned that women of Medina tore their aprons apart and covered their faces upon hearing the verse) than following specific commandments to the letter. In other words, she admired their willingness to interpret the verse broadly, without compulsion from anyone. This rendering of the story of the women of Medina resonated with her personal experience: she told me that she had worn a black niqab for a long time, but she liked "fun accessories," such as brightly colored purses and shoes. Dissatisfied with that, her first (now ex-) husband had insisted on her wearing all black, as well as gloves and an eye cover. Zahra told me she had felt this to be an imposition and divorced him because of his authoritarian inclinations. After that, she continued to wear the niqab in a style that she preferred. This indicates that modesty is a religious duty, and the niqab may be an embodiment of this duty if a woman chooses to interpret it this way. Mahmood noted the function that the referencing of the conduct of the key figures of early Islam had for the mosque participants in her study:

> The teleological model that the mosque participants seek to realize in their lives is predicated on the exemplary conduct of the Prophet and his Companions. It would be easy to dismiss this ideal as a nostalgic desire to emulate a bygone past, a past whose demands can never be met within the exigencies of the present. Yet to do so would be to miss the significance of such a telos for practical ethical conduct. Among mosque participants, individual efforts toward self-realization are aimed . . . at honing one's rational and emotional capacities so as to approximate the exemplary model of the pious self. The women I worked with did not regard trying to emulate authorized models of behavior as an external social imposition that constrained individual freedom. Rather, they treated socially authorized forms of performance as the potentialities—the ground if you will—through which the self is realized.
>
> (Mahmood 2005: 31)

Zahra's story indicates that choice and (what is normatively seen as) constraint may effectively coexist with each other, allowing for the formation of a pious subjectivity. This was eloquently expressed by Shafeeqa, a 46-year-old African American convert to Islam who had worn the niqab for three years but stopped due to harassment: "I firmly believe that just as, you know, putting on the niqab and wearing that is, is a part of the faith . . . the niqab is something that is an act of worship for a believing woman if she can also choose to take that path." Here, Shafeeqa, drawing on her experience of having to give up the niqab, observed that the path of the niqab may be closed to some women due to safety concerns, family pressure, or health reasons. (Some of these reasons are discussed in Chapter 5.) The constraint, in her case, came from the environment hostile to the niqab which prevented her from wearing it and, consequently, engaging in an act of worship.

Different Emanations of Discursive Tradition in the Context of Correct Practice

The historical aspect of face covering, situating it in the Islamic past (as illustrated by Zahra's narrative), was an important reason for adopting it by the participants. This historicity corresponds to Asad's concept of Islam as a discursive tradition (2009c: 21), as opposed to an ideology, a structure, or a heterogeneous collection of beliefs, practices, and morals:

> A [discursive] tradition consists essentially of discourses that seek to instruct practitioners regarding the correct form and purpose of a given practice that, precisely because it is established, has a history. These discourses relate conceptually

to a past (when the practice was instituted, and from which the knowledge of its point and proper performance has been transmitted) and a future (how the point of that practice can best be secured in the short or long term, or why it should be modified or abandoned), through a present (how it is linked to other practices, institutions, and social conditions). An Islamic discursive tradition is simply a tradition of Muslim discourse that addresses itself to conceptions of the Islamic past and future, with reference to a particular Islamic practice in the present. . . . Clearly, not everything Muslims say and do belongs to an Islamic discursive tradition.

(Asad 2009c: 21–2)

Indeed, Sedgwick (2013: 281) makes a similar point: "Islam is only one influence among many . . . and it is a classic methodological error to seek to explain everything that is done by a person or society that happens to be Muslim in terms of Islam." Conversely, practices should not be dismissed as purely "cultural" simply because there is no consensus about them in the global Muslim community. As they are historically and socially situated, bearing particular personal resonances, they may be interpreted as religious by some practitioners:

Nor is an Islamic tradition in this sense necessarily imitative of what was done in the past. For even where traditional practices appear to the anthropologist to be imitative of what has gone before, it will be the practitioners' conceptions of what is *apt performance*, and of how the past is related to present practices, that will be crucial for tradition, not the apparent repetition of an old form.

(Asad 2009c: 21–2)

Underscoring this point, the understanding of the niqab's origins as an Islamic practice, central for the women I interviewed, varied to a degree. They were all aware that there was a significant interpretive diversity in this regard and reflected on why they occupied different positions on this continuum. While in developing their understanding they were likely to be influenced by other women who wore the niqab (often family members), scholars, Islamic schools of thought (known as *madhab*) highly regarded in their communities, and their life experiences pre- and post-adoption of the niqab, their niqab journeys were usually complicated, marked by long periods of study, experiential learning, reflection, and, sometimes, doubt.

The debate on the Islamic nature of the niqab among the women who wear it and, more widely, in the Islamic *ummah,* is driven by the need for reassurance that compliance with the divine commandment has been achieved. The participation of women in various Islamic study groups and the popularity of female teachers/mentors therein (Mahmood 2005; Nyhagen Predelli 2008; Piela 2012) could be interpreted as a means to this end. Mahmood (2005: 29) linked a keenness for ethical formation through education to agency "[which] is predicated upon [one's] ability to be taught, a condition classically referred to as 'docility.'" The knowledge that one has complied correctly has spiritual benefits as illustrated by the following point made by Sumayah: "I've learnt a lot about religion throughout the years, erm, [in my] academic studies and er, it brings you more close to God because you know that God has guided you to this point in terms of the dress code, in terms of how to be" (Sumayah, 39, British Pakistani, emphasis added).

Aisha, a mathematics teacher at an Islamic school in West Yorkshire, like almost all the participants interviewed for this project, was aware of the general Qur'anic commandment for women to dress modestly. Demonstrating a commonly held view among the women I spoke with, she explained the niqab as "going the extra mile" in her worship, and noted that this logic was her own, in the sense that covering of the face was not mandated by the Qur'an. The following extract highlights Asad's observation that practitioners' conception of what is "apt performance" is crucial:

> Well the Koran does not mention wearing the niqab, erm, it says to cover the erm, cover your chests for the women. . . . *But erm, it's, it's not, it's not compulsory as long you're dressing modestly, but it's not compulsory to cover your face. However, if you, it's like, erm, once you're, you've been, when God tells you, and* Allah tells you to erm, cover your, cover your head, so *by covering your faces and so you're going one step closer to God* by saying that you've told me to cover my head, but I want to get even closer to you by covering my face as well. . . . I'm not drawing that from the Qur'an, and, that's just my own [understanding of the Qur'an]. I can't remember, but I think there's been some narrations [i.e., the Hadith] that say that erm, you should cover the face erm, I think it's, I'm not sure, I'm not going to say because I'm not sure [laughs].
>
> (Aisha, 24, British Pakistani)

Even though Aisha was not able to recall the particular Hadith that recorded instances of face covering, for her the practice was rooted in the Islamic tradition as one of many options related to modest comportment. The particular option she chose to enact reflected her religious sensibilities, that is, the yearning for the experience of being closer to God. This is a typical logic I encountered among the participants. They did not approach the Islamic scriptures as a blueprint for their lives—but actively mediated them through engagement and reflection on their underlying principles. It is essential to note that all the participants expressed the principle of citationality in their constructions of correct applications of Islamic teachings. Here, Wafa compared the process of interpreting the sources and deriving solutions applicable in day-to-day life situations to writing an essay:

> [I]n Islam we usually have a source for everything, wherever we get our erm, our narrations or anything from there's always a source. It's very, it's not very erm, liked to just say your own views. . . . Hmm. It's, you should have a source for everything that you're saying. Yeah, so it's, it's like, you know, how you have a bibliography at the end of an essay, it's like that, that you, you should provide yourselves with a bibliography for everything.
>
> (Wafa, 25, British Pakistani)

Sumayah saw the adoption of the niqab as occupying one of many positions on the interpretive continuum as far as the Qur'anic modesty verses are concerned but considered the example of the Prophet's wives as important in her daily practice. She shared the popular "one step further" view of the niqab:

> In the Holy Book, in the Qur'an, it says to cover yourself modestly, and to wear an outer garment. Now, the interpretation of that is different to every group of Muslims. To certain groups, and when we talk about the whole concept of covering ourselves modestly, some people believe it just to be the dress code itself. However, others believe it to be an outer garment as well as headscarf, they believe it to be erm the, the long robe, the gown. Whatever you'd like to call it, the abaya . . . Abaya. Abaya. So some people you know stick to that. However, erm, others would go further, one step further and of this they say it's covering, the face covering as well, because it says to cover yourself. And because the wives of our beloved Prophet Muhammad, peace be upon him, erm, he was the final messenger of Islam, and because his wives used to cover in that manner, many Muslim women take it from them as well that erm, because the Prophet, peace be upon him, was the perfect example for mankind, and therefore he taught the message of God, and the conducts of daily life to his wives, and therefore we practise what his wives did as females.

> (Sumayah, 39, British Pakistani)

Nabila, a British Muslim and one of the two Salafi participants in the sample, specifically talked about comparing Islamic evidence in favor of both positions (obligatory versus recommended). Her opinion was framed by Salafi perspectives, but she did not support the view (often considered as *the* Salafi view) that the niqab was obligatory. This dovetails with Inge's findings (2016) that the practice of niqab-wearing among Salafi women in Britain is common, but by no means ubiquitous. This pertains particularly to women who are employed outside the home, for example, in the medical profession— the uniform requirements preclude the adoption of Islamic dress. However, at the time of the interview, Nabila was a PhD student and free to wear the niqab. She underscored the significance of emulating the conduct of the wives of the Prophet as her main motivation:

> [W]ithin the Salafi community you have two different points of view or in terms of you know, we follow evidence. Where does the stronger evidence lie in terms of what you're going to follow practice with these sorts of issues. I myself tend to think that covering the face within niqab is not actually obligatory when you look at the textual evidence from the Koran. However we do think it's highly recommended it's more virtuous because the wives of the Prophet used to cover their face. So you know we want to excel in our good deeds.

> (Nabila, 43, British Pakistani and Salafi Muslim)

Many participants put a great deal of effort into educating themselves—often by attending classes and workshops online—on principles of Islamic reasoning as well as established Islamic knowledge. The two sometimes went hand in hand as the next examples show. Here, Sadiqa reasoned that since the Prophet criticized some actions of the early Muslims as too extreme (not marrying, not breaking the fast, not sleeping), but not others (face covering), this implied that the latter were not too extreme or discouraged:

> So this Hadith, it talked about how, you know, how the ayah [verse] of hijab just came down. The next morning, the women, they took their, I think they're like aprons of wool and everything, and they just put it all like this [shows], over their head. And they said, when they went out . . . no one could tell, who was who, everybody was covered. . . . And[there's a Hadith that says] you're not supposed to be too extreme with religion. One was the one sort of, like, some of the companions, like one was saying, you know, I'll never get married. Another was like, I'll never break my fast that almost like, I'll not sleep all night, this kind of thing. And [the Prophet] was like, why would you go to such extremes? It's like, I'm married, you know, I put in my, but I also go to sleep. I fast but I also break my fast, you know, you shouldn't go too far. *And so, with that idea, I was imagining, like, Okay, well, if the women were covering their faces, and it wasn't necessity. I, like I would already automatically assume like, the Prophet probably would have told them, if it's not a necessary thing.*

Another example of such reasoning was offered by Asma:

> [T]here's also another verse in the Qur'an, it states that . . . women shouldn't be stomping their feet while wearing anklets to draw attention to them and so it helped me to further understand that you know, women really . . . we need to wear niqab and that was a verse that helped me to see that Allah is concerned about that, drawing attention with anklets that no one can see—what about your face that draws attention? Your face is an adornment that everyone can see. You know, so if He's mentioning that about an adornment that's around your ankle, but no one can see, what about your face? So that just helped me to understand that it is highly recommended in even if it isn't obligatory.
>
> (Asma, 46, African American)

These examples from Sadiqa's and Asma's narratives could be interpreted as personal attempts at *ijtihad*, legal reasoning which allows one to derive law on the basis of the Qur'an and the Sunnah. Asad (2009c: 23) argued that argumentation was a part of traditional practice, therefore it was the first task of an anthropologist of Islam to "describe and analyze the kinds of reasoning, and the reasons for arguing, that underlie Islamic traditional practices," as this is where the "central modality of power" may be located, along with resistances to it. These are intrinsic to "development and exercise" of any traditional practice. The idea of the niqab as a practice that is essentially too extreme is, of course, common among those who refuse to recognize its historical and political contextuality. It is, more importantly, common among political and religious actors who wield the power to prevent women from wearing it. Thus, as in the story of Hajja Faiza in Mahmood's seminal study (2005), by situating their reasoning in the religious framework, some participants are able to claim that niqab wearing is one of the recommended positions that believing women are able to occupy.

In the dataset, Selina's narrative, a part of which is quoted below, was an exception in that she thinks it is compulsory based on her preferred scholars. She was, however, aware of a variety of opinions on the matter. She labeled the scholars she follows as conservative, but she was also aware that there were different views on whether the niqab was compulsory and appeared at ease with this interpretive diversity.

> [W]e were studying Islamic theology and obviously, there's a couple of Qur'anic ayahs, erm, verses in the Qur'an which point to, when you, as a believing woman when you leave the house, you should be covered. Now obviously the thing is that is interpreted, has been interpreted by scholars, now some, some would say that includes the face veil and some would say, erm . . . it doesn't, you know, it's everything but your . . . everything except your hands and your, erm, feet and your face. Obviously where I was born is quite a conservative area . . . so a lot of, if you ask scholars in our, where I grew up and that, they would definitely say wearing the veil is compulsory. It's kind of an issue of where you're living at the moment, you know, obviously, you know, predominantly Asian/Muslim area. Erm, and obviously where I was studying our, teachers and . . . they were from the same school, of the same way of thinking, erm, and I think it came, and I think it came, comes from that.
>
> (Selina, 29, British Indian)

Selina ascribed her views to the predominant scholarly opinion in her neighborhood. It was a highly diverse area which I visited several times to conduct interviews in different locations, including schools, study groups, women's gyms, and private homes. It was an area that covered, administratively, several different towns, and was seen by many researchers as one of the best locations to research Islam in the North of England, "the Asian area." It was rich in halal supermarkets, halal takeout restaurants, masjids, Asian fashion stores, and Islamic bookstores. However, while the proportion of face-veiled women was higher there than in an average English city, by no means were all women in the neighborhood wearing the niqab or even the headscarf. But, as Asad (2009c: 23) writes, "the variety of traditional Muslim practices in different times, places, and populations indicate the different Islamic reasonings that different social and historical conditions can or cannot sustain." Of course, the decision whether or not to wear the niqab is related to more conditions than the predominant scholarly viewpoint in that geographical location (to name a few, one's personal understanding of Islamic traditions, family dynamics, peer dynamics, diversity (or lack thereof) in one's neighborhood, health issues, employment), but it is an important insight into the process of distribution of discursive traditions.

Lived Religion and the Importance of Religious
Formation for the Adoption of the Niqab

For many women, adopting the niqab is not a straightforward decision—women often talk about years of reflection before they take this leap. It is rarely a conclusion that stems purely from studying the sources; women's narratives point to a lengthy process of spiritual discernment. Often, a specific event such as a pilgrimage or college graduation marks out the decision. The following extracts illustrate different approaches that informed participants' journeys: Sadiyah highlighted the role of her emotions, Sadiqa talked about developing the resilience necessary to wear the niqab prior to adopting it, and Asma described an event that could be understood as supernatural:

> I knew that it was something that God wanted me to do, and the people in my family were already doing it, like my sisters who are younger than me, they wear the niqab, I wasn't ready, I always knew that I was . . . that's right, I didn't have that strength in me . . . and there was this one day, and I woke up in the morning, and that's what it was, so basic, something God wanted me to do.
>
> (Sadiyah, 37, British Pakistani)

Sadiyah then reflected on her personal "mode" of adopting the niqab by contextualizing it in a particular type of discursive tradition that shaped her formation as a pious Muslim:

> I left Madrasah at a very young age, I was only eleven, when er, you know my Islam knowledge that I was gaining [trails away] . . . I left that at eleven and I didn't enjoy Madrasah at all. And whatever Islamic knowledge I did gain was my own, my, my father's and my mum's, we used to listen to lots of like lectures and things like that. That's why I think my, my look on things is slightly different. If you go through the whole system, learning everything and then practising it, and then [trails away] . . . I feel like I go with my emotion, that I know what's, I didn't look at Hadith and things like that even though I think it must have been, I thought it's, *God* has told me to do this and that is why it's right for me to do it. . . . God wants me to do it, and I did it in that way. And there's even variations within Muslims and people say you don't need to wear it. So it's different thinkings behind it, I think.

Here, Sadiyah positions herself as "slightly different" in terms of Islamic schooling which has affected her perspective on Islamic practices. Not having gone through "the whole system," that is, the institutionalized Islamic education of the madrassah often criticized for its focus on rote learning of the Qur'an rather than understanding it (Cherti and Bradley 2011), she comfortably draws from an affective religious repertoire that includes the sensation of being close to God, communicating with God, and being guided by God through emotion. In her case, this was fostered by a home-schooling approach to learning about Islam and, importantly, *how to be Muslim*. Based on Asad's notion of learning Islamic practices (2009c: 21), this mode of education is by all means Islamic. ("A practice is Islamic because it is authorized by the discursive traditions of Islam, and is so taught to Muslims—whether by an *'alim*, a *khatib*, a Sufi *shaykh*, or an untutored parent.") In this case, niqab-wearing, practiced by other family members, existed as an available option to Sadiyah, but was not required. She talked about "not having the strength" to wear it for a long time, and then experiencing a moment of illumination that this was God's will and gaining the strength.

Sadiqa grappled with this issue for six years. It was a lengthy discernment during which she developed the emotional maturity and resilience necessary not only to adopt the niqab but also to persevere with it. Notably, the notions of strength as well as God's involvement in the process also frame her reasoning:

> I think after six years [of soul-searching], I really understood exactly why I was going to do it. And it made me stronger. And also, I think because there was so much to happen along the way for six years that helped me grow up and be more mentally strong and emotionally strong and kind of like, you know, the things off more than it actually was for the better when I reflected upon it. Because I was thinking what could have happened if I hadn't waited? I might not have been able to keep it on I might have decided to take it off after a year or two. Whereas, you know, there's a lot more that's kept me on it. And for that I'm grateful, you know, as much as I wanted to do it for those years. You know, God probably kind of understood my intention in that, you know, as much as I wanted to do it, it was for the best.
>
> (Sadiqa, 25, African American)

Sadiqa also talked about her experience of Islamic education in this context, which was mostly based on her personal research. This scholarship-oriented approach was intertwined with her own life experiences as well as conversations with her older sister who also wears the niqab. Her account suggests that experiential knowledge does not necessarily have to stand in conflict with traditional scholarly interpretations of Islamic modesty rules:

> I want to look at more and more into it, there was a lot of scholars that have said, niqab is perfect hijab. . . . And they're all like, really, really old scholars from made from way back when and even some now. So the more I read into and stuff like those like, okay, well, if they're all saying that, . . . I'm not one to like, be against this, to challenge the scholars, I've nowhere near their knowledge, and I don't know as much as them . . . and they're, like, all known as the very few people who . . . spent the whole life studying. So that was what led me to that I was really looking more into the tafsir of like, you know, the Quran, and Hadith, and the scholars all together is what got me to a point where I was like, okay, *even though I've already worn it, it's not like my opinion's changed.*
>
> (Sadiqa, 25, African American, emphasis added)

Sadiyah's and Sadiqa's stories of niqab adoption and subsequent reflection contrast with Asma's. Asma, unlike Sadiyah and Sadiqa, was a convert from Christianity, but had always been drawn to different types of head-covering as an African American. Having initially learned about Islam through media coverage of the World Hijab Day, she struck up a friendship with a Muslim woman who was a fellow parent at her children's school. Step by step, through frequent interactions with her friend and her family members, Asma came close to accepting Islam which she finally did at her Muslim friends' dinner table. Gradually, she adopted a range of practices and finally was faced with the decision of whether to adopt the niqab, which she told me she had always admired as a beautiful form of worship. She decided in favor of it. On her first day as a niqabi, she was waiting for a friend near a playground when she noticed a toddler in visible distress because she could not get down from a spring rider:

> I picked her up, and I fixed her. And it was so cute. She said, Come sit down. And so she wanted me to sit down with her. . . . For the whole half an hour, she didn't want to go back to her parents. She stood with me the whole time was, she stood with me the whole time at the park, she wouldn't let go of my hand, she wouldn't let me take to her parents. So right there, that was a confirmation, *Allah told me that this, this is what he wanted me to do.* Because if a child is not afraid of me in niqab, that I shouldn't worry about anybody else. And from there on. I never took it off. Alhamdullilah.

> (Asma, 46, African American, emphasis added)

Asma's religious formation was influenced not only by her study of Islam, but also by a series of encounters with people whose reactions and behaviors she interpreted as a confirmation that she was "headed in the right direction" as far as the niqab was concerned. This conviction rests on the premise of a closeness with God that is shared by many participants. Moreover, Asma's narrative indicates that through the (traditionally gendered) act of caring for the little girl in distress, she encountered God, in a manner of speaking, as she could sense God's will, recognize, and enact it. This is an apt example of cultivation of an ethical disposition, since her story illustrates that one good deed leads to another.

Asma, along with almost all the other participants talked about the affective aspect of wearing the niqab—how it made them feel (spiritual, worshipful, connected to God, spiritually protected, or, rather, looked after) was a significant part of the reality of this religious practice. It appears then that the niqab is both inspired by pious disposition and also helps cultivate it by creating a particular emotive state (Mahmood 2005: 30). This also speaks to Orsi's (2005) point that embodied practices affect the everyday life of many people for whom the sacred is made vividly real and present by the experiencing body. Her connection with God helped her face the dilemma as to whether she should adopt the niqab, and this accomplishment illustrates well "[why lived religion] requires a practical coherence: It needs to make sense in one's everyday life, and it needs to be effective, to 'work,' in the sense of accomplishing some desired end" (McGuire 2008:

15). Finally, this one and several other anecdotes that Asma shared with me reveal the workings of the architecture of her life. The sacred, using McGuire's fitting wording (2008: 81), "regularly erupts" in the day-to-day existence, "producing miracles, prophecy, and other evidence of divine intervention in the course of mundane events."

Pious Disposition and Spirituality

While the most visible in the public, the niqab is just one of a whole gamut of embodied Islamic practices that are meant to orient the practitioners to cultivation of ethical disposition:

> My, my whole life is based on what God would want me to do. That's what I would work towards and if there are any actions which I know which I'm not working towards . . . that I know God wants me to do and that's something that I focus on. But, I do all the basics, like I pray Sunnah and all that and I think OK those are the commandments set by God that I have to do, but even my daily life I, I would hope that I'm living it according to how God wants me to live it. Like even my job, I would not be doing it and if, if it was not for God. Everything I do, like you know not talking to men and all that, that's my following of my belief. Erm, keeping my eyes low is my following of, my belief, even my interactions on a daily basis with females, it's my belief in God, this is the way I should behave. Erm, being truthful, you know, those kind of things.
>
> (Sadiyah, 37, British Pakistani)

Sadiyah's narrative bears many similarities to Asma's, as quoted earlier. Here, she framed both traditionally religious (prayer) and mundane tasks (employment) by the continuous process of anticipating, recognizing, and enacting God's will. This becomes a prism through which pious disposition ("the way I should behave") is cultivated. This dovetails with observations made by Mahmood who witnessed how women participating in the mosque movement educated each other on how to train their pious capabilities. Mahmood highlighted

> the economy of discipline at work . . . particularly the ways in which ordinary tasks in daily life are made to attach to the performance of consummate worship. Notably, when Mona [a participant] links the ability to pray to the vigilance with which one conducts the practical chores of daily living, all mundane activities— such as getting angry with one's sister, the things one hears and looks at, the way one speaks— become a place for securing and honing particular moral capacities.
>
> (Mahmood 2005: 126)

Orienting all mundane practices to God is a gradual process. By training herself to pray salat, keep her eyes low, and being truthful, Sadiyah, steadily formed her pious disposition. Modesty, achieved not just by covering up, but by avoiding unnecessary contact with men, and demure interaction with both genders, was an important part of the pious attitude, as "the veiled body becomes the necessary means through which the virtue of modesty is both created and expressed" (Mahmood 2005: 23). Mahmood emphasized here that wearing the niqab, or other embodied acts such as Islamic prayer, *salat*, are not simply an outcome of an already forming or formed pious disposition, but an essential practice that helps cultivate the desire to strengthen it in the wearer: "the outward behavior of the body constitutes both the potentiality and the means through which interiority is realized" (Mahmood 2005: 159). Sadiyah's narrative is further illuminated by Butler's concept of "enabling constraints" (1997: 16), especially her statement, "like even my job, I would not be doing it and if, if it was not for God." While she emphasized this pious qualifier, she did mention elsewhere in the interview that she really enjoyed teaching and it gave her a sense of purpose. Agency emerges clearly in Sadiyah's narrative as a modality of action. Furthermore, by working within the "enabling constraints," she becomes the moral subject who participates in the discursive processes that define her existence (Magnus 2006).

For Sadiqa, the niqab is also emblematic of her continued cultivation of ethical disposition. To a degree, it is a test of her resilience, but also a way to redeem her perceived shortcomings in other areas of life. Tellingly, she says that when she wears the niqab, she is the person "she aspires to be," even if she is "not that person yet." Thus, the niqab enables a project of ethical shaping of the current and future selves.

For me, this is just one of the physical manifestations of me trying to get better, because it's something I know, I can do better. You know, and I can persevere through this difficulty in hopes of getting better through another means. The reason I wanted to go into it, because I felt like you know, I know, I have so many faults of my own in different aspects. But, you know, there's a saying that, like, a good deed is followed by good deed. So, you know, if like, the more good you do the more like a lead to doing more good, you know? So, in my head, I was thinking, Okay, well, if I perfect, perfect this, maybe this will lead to me doing better in other ways. Cuz I'll also, in a way, also a conscious reminder in my face, you know *how to be* and *how to act* and like, *what kind of person I'm trying to aspire to be, even though I'm not that person yet.*

(Sadiqa, 25, African American)

The gradual process of self-improvement is facilitated by having a material reminder symbolizing her aspirations. Sadiqa's narrative hints at the conscious and difficult labor of shaping not just the present, but also the future ethical self. Perfecting a particular practice—wearing the niqab—makes way for a more encompassing approach to living out a pious existence to her satisfaction. Sadiqa's explanation, as well as Halima's earlier point about the primacy of faith as opposed to pragmatist reasons in adopting the niqab, resonate with Mahmood's notion that in contrast to "utilitarian, functionalist or symbolic explanations of veiling . . . [it] is, rather, a practice that is in itself constitutive of a disposition of shyness. To veil oneself is a conscious act of self-cultivation in which the body is an instrument utilized towards piety. In other words, one's body is both the potential for as well as means through which forms of interiority (such as, but not limited to, shyness) is realized and cultivated" (Bautista, 2008: 79). However, based on the interview narratives, it would sometimes be difficult to establish definitively how piety initially manifested itself in participants' lives; it is possible that pious disposition and practice are sometimes mutually constitutive. Many accounts produced by the participants were framed by the notion of growing spirituality, interwoven with interiority, resulting from an increased involvement in their faith. One of them is Ayaan's story (narrated in Arabic and interpreted to me by her daughter):

> [S]o *the more she learned about it, the more she felt like the deeper she went into religion, she became more and more spiritual the less involved and interested she was in a kind of what's going on in the world* like we're worldly gains. It was also kind of removal from the pleasure that she gets from her beauty. sort of distancing herself a little bit more from the world and focusing more on her spirituality. she says she feels closer to God, *she feels more spiritual and she says as long as her face is covered she's able to do things that are keeping her connected to her spirituality.*

> (Ayaan, 55, Somali American, interview interpreted by her daughter)

It is notable that in the interviews the notion of spirituality, in particular closeness to God, was integrated into the reflections on cultivating one's ethical disposition through embodied practices. This merits a discussion, given the fairly entrenched distinction between (organized) "religion" and "spirituality" in popular culture as well as sociology of religion until recently (Giordan, 2009). For instance, according to Pace (2011: 24), systems of belief are restrictive for believers because they "depriv[e] the individual of the power of direct experience or reduce the potentiality of meaning concealed within the sacred itself." Spirituality, including Buddhist traditions and neo-paganism, became a shorthand for departure from organized religion, including doctrine and organizational structure, and privatization of the relationship with the transcendent. A common view of the relationship between religion and spirituality in Islam situates spirituality in minority Islamic traditions such as Sufism and Shi'ism, while the majority Sunni tradition is viewed as dogmatic, authoritarian, and legalistic. Nasr (2006: 59) discusses the similarities between Sufism and Shiism by drawing on the example of the "spiritual essence of the saints" revered in both traditions and a "deep sense of spiritual and emotional attachment" that believers develop toward shrines. Due to Sufism's commitment to spirituality and mysticism, it was often perceived as not "real" Islam, and thus spirituality was relegated outside of the Islamic imaginary along with Sufism (Cornell, 2007). Reformers of Islam attempted to excise the "idolatrous" and sought to extract the "pure, rational, ethical, monotheistic core" (Woodhead 2011). For example, Sayyid Qutb, the author of the famous religious/political manifesto *Milestones* that inspired revivalist Islamic movements globally, understood piety as a means of protection against Western knowledge, rather than a spiritual connection to God ([1964] 1990).

However, trying to escape this distinction, some authors point to the existence of spirituality in all Islamic traditions (including Sunnism) as a useful direction of research. For example, Cornell (2007: xix) in his introduction to *Voices of Islam: Voices of the Spirit* wrote that "outside of Sufism, no aspect of Islamic thought and practice has been more overlooked in recent studies of Islam than spirituality." He reasons that interpreting Islam (and identifying a presumed "essence" of it) on the notion of exteriority (practices, traditions, laws), while neglecting the notion of interiority (spirituality, belief, theology) allows for representing Islam as a religion without a mind (theology) or a soul (spirituality). As such, Islam "would pose no challenge either to Western religions or to secular notions of ultimate truth" (Cornell, 2007: xx).

This well-founded concern with acknowledging the significance of spirituality in Islam more widely reflects what Swatos and Giordan (2011) call a "spiritual turn" in the study of religion. A theoretical nod toward spirituality, however, would not explain the degree to which traditional religious notions, such as acts of worship or engagement with holy texts are integrated with spiritual aspects of the religious experience (a sense of closeness to God, feeling love for God) in the context of niqab-wearing in participants' narratives here. Consider the following extract in which Sumayah talks about the niqab in terms of it being a "faith boost" that increases the wearer's spiritual *and* traditional worship repertoire; the niqab increases her ability to have a religious experience that combines spiritual and "traditional" religious aspects:

> [W]hen you're dressed in a particular way, spiritually it connects me back to God, it's a kind of boost I guess. It makes you, *it connects you more to erm, God's path, to your religion, to your holy book, to your guidance, and you study a lot more, and you practise a lot more of er the religious aspects such as the five prayers, erm, you know such as erm, extra voluntary fasts,* erm you know there's so many other things that you can, that, that you start doing as a Muslim, erm, but to bring it back down to the veil *I think the connection between the veil erm and the spirituality is, is amazing in itself.*

> (Sumayah, 39, British Pakistani, emphasis added)

Sumayah makes two important points here: wearing the niqab connects her to God, which is a concept underpinned by the notion of interiority, personal experience of the transcendent, *and* to "God's path" framed by exteriority, that is, external religious practices: the study of the holy book, prayers, fasting. Thus, it is the covered *body* that connects the interior and the exterior, or, in other words, the spiritual and the (traditionally understood) religious aspects of piety. This integration sits very uneasily with theorizations of religion and spirituality that rely on a conceptual dualism and opposition, for example, Wuthnow's (2001: 2005) distinction between "dwelling spirituality" that relies on rigidity of codified pratices, and "seeking spirituality" that is situated in everyday life and one's own self. More recently, Giordan (2009: 232) proposed that "we may define 'spirituality' as a modality of referring to the sacred that is legitimized no longer by obedience to the external authority of a religious institution, but rather by the subject himself/herself, by the free expression of his/her creativity." Niqab-wearing appears to connect the two aspects, or, rather, constitutes an embodied interface between both these analytic categories and shows them to be more malleable than previously conceptualized.

Concluding Remarks

In my analysis, I examined the question pertaining to the Islamic foundations for the practice of niqab-wearing. By adopting Asad's approach to the study of Islam and the practices in it, focusing on the linkages between the past (the historical context of institution of the practice), the future (the aim and transmission of the practice) through the present (especially, how it is linked to other practices, institutions, and social conditions), I was able to explore the implications that the niqab is, as a practice, rooted in the Islamic discursive tradition. I concluded that it connects with the "formation of moral selves . . . and the production of appropriate knowledges" (Asad 2009c: 10). I assert that, therefore, in the case of participants in this project, the niqab cannot be dismissed as un-Islamic or simply "cultural."

Further, I traced the ways in which the niqab as an embodied practice functions as an interface between the notions of religion and spirituality. I argue that by integrating exteriority and interiority, it indicates that the entire family of "religion versus spirituality" dualisms may have outlived its usefulness. Similarly, the narratives presented here collapsed the categories of doctrinally authorized knowledges and lived religion. For the participants, established religious practices operated hand in hand with affect and a sense of transcendence. Dovetailing with Asad's (2009c) critiques of various anthropological representations of Islam, McGuire (2006: 6) points to power dynamics that underpin distinctions used to question legitimacy of minority, "folk," and radical practices:

> In recent decades, many people have made a distinction between "religious" and "spiritual" in describing their own religious lives or the spiritual attributes of others. We should not accept those distinctions at face value. We need always to be alert to the social meanings behind such distinctions, because making distinctions involves trying to delineate acceptable from unacceptable beliefs and practices, desirable from denigrated identities and statuses, and worthy from unworthy ideals and values. Religious organizations routinely try to shape such boundaries, exerting their authority to distinguish what they approve as proper individual religious practice from all else.

At this point, I would like to return to the discussion of the usefulness of the notion of agency in relation to religious subjectivity. Asad suggested that "contrary to the discourse of many radical historians and anthropologists, agent and subject (where the former is the principle of effectivity and the latter of consciousness) do not belong to the same theoretical universe and should not, therefore, be coupled." Bilge (referring to Asad's work) asked (2010: 22), perhaps rhetorically: "Why does it seem so important to us to insist that veiled women are 'agents'? What kind of theoretical and political work do we achieve by insisting on their agency and by avoiding their claim that they were 'made into' (veiled) Muslims by a supernatural force?" It would appear that by shoehorning the veiled women into particular versions of agency, secular-liberal actors achieve false gratification of ostensibly having made them intelligible in ways that speak to secular values, sensibilities, and affects. By assigning to the veiled women particular subjectivities—those of victims, extremists, or resisters—secular actors assume that they are able to slot them neatly into appropriate slots within the social system, assign loyalties, ascribe roles and responsibilities, and bestow (or remove) rights and freedoms. This would explain the incessant, relentless belaboring of the issue of the legitimacy of the veil.

Could the niqab-wearing women try to explain the niqab's religious origins a bit better, in a manner more accessible to the secular public? As demonstrated in Chapter 2 of this book, many niqabis take the role of the spokesperson in this debate and state repeatedly that 1) the niqab is their choice, 2) they see it as a religious practice, and 3) as such, they expect it to be protected on the basis of freedom of religion. Yet, this argument does not seem to satisfy their fellow citizens.[4] Fernando (2010) in her article about debates around the time of the introduction of the ban on hijab in public institutions suggested that a discourse which does not contrast choice and constraint, or autonomy and regulatory authority (and this is a discourse mobilized by veiled women), is simply illegible in the dominant legal, political, and ethical frames of reference. Despite women's explicit framing of the niqab in religious and spiritual ways, scholarly analyses of veiling, policy discourses, and the media inordinately focus on motivations for niqab-wearing that are different from faith-related ones. This would also appear to be the case of the women whom I interviewed: niqab wearers living in the United Kingdom and the United States, the political and cultural differences between these contexts and France notwithstanding. This study suggests that such persistent secular reconfigurations of the niqab may lead to two previously undocumented outcomes: on the one hand, many women themselves transfigure their narrative repertoires to fit in with the expected secular-pragmatist framework in their interactions with non-Muslims, and on the other, some conclude that it is impossible to be intelligible and acceptable on these terms, and therefore refuse to participate in the project of de facto moral (and, in many cases, legal) delegitimization of the niqab in the secular-liberal West, central to the wider ideological enterprise of "Western nation states' condemnation of the Muslim 'other'" (Edwards 2016: 52).

---

[4]This led me to realize that the fact that the participants wished to discuss the religious aspect of their lives with me, a White non-Muslim feminist, was a privilege. Opening up about their religious sensibilities rendered them vulnerable to misrepresentation, judgment, dehumanization, and bullying. And yet, they were willing to engage with me so that they could present their views and address issues that affect them. The enormity of the responsibility related to representing these women and their priorities struck me fairly while reading about a sociological study conducted in Egypt in which the author, despite the participants' clearly expressed religious motivation for covering, ascribed the practice to socioeconomic benefits resulting from the adoption of the veil (Mahmood 2005).

CHAPTER 4
TRANSLATING THE NIQAB FOR SECULAR AUDIENCES

While in Chapter 3, I analyzed women's religious narratives regarding why they wear the niqab, here I focus on their "secular" reasoning pertaining to their right to wear it in the secular-liberal Western public sphere. By drawing attention to the necessary discursive shifts executed by niqab wearers, I reframe the discussion of constraint experienced by Muslim women who veil in the West from that traditionally associated with an ostensibly patriarchal Islamic culture to constraint imposed by secular-liberal actors. This theoretical differentiation between different types of constraint is necessary to further the discussion of agency enacted by these women which is a necessarily slippery category (Hitlin and Elder 2007). In Chapter 3, I argued, drawing mainly from Mahmood's seminal work *The Politics of Piety* (2005), that the religious agency they manifest is not founded on resistance to social norms, which challenges secular-liberal assumptions regarding the operating of agency. My conceptualization of niqab wearers' agency hinged on Mahmood's notion of agency through submission to norms formulated in the context of the Islamic tradition. However, Mahmood's discussion, although it acknowledges global trends impacting on the micro-level Islamic practice, focuses on the sociopolitical context of Egypt. It is a Muslim-majority country where the veil, whether the headscarf or the niqab, is generally accepted as an emanation of Islamic practice, despite occasional rebukes from Islamic scholars who rule against the practice of niqab-wearing.

The situation of veiled Muslim women living in the West is different[1] in that they need to engage, to a greater degree, with secular-liberal discourses that seek to restrict their religious autonomy. Fernando (2010) argued that the religious discourse of piety is often unintelligible to secular actors; thus, women who veil often mobilize the secular language of rights and freedoms, as well as the notions of rationality, common sense, and social cohesion to advocate for their right to wear the niqab. Thus, Mahmood's theory of pious Muslim women's agency stemming mainly from religious commitment has to

---

[1] By differentiating the Egyptian context of Mahmood's research and the notion of the West, I do not mean to contrast Egypt as "essentially" religious (dramatic, irrational) with the West as "essentially" unreligious (reasoned, secular, scientifically driven). Such distinctions are critiqued by Asad (2009b, c) as emblematic of anthropological analyses which cast both contexts as fixed, unmovable, and necessarily different. On the contrary, I argue that it is important to read the Western approach to religion as historically rooted in its relationship with the dominant and minority religions.

be complemented by alternative conceptualizations of agency that recognize particular demands on pious Muslim women in the secular-liberal West. In Mahmood's own words (2005: 157), "agency is a modality of action"; this modality is situated in the power dynamics of any given setting.

Fernando (2010) outlines the discrepancies between conceptualizations of the headscarf in the mainstream public discourse and those of the headscarf wearers during the 2004 "headscarf affair," when religious symbols were banned from public schools in France. While France is not a context investigated here in this book, it is bound by European law along with the United Kingdom (no longer a EU member at the time of writing). On a more universal level, political systems of all three countries are informed by the concepts of, among others, freedom of religion, right to conscience, and right to expression of conscience. Similarly, in all three, the Islamic dress code appears to engender, to different degrees, political controversy that leads to disavowals, ban proposals, or actual legislation banning the niqab (the latter just in France). Therefore, Fernando's conclusions (2010) illuminate dilemmas experienced by British and American participants in this project.

Legal Debates Pertaining to Islamic Veiling in the United Kingdom and the United States

The legal framing of religious attire in France is problematic for the Muslim women who wear the headscarf there (Fernando 2010). It is based on the distinction between the inalienable *right to conscience*, and the *right to expression of conscience*, subject to restrictions. Only the former is protected by the French Declaration of the Rights of Man and Citizen, the European Convention on Human Rights and Fundamental Freedoms (ECHR), and other international conventions. Arguments formulated during the headscarf affair underscored the point that this distinction informed another familiar binary: that of religious belief and practice. Religious belief was considered to be an internal state, a state of conscience thus protected by law, while practice was understood to be a semiotic expression of the conscience, and ultimately restricted or banned.

> Everyone shall have the right to freedom of thought, conscience and religion; this right includes freedom to change his religion or belief and freedom, either alone or in community with others and in public or private, to manifest his religion or belief, in worship, teaching, practice and observance. . . . The freedom to manifest one's religion or beliefs shall be subject only to such limitations as are prescribed by law and are necessary in a democratic society in the interests of public safety, for the protection of public order, health or morals, or for the protection of the rights and freedoms of others.
>
> Article 9, European Convention on Human Rights. Council of Europe (1950)

Unsurprisingly, the headscarf during the 2004 affair and the niqab during the controversy preceding the 2010 ban were classified by many scholars, activists, and political actors as expressions of the conscience, rather than an act of conscience. Fernando notes that this distinction, which informs French and international law pertaining to rights to conscience and its expression, did not simply emerge in an ideological vacuum—it stems from the "imbrication of Protestant epistemologies and sensibilities with the development of modern secularity" (Fernando 2010: 26). One example of such influence can be found in Mahmood (2005) who cited Targoff's study (1997) on the conflict within the Church of England during the Renaissance period, where on the one hand, there was a push for a separation between a public exteriority of religious experience and individualistic interiority, and on the other, attempts were made to reestablish a connection between outward practice and the inward belief. The latter faction regarded the integration of visible forms of prayer and internal faith as a "vehicle of inward change" (Mahmood 2005: 135). Mahmood (2005: 135) explained that this understanding of exteriority and interiority working in unison to create "devotional attitudes and dispositions" stem from the Aristotelian formulation of habitus in which such ethical cultivation leads to creation of moral character.

The incompatibility between the two interpretations of religious dress rooted in these dualisms—that is, the modern secular reduction of the headscarf, the niqab, or the Sikh turban to a mere sign of religious belief and the contrasting notions of adopting these garments as acts of worship—haunts religious individuals' lived experience not only in France, but also in many secular-liberal nations, including the United Kingdom and the United States. Regulatory practices that pertain to veiling in every country depend on the social, legal, and historical contexts that involve, in particular, differing approaches to protection of minority religious rights and accommodating new citizens (Moore 2016). Here I provide a brief outline of these approaches, as well as some landmark legal cases that concretized the application of freedom of religion and freedom of conscience legislation in the United Kingdom and the United States.

Approaches to Religious Veiling in the United Kingdom

As mentioned previously, the United Kingdom is a signatory of the European Convention of Human Rights.[2] It was the very first nation to sign it in 1951. Further, the Human Rights Act 1998 formulates freedom of religion as "a right and fundamental freedom." Notably, Muslims as a religious community are not protected by the 1976 Race Relations Act which prohibits racial and ethnic discrimination. In spite of recommendations made in the Runnymede Trust report (1997) and the Derby report commissioned by the Home Office (1999), the Labour government considered that the Human Rights Act provided sufficient protection for Muslims and refused to amend the Race Relations Act (Kiliç 2008).

---

[2]The withdrawal of the United Kingdom from the European Union (Brexit) on January 31, 2020, does not impact United Kingdom's membership in the European Convention of Human Rights (ECHR). The ECHR is an international treaty signed by member states of the Council of Europe, rather than the European Union.

As in France, it was a school that emerged as a site of contestation in the *Begum vs Headteacher and Governors of Denbigh High School* case (2006).[3] This landmark case concerned fourteen-year-old Shahbina Begum's wish to wear a jilbab to school, in contravention of the school's uniform policy. The High Court's ruling in favor of the school was based on a questionable assertion that "insistence on wearing religious dress does not constitute a manifestation of one's religion or belief per se" (Sandberg 2009: 272). A series of appeals followed. While some legal scholars praised the final ruling upholding the school's position as "sensible, careful, and contextual" (Bennoune 2007: 413), others raised the objection that the judicial deliberations at three court levels in this case constituted "a confusing and unhelpful precedent" that restricted religious liberty in England and Wales (Hill and Sandberg 2007: 498).

In 2007, two years after the 7/7 London attacks, a student was prevented from wearing the niqab, even though her three older sisters who wore the niqab attended the same school without any hindrance (Kiliç 2008). The judge, drawing from the *Begum* case, ruled in favor of the school, reasoning that the niqab was an obstacle for communication and learning; the students needed to be able to express a sense of "equality and identity" through the school uniform; the niqab compromised security at the school; and that allowing it might facilitate peer pressure on other students to wear it as well. The student was offered a place in another school that allowed the niqab. Distancing himself from any general comments about the niqab and its appropriateness, the judge stressed that "nothing that appears in this judgement seeks to resolve or to throw any light on this problem or the circumstances in which a veil [*niqab*] should be permitted to be worn in schools or any other arena in this country" (Kiliç 2008: 447). Neither this nor the *Begum* case was meant as a "blanket rule" on the niqab and jilbab. However, it is argued elsewhere that, while prior to the *Begum* case, British lower courts and tribunals generally followed the "classic human rights approach" (Langlaude 2006: 345), after *Begum*, lower courts and tribunals generally interpreted the Article 9(1) right in an unduly restrictive manner (Sandberg 2009).

Kiliç (2008) further points out that practice regarding accommodating the niqab is not uniform across the United Kingdom, as there are schools, workplaces, and courts and tribunals that allow it. She provides, as an example, the Judicial Studies Board Equal Treatment Advisory Committee's policy, *Guidance on the Wearing of the Full Veil, or Niqab, in Court* (2008). The document states that legal representatives (advocates, barristers) should be allowed to wear it as long as this does not impede the interests of justice. This leaves the final interpretation of the "interests of justice" to the judge. It is imperative that the legal norm of proportionality that involves balancing freedoms of different parties and the common good (religious harmony, tolerance, broad-mindedness) guides decisions and rulings. These cases demonstrate that the lack of

---

[3]Notably, in both the French and the British examples, the rulings banning or upholding bans on these particular types of religious dress in schools claimed to protect religious freedom of other students who might be coerced into (stricter) religious dress on the basis that it is allowed.

uniform legal regulation of the niqab in the United Kingdom, while, at least in theory, allowing for more flexibility to accommodate particular parameters of each case, leads to a situation where individual judges wield a great deal of power over the assessment of what is an acceptable expression of religious belief.

Approaches to Religious Veiling in the United States

Despite the completely different evolution of the American political system, there are many similarities between the outcomes of American and British court cases involving the right to wear the niqab. Based on the First Amendment to the United States Constitution, the government is prohibited from passing laws which respect an establishment of religion, prohibit the free exercise of religion, or abridge the freedom of speech, the freedom of the press, the right to peaceably assemble, or the right to petition the government for redress of grievances. What it means in practice is that no religious tradition may be supported by the American government as state religion (Ajrouch 2007). This approach has been termed "negative secularism" (McClay 2001: 59). Killian (2011: 39) explains that "negative secularism in the U.S. allows politicians to proclaim 'God Bless America' as long as they do not name a particular God." According to Warner and Wittner (1998), it was the fact that immigrants were not expected to assimilate in religious terms that has laid the foundation for the emergence of hyphenated identities. Thus, the headscarf in the United States is seen by some as "the pathway to developing an American Islam" (Ajrouch 2007: 323).

However, early Supreme Court rulings clarified that restriction on the free exercise of religion were seen as necessary. In *Reynolds v. United States* (1878), an appeal of a Mormon man's criminal conviction for maintaining a polygamous union (Boaz 2019), the Court ruled that "freedom of religion means freedom to hold an opinion or belief, but not to take action in violation of social duties or subversive to good order." Interestingly, the ruling had strong racial overtones, as the judges asserted that polygamy was "odious among the northern and western nations of Europe . . . [while] almost exclusively a feature of life of Asiatic and of African people" (Reynolds 1878: 167–8). While the First Amendment originally applied to Congress legislation, in 1925 the Supreme Court began applying it to state legislation which was known as the process of incorporation, based on the Due Process Clause of the Fourteenth Amendment. Subsequently, in *Cantwell v. Connecticut* (1940), the Court held that the Due Process Clause of the Fourteenth Amendment applied the Free Exercise Clause to the states: "While the right to have religious beliefs is absolute, the freedom to act on such beliefs is not absolute."

One of the landmark American cases related to Islamic dress in public spaces focused on the headscarf as a breach of school uniform policy (Moore 2007). The features of this case illustrate the difference between the approaches of the American and French states to sartorial expressions of religion, at least as far as the hijab is concerned. In this case, a sixth-grade student was suspended twice for wearing the headscarf at school. This was considered to be in contravention of the policy, as the headscarf was equated to a bandanna or a hat. After the student's parents sued the school district, the Department of Justice supported their position in federal court. Assistant Attorney General for Civil Rights Alex Acosta, representing the Department of Justice, said in his statement: "No student should be forced to choose between following her faith and enjoying the benefits of a public education" (Frieden 2004: np). According to the government, the 14th Amendment prohibits applying dress codes in a discriminatory manner on the basis of the equal protection clause. The school, therefore, ought to revise its dress code to accommodate that. Two months following this intervention, the case was settled in favor of the claimant (Moore 2007). Such an interpretation did not hold in two legal cases, the first of which was determined as one of the four most important cases related to freedom of religion in the United States in the last forty years (Boaz 2019), *Freeman v. Department of Highway Safety & Motor Vehicles* (2006). After four years of wearing the niqab and possessing a driver's license with a photo of her with a veiled face (first in Illinois (1997–2000) and then in Florida [2000–1]), Sultaana Freeman was challenged by the DMV who threatened to cancel her license if she did not supply a photo of herself with her face uncovered.[4] Asserting that her right to free exercise of religion was being compromised, Freeman filed a suit against the DMV. Specifically, in her public statement, she claimed that the niqab was fundamental for her religious practice: "I wear the niqab because I believe that according to The Qur'an and Sunnah, Allah has legislated for the believing woman to dress in this modest way" (Schwartzbaum 2011: 1542). Further, she argued that her religious belief prevented her from producing likenesses of her face, such as photographs, and the niqab helped her mitigate this limitation for purposes such as procuring official IDs. The case appeared to be in favor of Freeman, as according to Florida law, the government must show a compelling interest before placing a "substantial burden" on free exercise rights (Boaz 2019). However, the court concluded that having a photograph taken while unveiled was not a substantial burden on Freeman, and that her belief pertaining to a religious prohibition on photographs was not sincere. As a result, she lost her case. Boaz points to two questionable aspects of the case: the court called its own expert witness who argued that it would be permissible to take off the niqab for this purpose, and disregarded Freeman's and Freeman's own expert witness's opinions which stated the opposite; and, Freeman's sincerity was evaluated on the basis of her husband's less stringent attitude to religious worship (Boaz 2019). Therefore, the court engaged in the unconstitutional activity of defining what constitutes permissible and required religious practice for Muslim women (Yildirim 2010: 300).

Another American court case involving the niqab which acquired some notoriety was that of Ginnah Muhammad, an African American convert to Islam who refused to take off her niqab during her testimony in court in 2009. The judge insisted that he had to see her face in order to assess her truthfulness, demeanour, and temperament. When Muhammad contested that opinion, the judge suggested that the niqab was a custom, rather than a religious thing, effectively making a theological judgment (Schwartzbaum

---

[4]The timing of the letter appears to be significant, as the Florida DMV first contacted Freeman three months after 9/11.

2011: 1534). Eventually, the case was dismissed, because Muhammad refused to remove the niqab, but she later sued the judge in a district federal court which declined to exercise jurisdiction, and she subsequently appealed against this outcome in the United States Court of Appeals for the Sixth Circuit, but withdrew the suit before oral argument was made (Schwartbaum 2011). Schwartzbaum, in his sensitively and eloquently mounted analysis of the case and its implications (which also illuminates the Freeman case), argues, citing previous relevant cases and Supreme Court rulings:

> Muhammad's testimony suggests she would pass the initial requirement of the Free Exercise Clause that a belief be sincerely held. Once a belief has been deemed sincere and religiously motivated, "the factfinder may not delve into the question of religious verity, or the reasonableness of the belief." The Supreme Court has made clear that "[i]t is not within the judicial ken to question the centrality of particular beliefs or practices to a faith, or the validity of particular litigants' interpretations of those creeds." As Justice Antonin Scalia noted in Employment Division v. Smith, the leading case on these issues, "Repeatedly and in many different contexts, we have warned that courts must not presume to determine the place of a particular belief in a religion or the plausibility of a religious claim." Judges Paruk and Corrigan's hairsplitting over whether the niqab represents religion or culture runs afoul of this clear rule. Even if some Muslims find Muhammad's refusal to remove the niqab in court to be inscrutable, "religious beliefs need not be acceptable, logical, consistent, or comprehensible to others in order to merit First Amendment protection."
>
> (Schwartzbaum 2011: 1541–2)

Thus, despite the Supreme Court's opinion that courts should not undertake theological assessments of religious practices, it is evident that some individual lower court rulings ignore this warning. We can see that in the American context, secular actors (trial court judges) tend to intrude in the areas of both theology and lived religion where Muslim religious dress is concerned, creating unnecessary restrictions on expression of religious belief and, consequently, limiting veiled women's access to the legal system.

These snippets illustrate the various interpretations of the right to conscience, religious liberty, and freedom of religion in three legal systems. They also demonstrate justifications for differing interpretations of why and how restrictions may be placed on the expression of those rights and freedoms. They provide a necessary context for understanding the incompatibility of the way secular law operates within the ambit of religion and the ways pious Muslim women may experience religion though dress. In the following extract, Shafeeqa (46, African American), reiterating Muhammad's view, unambiguously formulated the parameters of that experience: "I firmly believe that just as, you know, putting on the niqab and wearing that is, is a part of the faith, . . . the niqab is something that is an act of worship for a believing woman." In Shafeeqa's experience, faith pushed to the realm of the individualized interiority and stripped of its external aspects is simply implausible.

The Biases Inherent in the ECHR

European law does make an exception for practices (manifestations of conscience) "required by religion" which retain protection under Article 9 of the ECHR. However, the challenge lies in evidencing a strong link between belief and practice: to appeal for protection under Article 9, applicants must "show that they were required to act in a certain way because of their religion or belief" (Evans 2001: 115). This wording (which appears to be founded in the Judeo-Christian traditions) and the manner in which it is interpreted in the European Commission and European Court of Human Rights have unfortunate implications for women who veil. Both institutions have preferred to interpret the concept of religious requirement either on the basis of consultation with religious authorities, thus adopting dominant (and usually male-biased) perspectives, or developed their own definitions of religious requirement (Langlaude 2006; Fernando 2010), making a secular intervention in the fields of theology and lived religion.

In addition, an approach that relies on dominant understandings of religious teachings for granting protection inevitably favors hierarchically structured and centralized denominations with a clearly delineated body of authorized knowledge. Believers of Islam, a less centralized and more pluralistic system of belief than Catholicism or national Protestant churches, have therefore less recourse to legal protection under European law than the former. It is striking that individual understandings of religious obligations seem to have little bearing on legal rulings. Courts and tribunals would do well to revise their definition of religious authority by recognizing that privileging established authority, structure, and centralization in formulating rulings not only privileges Christianity, an already dominant religion in Europe, but also curtails protection for believers of minority religions (and, particularly, minorities within minorities, such as the niqab wearers) who experience structural inequality and individual prejudice on a daily basis.

The second challenge (this applies only to the jurisdiction of the ECHR, so this includes the United Kingdom, but not the United States) for the women who veil stems from the distinction, in this case a very unhelpful one, between "religious requirement" and "religious choice." As demonstrated earlier, many Muslim women who veil argue that it is their choice to cover. This was certainly expressed by participants in this project: "Nobody's telling me to do this, I'm doing it, so, so it's my choice" (Nuzzat, 54, British Pakistani). "It's my personal lifestyle choice to wear my niqab and that shouldn't be, you know impinged on" (Semaab, 29, British Pakistani).

My interviewees felt the need to broaden their defense of niqab wearers' husbands by highlighting that the latter had no involvement in their decision to adopt it. Sadiyah (37, British Pakistani), recognizing that Muslim men are assumed to have coerced their wives or daughters into covering up, was at pains to explain that her husband was indifferent to her niqab: "nobody is telling me to do this, I'm doing this, it's my choice. . . . I just got married, everyone was like, oh your husband told you to wear it! I just laughed at the idea, why would my husband tell me to wear it? Like when I first put it on, he was like: 'What? You're wearing it today?' And I went like, 'Yeah.' He said 'OK' and he went with it."

I would argue that the reason why oftentimes women highlight the notion of choice and personal autonomy is that they recognize that they need to slip out of the religious discourse to challenge the framework of submission (Bilge 2010) effectively, that is, mobilizing the secular-liberal notion of agency to be intelligible to the Western public. A well-contextualized example of the choice narrative was offered by Sidrah who simultaneously formulated a very individualistic definition of freedom here:

I don't approve [of] what is happening in France. I do not approve what is happening in Saudi Arabia and all that. Because, it's everyone individual's choice. . . . It's not up to any government or people to tell you what to do. . . . I think the Islamic extremist and the socialist extremist, they are, they are just fighting for their own thoughts and *we Muslim women are, you know, sandwiched between them*. They . . . think that they are giving us freedom. I don't know what is freedom? I feel, I believe, that freedom is what I want to do.

(Sidrah, 27, Pakistani living in the UK, emphasis added)

Yet, by distancing themselves from the idea that the veil is forced on them by the ostensibly patriarchal Islamic culture or actual individuals, women who veil lose the legal protections that stem from the idea of requirement that is closely related to the idea of the veil being forced on them. Put simply, if it were, indeed, forced on them on the basis of religious duty, it would be legally protected. This means, as Sidrah correctly observed, that Muslim women who veil find themselves in a double bind. My analysis of the narratives about the motivations for wearing the niqab suggests, however, that the argument of choice runs concurrently with the argument of a certain type of a religious obligation (as many women said clearly that they adopted the niqab as soon as they realized that God wanted them to do it).[5]

These narratives clearly show that the notion of choice is mobilized to discount the allegations of forced wearing of the niqab, but it exists simultaneously with the sense of religious duty to veil (which the interviewed Muslim women who do veil embrace willingly), not to distance themselves from God's call to veil which they experience. (The duty, importantly, is not universal for all Muslim women, according to the vast majority of the participants, but pertains to individual women who interpret God's will as requiring them to adopt the practice. It is anchored in an internally experienced relationship in which an individual is the subject, as opposed to an institutional edict which would make her the object.) The women choose to submit to what they believe is the will of

---

[5]Many such statements highlighting choice and freedom made by face-veiled women are dismissed as "false consciousness." This is a dishonest charge which assumes that Western liberal subjects enjoy a personal freedom untainted by religious or cultural limitations. Even when the premise is that we are all constrained by societal expectations, Western liberal choices are constructed as "freer" than those made by others. Muslim women, on the other hand, are framed as "intrinsically suffering from diminished rational capacity or destructive behavior" which "saturates their public sphere and formal law" (Vakulenko 2012: 70).

God, which is exactly what Mahmood theorized as a particular modality of religious agency (2005). Furthermore, this complicated symbiosis between choice and duty that emerges from the narratives indicates that the distinction between obligatory (*fard*) and recommended (*mustahhab*) practices in Islam which operates as the lynchpin of Islamic theological debates over the niqab has potentially more far-reaching consequences for the women than simply guiding individual decisions whether to wear it; in Europe, it defines a basis for legal protection, or, in this case, a lack thereof (Fernando 2010).

In a convincingly formulated recent article, Van Engeland (2019) called for the European Court of Human Rights to center religious narratives and experiences of discrimination of Muslim women who wear the niqab in adjudicating cases that involve them. Citing a previous ECHR ruling, she points out that the Court itself emphasized the value of "a cultural diversity of value to the whole community" (Van Engeland 2019: 215). Further, she argues that the niqab acts as a passport for the women who wear it, that is, it facilitates the crossing of private–public, and religious–secular boundaries. Based on her analysis of EHCR case law pertaining to women's Islamic dress, she concludes that the former has often stereotyped the latter in line with common perceptions of it as a tool of oppression and upheld national bans. Opposing this construction of the veil, she calls for its decriminalization, as it enables the construction of women's identities in the public sphere. Indeed, the complainant in *SAS vs France* stated that as a result of the French ban, "she is denied the right to exist as [an] individual in public" (in Van Engeland 2019: 219).

Translating the Niqab into Intelligible Discourses

Virgin Mary, Nuns, and Michelle Obama: Referencing Christianity

Niqab-wearing women correctly recognize that in the West, it is Christianity which constitutes a benchmark for other religions in the popular imaginary as well as legal systems (either explicitly or tacitly, operating through mobilizations of particular concepts, associations between them, or individual judges' interpretations). Therefore, referencing Islamic history and key figures, such as the wives of the Prophet, may not be a particularly helpful discursive device to explain veiling to secular-liberal audiences in the West. Instead, women often make references to veiling in Christianity. Consider Sidrah's argument:

> You know in Christianity, it's, if you just [think] about religion, in Christianity, I've seen in the churches also and when, when they portray, the mother of Jesus, Mary, she has a head covering. . . . And I have heard that Michelle Obama, when met the Pope, she has covered her head. . . . I don't think it's not compatible with the British society, why not? If they're following Christianity, the nuns in the church, they cover their head, they're covering their whole self, to obey God and to please him, why not Muslim women?

> (Sidrah, 27, Pakistani living in the UK)

Like nuns wear [the veil] . . . we do respect them and they are nuns, you know. Like the way we wear it we get rewards like nuns, so . . . And even . . . I watched a . . . Moses movie and a Jesus movie and all people were covered up like Muslims, everybody's wearing, even women, like a big, you know, veil over their hair and they're a lot like us, so beautiful, you know, with the clothing and everything.

(Nuzzat, 54, British Pakistani)

The Italian Prime Minister or Secretary or whoever, said, how can you ask me to put the ban on the veil when in every picture of Virgin Mary, she's in a veil? And it's a very Catholic country. Orthodox Christians in Russia still wear it too.

(Soraya, 52, Scottish convert)

While the concept of veiling has often been represented as a practice in various religious traditions to aid interreligious dialogue (see Muslim Women's Council 2014), here, such comparisons to Christian practices of veiling are an attempt to translate the practice of Islamic veiling for secular-liberal Western audiences who are usually at least culturally familiar with Christianity and its basic theological framework. By attempting to make veiling intelligible by pointing to the fact that veiling is not a contested practice in the case of nuns, visitors to the Pope, or representations of Mary, they argue for a corresponding right to veil.

This reasoning is further illuminated by Asad's ruminations (2009a: 189) on cultural translations in anthropology: "All successful translation is premised on the fact that it is addressed within a specific language, and therefore also to a specific set of practices, a specific form of life." While ostensibly similar in its form (drawing a covering over a woman's head), the act of veiling stemming from the Islamic discursive tradition had to be translated by Sidrah into the corresponding practice stemming from the dominant Christian tradition. This echoes, to a degree, the emotional turnaround that affected the vocabulary currently predominantly utilized in relation to Islam that was traditionally applied to Christianity; Robert (2005: 230) observed: "there are so many words that we use regularly in Islamic parlance that have negative or pejorative connotations in the modern Western context, among them, 'submission,' 'obedience,' 'righteousness,' and 'piety.'" What is at play here is the power differential between the two that renders the same practice or discourse unintelligible in Islam and intelligible in Christianity, respectively.

There is a marked contrast between the enormous public attention drawn to Muslim women who wear the hijab and the niqab, and the scarcity of debate regarding the history and modern-day practices of other religious women who cover their heads, such as nuns or Orthodox Jewish women. Yet, only the Islamic veil is embroiled in sustained, global controversy. This suggests that it is not the head-covering itself but, rather, its context—here, its associations with Islam's apparent patriarchy, submission, or a threat, that determine the increased focus on Muslim women.

"My Body, My Choice": Referencing Pro-Choice Arguments

The following two extracts illustrate a common argument that hinges on the right to self-determination. Soraya's comparison of the niqab to a miniskirt disenchants the niqab somewhat, but she compared both garments to indicate that they are valid sartorial options, regardless of the controversy they may engender. Just as the right to wear a miniskirt is not contested in secular-liberal public space, so should not the right to wear a niqab:

> I feel that's not fair on us. 'Cos if a person is allowed to wear, if a White person, or a non-Muslim is allowed to wear whatever they want to wear, erm, you know, if they want to wear short clothes . . . miniskirts, whatever, they have the right to wear whatever they want to wear. We as Muslims, if we want to wear a niqab that's our right to wear a niqab. We should be allowed to wear it, you know, 'cos we feel comfortable in it.
>
> (Soraya, 52, Scottish)

> If you want to cover your whole body in a tattoo . . . I will not mind it because it's your choice, it's something you wanted to do. But if I'm covering my body with a piece of cloth you shouldn't mind it.
>
> (Sidrah, 27, Pakistani living in the UK)

In her discussion of the right to bodily integrity, Sidrah drew a striking parallel between a niqab and a full-body tattoo. This is actually a very apt rhetorical device, given tattoos' long history of religious symbolism—stigmatization and subversion—and becoming mainstream in the recent years (Kosut 2000; Rush 2005). Both niqab wearers and extensively tattooed persons attract attention because of a particular cultivation and display of bodies that is crucial for the production of identities. In many women's narratives, the niqab emerges as a "second skin" that cannot be easily shaken off, reminiscent of the inscription of tattoos on the body. However, the key point Sidrah seems to be making here by singling out the practice of tattooing as a reference point is that deviance bias operates in readings of both veiled and tattooed bodies, but only the right to veil is contested.

Furedi (2016: 111), writing about the genealogy of pro-choice arguments, notes that the "right to inherent respect for the integrity of one's own body follows from Kant's imperative that we should act in a way that we would wish to see generalized throughout society." Further, two principles flow from it: "(i) that it is wrong to violate the freedom of another to act according to their personal autonomous decisions (unless these would harm others); and (ii) that our bodies are our own and we have the right to live free from physical harm by others. This latter principle is sometimes referred to as 'bodily integrity'" (Furedi 2016: 111). Personal autonomy and the right to self-determination underpin the expectation of inviolability of the body. This means that one has the right to make decisions about one's body, in life and in death—only organs from those who have consented to be donors can be used for transplants. This right, unlike the right to terminate a pregnancy or to veil, is undisputed, despite the fact that the owner of the body has passed away.

The Kantian imperative also undergirds the "belief that people should be entitled to live for themselves and not as a means to others' ends" (Furedi 2016: 111) This belief, represented by pro-choice activists, is echoed in arguments put forth by many niqab wearers responding to challenges that the niqab hinders social communication. It is, after all, a vehicle which structures social interaction by obscuring some facial features and cues. The point that they make, however, is that even with the niqab in place, the essential communication (as Soraya put it, "don't view my outer, listen to the inner" can take place). Sumayah said:

> I know in the media sometimes they say that when you're talking to a woman in the veil you can't communicate because you can't see her facial expressions, etcetera, but I am surprised at that because whenever, all these years I've been going to shops, I've been going to supermarkets I've been communicating with the world out there, you know, they've always recognised me for who I am.
>
> (Sumayah, 39, British Pakistani)

It is precisely because of her individual interactive style—the timbre of her voice, accent, facial cues on the visible part of her face, body gestures, gait, and so forth—that Sumayah is recognized "for who she is." This account resonates with Hollywood's (2002: 95) argument that "the subject is formed not only through the linguistic citation of norms, but also by the bodily subject's encounters with other bodies in the world and by its practical or bodily citation." Giddens (1999: 99) similarly draws attention to the interactive, disciplined, socially immersive aspect of the body "[which] is not just a physical entity which we possess, it is an action system, a mode of praxis, and its practical immersion in the interactions of day-to-day life is an essential part of the sustaining of a coherent sense of self-identity." It is exactly the system and mode of interaction between Sumayah's body and its surroundings fashioned in a sartorial and interactive way according to Islamic principles which creates the foundation for her subjecthood, or identity.

Referencing Feminist Arguments About Sexual Objectification

Noting various feminist debates about the role of clothing in women's social lives, Soraya, reiterating views of many other participants, observed that gendered sartorial pressures exist not just in relation to Muslim women, but culturally apply to all women, regardless of religion and background.

> There are women in this world who are oppressed, and they're forced to wear certain dress, whether a business suit with a tight skirt to fit in the office, or the burka on the streets of Afghanistan.

Treat me for who I am; don't view me as . . . as a sexual object or non-sexual, we're put it in categories, she's hot or she's not, as woman. How we're viewed by others— men or women, as we were discussing earlier, we . . . society has nowadays become so sexualised, for even . . . a very tiny eight year old seems to think "I look sexy!" It's crazy! I thought O my God . . . this is what I've been thinking as a feminist, for years, don't view my outer, listen to the inner.

(Soraya, 52, Scottish)

When I put the niqab on it was totally about what I'm saying. For the first time, because up until then, being in the music business, everything was about the way that I looked . . . because you realise at this point how much this society affects us in how . . . we are being oppressed by society because we're being told how to look.

(Semaab, 29, British Pakistani)

Semaab's observation that bodily display is expected in Western societies, with agency habitually linked to the freedom to reveal; this is also noted by the literature and defined as "post-feminist forms of sexual liberation" (MacDonald 2006). However, the reverse freedom, freedom to conceal one's body, is increasingly curtailed by liberal democratic states. As Asad notes (2009c: 30–1), one's existence in the West is inevitably shaped by state interference in the life of an individual. Consequently, covering in the liberal democratic context becomes denaturalized and ultimately stigmatized, because it removes Muslim women from the constant scrutiny of others. Covering up is seen as problematic in Western societies increasingly dependent on constant observation of others as well as self-scrutiny (Foucault 1988). This argument is poignant in the context of how Muslim women were perceived historically, in particular in Orientalist art and literature where they were eroticized and gazed at (Kahf 1999). Adopting the niqab may be interpreted as "gaze reversal" and power relations reversal, as niqab wearers are no longer seen but can still observe others.

These examples further serve to indicate that the commonly invoked binary of the West as a mainstay of personal autonomy versus the Orient as a mainstay of patriarchal tyranny is an inherently ideological construct. This binary is deeply entrenched as demonstrated by Dowler (2002) who tested feminist pedagogies in the classroom by showing images of veiled Muslim women alongside extremely skinny fashion models—the students, unable to transcend their moral code, still assessed the veiled women to be more oppressed than the pictured models. Yet, research suggests that in the West, double standards operate regarding clothing norms. To illustrate this phenomenon in the Netherlands, Duits and van Zoonen (2006: 104) wrote about how moralistic argumentation pertaining to both headscarves and revealing clothing affected the way girls' "deviant clothing" was often regarded as deviant and subjected to societal regulation and intervention, while boys' "deviant clothing" was framed by the "freedom of expression" rhetoric and therefore exempt from intervention.

Many women I interviewed spoke with a degree of resignation about the sexual harassment they experienced prior to adoption of the niqab and how it ceased as soon as they started to veil. Halima told me that she was frequently harassed at work by her male colleagues: "crude comments and gestures were the norm, and I got smacked on my butt as well." Reporting these behaviors did not yield any positive results, rather, the situation became aggravated. As soon as Halima began to veil, all sexual harassment stopped (and Islamophobic comments started). While the point is often raised by niqab wearers that loose, opaque clothing protects against sexualization in the public sphere, a small number of women told me that even when covered by the niqab, they occasionally experienced stalking and sexual harassment in public. Sajida (26, Jewish American) was hassled by her mailman: "He commented on my dress a few times, he said, 'I bet you look really good under that.'" Nazneen (58, British Indian) eventually resigned from her job selling Indian food out of a food truck because "men kept making me sexual offers, even though at work I was wearing the niqab and kept asking them to stop."

Counterintuitively, in one case, the adoption of the niqab led to aggravation of body issues. Ambivalent about her body image, Noreen (33, Indian American) was constantly rebuked by her mother (who did not wear the niqab or headscarf) for "letting herself go" and "not taking care of herself underneath." Things got even harder after Noreen gained eighty pounds after a pregnancy. Her husband accused her of using the niqab as a "cover up" and "excuse to avoid taking the initiative to get back to how she was." At the time of the interview, Noreen was ruminating whether she should, indeed, give up the niqab in the process of "getting back to her original self," to placate her relatives. This account suggests that the niqab may not be a straightforward solution as far as developing one's self-esteem is concerned. This was not a straightforward choice between a pious and a material path; marriage in Islam is generally perceived as a religious duty (Hassouneh-Phillips 2001), therefore both wearing the niqab and cultivating a happy marriage may constitute ways of forming a pious subjectivity. While religious dress (or rather, the ethical values behind it) appears to be a protective factor against the unhealthy Western drive for thinness for American Muslim women (Dunkel, Davidson, and Qurashi 2010), Noreen's example indicates that gendered pressures stemming from normative body politics in the West continue to operate, at least in family settings, in the case of niqab wearers as well.

For Zahra, whose story I mentioned in Chapter 3, the niqab became a focal point in articulating her attachment to feminist ideas:

Originally some of my feminism started coming in because I could tell the difference between when I chose to cover my way, based on my understanding, and my idea of spirituality, versus a man coming along and telling me what to do . . . sexism and misogyny and all kind of issues don't come from Islam itself. They come from people that created interpretations of Islam that aren't always accurate . . . So in my work, when I have addressed these issues much about . . . going back to religious texts and teachings and proving that this is not justified and this is wrong. And we need to change things in our community and fight against sexism and toxic masculinity and patriarchy that causes all these issues.

(Zahra, 41, Canadian Muslim)

While this framework is undoubtedly religious, discursively, Zahra clearly references classic feminist arguments when she says she does not need "a man coming along and telling her what to do," or that there is a need to "fight against sexism and toxic masculinity and patriarchy." Her definition of feminism is compatible with the key principle of the movement known as Islamic feminism: rereading Islamic sources with attention to gender aspects of the early Islamic vision of society. The movement is characterized by a degree of variance in claims pertaining to gender relations; while some writers have contested patriarchal readings of the Qur'an (Barlas 2002) and the Hadith (Mernissi), others have formulated innovative frameworks for women's gender activism, such as "gender jihad" (Wadud 2006). What they all have in common is that they trace the origins of gender-oppressive practices in Muslim societies to biased interpretations of Islamic texts, rather than the texts themselves. They also argue for the need of women to engage with these texts in order to formulate their own conclusions as to what is required of them by God. What is notable in Zahra's case is her self-identification as feminist. The label of Islamic feminism is frequently contested among women it allegedly refers to precisely of their disavowal of the "feminism" label, associated by those who prefer other identifications (such as non-Western gender activists) with colonial, neo-colonial, and other hegemonic practices (Badran 2001, 2005, and 2009; Moghadam 2003; Mahmood 2005). Lamptey (2018: 2–3) draws attention to these tensions experienced by Muslim women: "There is . . . widespread ambivalence toward the general norms, terminology, and approaches of feminism and feminist theology. This ambivalence in part arises from the concern that dominant forms of feminism and feminist theology are not expressive of—and are potentially oppressive to—the experiences, challenges, and liberative strategies of Muslim women."

However, there are some alliances across these lines. Badran (2005 and 2009) argues that secular and Islamic feminisms are increasingly imbricated in the Middle East where the political situation often requires unexpected alliances, but this may be less pronounced in the West. In my previous work (Piela 2012), I identified women who tried to build bridges between analytical positions of gender egalitarianism and traditionalism, and, perhaps, Zahra adopted such a position in her narrative quoted here. Her commitment to Islam leaves no doubt that her priorities lie in the religious sphere—but recognizing that her audiences are equally as likely to be secular as religious, she blended the Islamic feminist and secular feminist discourses, eager to call out gender injustices in both Muslim and non-Muslim settings.

Referencing Health and Well-Being Cultivation Arguments

The niqab has attracted some attention from medical researchers interested in its impact on health. Evaluations of Vitamin D levels in niqab wearers seem to be of particular interest (El-Kaissi and Sherbeeni 2010; Fuleihan 2010; Al-Mogbel 2012), along with effects of the face veil on pulmonary function (Alghadir, Aly, and Zafar 2012). These studies generally find that the niqab has a negative impact on both Vitamin D absorption and pulmonary function (functioning of the lungs and breathing). A few of the women

I interviewed reasoned that since the niqab was a physical barrier between their bodies and the environment, it was a protective factor against negative factors, such as pathogens or severe weather conditions.

> [S]he says she feels, when there's a virus or something like that going round, she, says "I'm good!" she said "imagine a world in which everyone is wearing niqab like, yeah, to protect themselves from the contagions, and viruses, and bacteria."
>
> (Ayaan, 55, Somali American, interview interpreted by her daughter)

> I don't get nearly as many colds since I started wearing it. I assume I don't pass germs as easily either; when I sneeze, my nose is covered.
>
> (Rana, 26, Arab American)

These are not unique cases of the use of the niqab to prevent infection. Alqahtani, Sheikh, Wiley, and Heywood (2015: 33) investigated Australian Hajj pilgrims' beliefs and practices pertaining to infection prevention and found that women traveling to Saudi Arabia preferred to use the niqab rather than a cloth mask which "has potential public health importance, as a recently published randomized trial identified that cloth masks actually increase the risk of ILI [influenza-like illness]." The medical literature, however, is ambiguous about this relationship; an earlier study (Choudhry, Al Mudaimegh, Turkistani, and Al Hamdan 2006) concluded that the niqab was not a protective factor during Hajj since it was not used consistently (for example, it was discarded in women-only gatherings).

Inconclusiveness about the niqab's protection from contagious conditions notwithstanding, for some women the niqab facilitated managing a wider range of health issues. Sajida (one of only a handful of participants who did not trace their initial adoption of the niqab to a sense of piety) told me that wearing the niqab helped her self-manage her panic attacks:

> And so when I started going to seminary, and when I had been going to like lectures at the mosque, I was getting extremely ill, like, I was fine the entire way there and while I was there, but then on the way home, I would get so ill that I would actually throw up. I was having panic attacks for because I was attending these, you know, large gatherings with people I don't know. . . . Um, so I have known other people to wear niqab, Muslims and non-Muslims, to deal with like, social anxiety or other forms of anxiety disorders. So I started wearing the niqab every day that I had school on, and it stopped my panic attacks. And then so like six months later, and it was New Year's. And so I was just like, I'm going to wear it every day.

Gulamhussein and Eaton's (2015) findings pertaining to the relationship between psychological well-being and explicit religiosity, which they defined as veiling and wearing loose-fitting clothing, resonate with Sajida's account of the protective quality of the niqab. Having surveyed fifty women who wore the headscarf and loose-fitting clothes and twenty-five others who did not, they reported that both the wearing of loose-fitting clothing (i.e., such that conforms to the requirements of Islamic dress code) and self-reported religiosity were negatively associated with both depressive and anxiety symptoms. Further, the authors found that higher religiosity predicted lower levels of anxiety and depression symptoms. Thus, religiosity was suggested to be a "buffer against psychological distress" (Gulamhussein and Eaton 2015: 36). However, such results should be treated with caution: niqab wearers are more conspicuous than other Muslim women; therefore, the adoption of the niqab in an attempt to self-manage mental health problems such as anxiety may result in one kind of stigma (mental health-related) being replaced by another (Islamophobia-related). Based on the interviews I conducted, the niqab, indeed, appears, in and of itself, to be a positive factor for both mental health cultivation and a more general sense of well-being, as illustrated by the following quote (whose sentiment was echoed by almost all participants): "The niqab makes me feel better, like it's a dress on my face. I wear loose niqabs to feel the wind on my face, it makes me feel good" (Amalfi, 24, White American convert).

The mobilization of the health and well-being discourse in the participants' narrations of the niqab is not very surprising if we consider that the pursuit of these states of being has been a central concern in the Western world since the 1970s (Crawford 2000). Public health discourses, including those pertaining to "individual behaviors, attitudes, dispositions or lifestyle choices" (Crawford 2000: 219) have entered the modern-day imaginary, resonating strongly with neoliberal sensibilities such as self-responsibility, individualism, and marketization of healthcare. As public health discourses increasingly shape our modes of being, delineating desirable and undesirable practices, we are molded into "reflexive subjects" who monitor their health and "self-reform" in a process of maintaining a disciplinary social order. Crawford (2000: 220) uses the notion of ritual in his analysis of health promotion practices in this context. Here, it provides a helpful framework for examining how the discursive deployment of the niqab as a positive influence on health and well-being aids in explaining the niqab to secular-liberal actors. In other words, Crawford's work suggests that in the interviews from which I quoted earlier, the niqab may be understood as a particular ritual of health promotion, recognizable in the context of prevailing (secular) public health discourses:

[Rituals] are a means for extending power through incorporating individuals within institutional projects. However, as stylised evocations of experience, rituals also rehearse and provide repertoires for making sense of widely shared conflicts or dilemmas. Rituals are employed as a means for situating individual experience in relation to the experience of others. They provide moral commentary on the conditions and possibilities for a "good life" and equip people with practical rules ("models of" and "models for") of living. Thus, rituals not only extend or revitalize system 'imperatives'; they are also practices the outcomes or significance of which are ambiguous.

(Crawford 2000: 220, emphasis added)

The religious discourse of "the niqab as divine protection" was ubiquitous among the participants. However, when they told me how they explained this to others, they resorted to using mundane registers, just as Sofia, mentioned in Chapter 3, did when she engaged in banter with driving examiners and instructors. Tazmeen's observation bears a striking similarity to Sofia's: "I agree completely that the niqab is meant for Muslim women as protection. I often explain it like this: in winter, we tell the kids: 'put the gloves on, or you get frostbite.' If they won't put the gloves on, they will get frostbitten and then they come back to mama and ask for the gloves in the end because their hands are hurting" (Tazmeen, 44, Polish Muslim living in the UK).

Arguments in favor of the niqab such as this are a prime example of employing a new, pragmatic repertoire that can help others make sense of the ambiguous, and at times controversial, presence of the niqab in the secular public sphere. By discursively "situating" the niqab in the common (and commonsensical) experience of avoiding frostbite, anxiety, or infections, these participants intentionally provide a possibility for others to recognize a temporary connectedness they may share. The reference to the non-controversial activity of managing harsh weather conditions demystifies the niqab here. Crawford's definition of a ritual applied to women's narratives suggests that the niqab is translated by the women from the discourse of divine protection, bestowed by the transcendent and affecting both spiritual and embodied aspects of niqab wearers' lives, into a secular ritual of health and well-being promotion. The latter discourse is definitely more intelligible and acceptable than the former, given that it permeates the Western public sphere and shapes individual dispositions.

Referencing Diversity and Cultural Citizenship Arguments

Werbner (2007: 173) argues that Islamic dress brings into closer focus questions "about meaning, diasporic mobilizations, identity, multiculturalism, cultural difference, political Islam, gender, agency, transnationalism and globalization." One of the most common charges against the niqab in the West is that it is "culturally alien," or incompatible with the British and American values and/or cultures (Cesari 2013). This view assumes that the nature and boundaries of national cultures are ahistorical, reified, exclusive, and evident to those who share it, drawing on a variety of arguments that mobilize the notion of diverse cultural citizenship. Soraya (52, Scottish convert) vigorously contested these hegemonic assumptions by pinpointing how concepts of normativity and deviancy are employed to stigmatize women who wear the niqab: "it's very colonial Britishness. This is the norm, everything else is deviant, negative or positive. Taking that Britishness, or colonial, White, Anglo-Saxon male view of life as the norm, anything outwith is deviant." It is notable that this critique is offered by a woman identifying as a Scottish Muslim, for whom both parts of her hyphenated identity represent a complicated relationship with the British colonial history and cultural baggage. Such a subjectivity allows her to observe that, in Jouili's (2019: 210) words, "promotion of a national cultural identity is directly connected to a discourse of defense against an alien—Islamic—culture."

Contrasted with that essentialized Britishness as a fixed national identity is a sense of belonging that transcends singular national or cultural identities. Affectively, it may operate in ambivalent ways: "I feel more English and British than I feel Pakistani, to be honest. Yeah, I might like the clothes and food, but I feel more British and more English. I'm comfortable here, you know, actually I'm not that comfortable here, to be honest with you, I am *more* comfortable here. . . . Actually, I have lived in Pakistan. When I was sixteen, I went for three years, and I was in culture shock for a good two years" (Nabila, 43, British Pakistani and Salafi Muslim). Despite a growing feeling of unease following a series of Islamophobic incidents, Nabila linked her sense of belonging to notions of comfort: having spatial familiarity with her neighborhood, social networks, language (although she speaks Urdu, her kids do not). She described that as "the places nearby that are just home and people are just used to it [the niqab], it is just daily life." Johnson (2017) defined comfort as "an affective encounter between our bodies and the audiences, objects and spaces which we negotiate. . . . It is both the product of this affective encounter as well as the process through which the sensation is produced." This definition illuminates Nabila's account of different degrees of (dis)comfort in both Britain and Pakistan. It communicates that they stemmed from the emotional power dynamic between her body and the people she interacted with, objects (food and clothes), and cultural contexts in both countries. Throughout the interview, she struggled to negotiate this conflicted perception of relative comfort in Britain compared to Pakistan and discomfort caused by the rise of Islamophobia in the United Kingdom. What emerges from this account is the problematic position of a stranger, theorized by Simmel in *The Stranger* (1950[1908]), one who complicates the social relationships that are based on agreed-upon ways of navigating closeness and remoteness; in the United Kingdom, Nabila remains close and remote at the same time which leads to dissonance and tension in the host society (Levine 1977). This is highlighted by a different moment in the interview when Nabila attributed her sense of displacement to reactions she received after she started wearing the hijab while at university: "I think for me as soon as I put the hijab on . . . I felt a bit displaced. I didn't feel comfortable here anymore. I do feel comfortable like I know this place, but I don't feel I don't know . . . whether I really belong here or whether I'm really wanted here." In other words, Nabila realized that overnight, she transformed into a stranger whose appearance was bound to create dissonance on campus. She talks about the emotional fallout of the loss of cultural citizenship:

> the right to be "different," to re-value stigmatised identities, to embrace openly and legitimately hitherto marginalised lifestyles and to propagate them without hindrance. The national community, in other words, is defined not only in formal legal, political, and socioeconomic dimensions, but also increasingly in a sociocultural one. Full citizenship involves a right to full cultural participation and *undistorted representation* [emphasis added].
>
> (Pakulski 1997: 83)

Traditional conceptions of citizenship inevitably construct women who wear niqab, and, indeed, Muslims more generally, as suspect. They are at a constant risk of having their symbolic citizenship revoked, as I later discuss in Chapter 5.

Bhimji (2012) offered in her analysis of British South Asian women's identities a useful framing of such subjectivities. She observed (2012: 3) that her participants "do not simply inhabit . . . spaces in narrow and limited ways, but rather participate in ways that serve to further make these spatialities open to differences and fluidity." Although Bhimji's focus was on British Asian Muslim women, her observations regarding the ways in which women cultivated cosmopolitanism by creatively constructing a variety of political, transnational, religious, and cultural spaces also illuminate comments such as Noreen's (33, Indian American): "[the niqab] brings in diversity. Erm and I think that's what makes America special and erm, even London or erm, Canada, like, Toronto . . . But erm, I think it brings about diversity." Here, Noreen refers to the popular perception of particular physical spaces: cities or even countries as a whole that enjoy a "special" cosmopolitan status. As destinations for global flows of migration, information, capital, and social inequalities, they transcend purely "nation state imagination" (Beck and Beck-Gernsheim 2002: 17). The niqab is particularly fitting for these cosmopolitan places, as it teaches others about "an alternative way of viewing lives and rationalities which include the otherness of the other" (Beck and Beck-Gernsheim 2002: 18). Noreen hopes for an educational quality of the niqab—that those who experience diversity on a daily basis, develop the dialogical imagination that underwrites cosmopolitan perspectives (Beck and Beck-Gernsheim 2002).

Diversity, a necessary component of cosmopolitanism, has a great deal of appeal for women who wear the niqab. They tend to classify diverse locations (streets, neighborhoods, cities) as welcoming and safe for them to just be: move around, interact, and produce space. However, my interview with Nabila (who lives in one of the largest and most diverse English cities outside London) drove home how adoption of religious dress transformed her into an "abject being," who was expelled from the social reality she marked as "home," or from the "domain of the liveable" into the "uninhabitable zone." This spatial rhetoric used by Butler (1997: 3) to analyze the process of abjection of some bodies resonates strangely with Nabila's emotional question regarding hostile attitudes directed toward her in diverse public spaces such as city centers and transportation hubs: "Should I get my bathrooms repaired? What's the point? I might have to just pack my bags and run in the middle of the night." Here, she recognized that her embodied piety jeopardized her status as a subject who has the right to existence in the liveable zone (where a bathroom symbolizes stability and comfort). Running in the middle of the night is therefore shorthand for abandoning stability while being catapulted into the uninhabitable zone. Therefore, the notion of cosmopolitanism also presents dilemmas: it is not necessarily derived from diversity. Cosmopolitanism fails to live up to its lofty ideals, as not everyone is willing to experience a learning moment facilitated by an encounter with a woman in a niqab.

Bhimji's analysis of British South Asian Muslim women's cosmopolitan practices can be extended by feminist arguments regarding citizenship as practice (Lister 2003). Building on the critique of the public/private divide (Johnston and Valentine 2005), these arguments identify citizenship at the intersections of politics, economy, society, culture, religion, home, and intimate relationships. Importantly, human agency is central to this understanding of citizenship. Lister (2003: 6) argues that from this

111

perspective, "citizens appear on the stage of both theory and practice not simply as the passive holders of rights, but as actively engaging with political and welfare institutions, both as individuals and in groups." Further, "the way we define citizenship is intimately linked to the kind of society and political community we want" (Mouffe 1992: 25). Based on these frameworks, I propose that the reasoning offered by the participants when they considered their role in society could lay the foundations for a hybrid notion of cosmopolitan citizenship that pays particular attention to grassroot voices. The women I interviewed for this study paint a consistent picture of a society and a political community they wish to live in. Ayaan (55, Somali American), who migrated to the United States in her thirties, referenced the desire for rights and freedoms: "The reason why people migrated to the US was because of [the American] explicit commitment to freedom of religion, protection of your rights, freedom of expression." In expressing this, she exemplified Berlant's (1997: 195) observations that "the immigrant is defined as someone who desires America," and "women especially are valued for having the courage to grasp freedom." Berlant is critical of the belief that the United States offers "symbolic evidence for the ongoing power of American democratic ideals" (1997: 195), the chief among them (as seen by the immigration discourse) being to escape their patriarchal family arrangements and freely find an object of love. This distinction between the United States and "beyond" (where the migrants hail from), reinforces the false notion, contested by postcolonial feminists (Mohanty 1991; Mojab 1998; Abu-Lughod 2013), that the former is where women unequivocally experience freedom from patriarchal oppression, while the latter is the mainstay of such oppression for women who live there. While Ayaan, indeed, desired some American freedoms, they were not framed by this gendered conception of what drives immigrant women. She sought a place where she would be able to freely practice her religion (along with her family), and in an act of cosmopolitan citizenship, she decided to immigrate to a place where she imagined she would find that.

Taking a step further than Noreen, Mahdia (32, Irish convert) offered a vision of a harmonious society that goes beyond diversity and closer to the definition of pluralism, where there is not just recognition, but also engagement with difference: "I think it's about people meeting, I think it's about faith, different faiths meeting, people not having faiths. I think it's about people communicating, whether you have faith or you don't have faith, I think it's about communication. And human beings *really seeing each other*, rather than seeing know, the visual exterior." Mahdia's notion of "really seeing each other" introduced here resonates with Eck's concept of engagement across difference in her definition of religious pluralism:

> Pluralism . . . is not just another word for diversity. It goes beyond mere plurality or diversity to active engagement with that plurality. . . . Pluralism is the dynamic process through which we engage with one another in and through our very deepest differences. . . . It does not displace or eliminate deep religious commitments or secular commitments for that matter. It is, rather, the encounter of commitments. . . . Such dialogue is aimed not at achieving agreement, but at

achieving relationship. . . . Finally, the process of pluralism is never complete but is the ongoing work of each generation.

(Eck 2001: 70–2)

In addition to these three axes of analysis, Eck (2007) formulated a fourth one: active seeking of understanding across lines of difference (Eck 2007). Mahdia's statement hinted that true communication between human beings involves more than observing each other's faces; rather, it requires interlocutors to be able to listen to each other and empathize. Razack (2018: 173) described the preoccupation with the face visibility that characterizes critics of the niqab as based on flawed logic, distinguished by "emotional outbursts, exaggerated claims, and an openly sexualized discourse, revealing the desire that marks the encounter." Mahdia argues for engagement involving niqab-wearing women whereby they are no longer stripped of subjecthood as a result of demands on them to unveil in order to be a conversation partner in the public sphere.

I argue that citizenship enacted by women who wear the niqab should be viewed as an agentic emanation of religious pluralism. They not only acknowledge the existence of diverse lifestyles, values, and interests in the public sphere—they engage with others in multiple ways, for example, through formal and informal education, professional activities, casual interaction with the public, and acts of charity. Weinstock (2002: 239) states that the emergence of new understandings of citizenship is a result of social phenomena that "fall under the rubric of pluralism." Crucially, under the conditions of pluralism, citizens can freely associate around an issue of common concern, and act in order to realize a shared interest (Weinstock 2002: 252). Women's speaking up for their rights in public is a good example of their enacting such citizenship while simultaneously acting in the interests of religious pluralism. Ultimately, for all the interviewed women, wearing the niqab was their choice—they emphasized the freedom they felt the niqab gave them within their existential ethical framework of piety. This may seem paradoxical in a "social context that is saturated by the demands of a secular existence" (Mahmood 2005: 83) to liberal sensibilities. However, the realization that a liberal, non-religious existence in the secular state is also subject to frequent interventions that curtail rights (for example, to privacy) demonstrates that the secular-liberal polity is not the ultimate space of personal freedom.

Concluding Remarks

The landscape of broad legislative frameworks regarding human rights and freedoms, as well as individual court rulings, presents a dilemma for niqab wearers, because the argument that the niqab is a personal religious choice, necessary to contest the notion that the niqab represents patriarchal oppression, prevents them from enjoying legal protection afforded only to religious practices firmly established as a religious requirement. The religious freedom provisions are incompatible with Muslim women's multilayered reading of the niqab and the hijab as a religious obligation that stems from freely chosen submission to God. As Jacobsen (2011: 76) put it in her reflection on multiple subjectivities of young Norwegian Muslim women, "'choice' was thus constructed as intrinsic to their moral agency as Muslims; 'obeying Allah' was an act of faithfulness and worship only to the extent that it was 'willed.'" Put simply, European and American legal systems appear to privilege centralized, hierarchical religious traditions that make it easier to argue in favor of there being such a requirement.

Despite this bias, in both Europe and the United States, Muslim communities have developed strategies of public presentation of self that are "defined entirely by the legal-political norms and expectations of the American public . . . it is as citizens that Muslims intervene in the numerous controversies [involving Islam]. . . . It is in the name of respect for citizen equality and for the First Amendment, not with verses from the Quran, that they claim their rights," argues Marzouki (2017: 21).

Dovetailing with this argument of Muslim citizens' fluency in secular-liberal rhetoric, British sociologist Tariq Modood (2006: 39) notes the rise of the concept of multicultural, diverse equality, whereby the basic concepts of civil rights and civic equality have been replaced by "equality as difference." This new notion of difference as not only recognized, but also celebrated in the public sphere, has, to a degree, successfully challenged liberal individualism. He observes that diverse equality underpins three types of policy demands (each of which, he asserts, is "progressively thicker" in relation to the previous one) formulated by Muslim groups and individuals as part of Muslim identity politics. This classification offers an interesting benchmark for inclusion of niqab-wearing women, a minority within a minority.

It is striking how these demands are aligned with the claims made by niqab-wearing participants in this project. First, Modood (2006) lists a demand for no religious discrimination, which is especially reasonable in the United Kingdom, where religious identity was not a protected category under the law until December 2003, when The Employment Equality (Religion or Belief) Regulations came into force. (The regulations extended the protection in the area of employment previously afforded to the categories of race and gender.) This is reiterated by niqab-wearing women who referenced the discourse of rights and freedoms to argue for the ability to wear the niqab, as demonstrated earlier in this chapter. The second demand mentioned by Modood (2006: 44) is "even-handedness amongst religions." He referred to efforts by minority faith advocates to extend state support, previously afforded to "longer established religions," to initiatives within minority faiths. Modood used the example of faith schools—in England in 2016, the state funded 4,381 Church of England schools (26.1 percent of all state-funded schools), 1,649 Roman Catholic schools (9.8 percent of all state-funded schools), and 53 non-Christian schools (0.3 percent of all state-funded schools)[6] (Andrews and Johnes

---

[6]Prior to 1997, when the new Labour government extended the eligibility of state funding, only Christian schools received it. In 1997, one Muslim school was granted it; in 2007, this number grew to seven (Walford 2008), and in 2016, to twenty-eight (Coughlan 2016). Some Muslim state-funded schools are high achievers in their categories; for example, in 2019, the Tauheedul Islam Girls' High School topped the secondary school ranking in England (Gov.uk 2019).

2016). This disparity simultaneously legitimizes the former and delegitimizes the latter. Discussions of the veil practices in Christianity among participants in this project echo this effort. Finally, Modood observes that Muslims appeal for "positive inclusion of (minority) religious groups" (2006: 44) which is also demonstrated in the section of this chapter discussing diversity and citizenship. This last claim, Modood contends, is the hardest one to accept for "radical secularists," as it calls for fair Muslim representation in all walks of life including political institutions.

I argue that the particular modality of agency that can be identified in the material presented in this chapter is rooted in the ability to switch between discourses based on the requirements of the situation: space, time, and audience. This kind of agency is constituted, so to speak, by the condition of secular-liberal polity, where religious argumentation, in both legal and everyday contexts, may be simply unintelligible. By formulating non-religious justifications for the niqab, as demonstrated in this chapter, women attempt to engage with their secular audiences in order to safeguard their rights, claim their stake in the public sphere, and construct their position as rational individuals. This shift represents "an effect of a particular form of liberal governance, a mode of relating to the self in which the individual is responsible for creating his/her own identity and future and where the value of autonomy and free choice serves as a basis for evaluating the good, moral person" (Jacobsen 2011: 77). This discursive position the women sometimes take does not, of course, preclude the religious (and, as most participants argued, the foundational) aspect of the practice of niqab-wearing. Mills (1949: 907) in his work on motives argued that motives are fluid and contextual, and where they are multiple, they do not negate each other. The women simply recognize that in order to be heard and understood, they need to translate the niqab from religious into secular discourse. As Moore (2007: 323) noted, claiming the right to veil is justified by the "recourse to the language of rights, and thus, of citizenship. Hence, the debate over the wearing of the headscarf in public settings asserts the Muslim as a subject of governmentality and, therefore, as a citizen." The question that remains is whether the non-Muslim majority will be able to accept the need for dialogue even if it is conducted within a framework they consider their own? The risk inherent in such dialogue is that one's own limitations are highlighted. As Tiryakian (1973: 57) wrote: "The stranger brings us into contact with the limits of ourselves . . . he makes us aware of ourselves by indicating the boundaries of selfhood."

The fact that the secular-liberal majority is a significant interlocutor in the niqab debates which shape women's modes of engagement is the main difference between the findings of this study and Mahmood's (2005). Addressing the differences between Muslim-majority and Muslim-minority contexts, Jacobsen similarly noted (2011: 79) that "'piety' cannot easily serve as a counter model to a liberal ethics of autonomy and authenticity. Rather, subjectivities and modes of agency are shaped at the intersection of different conceptions and techniques of the self, creating both convergences and tensions as people's relationship to norms and ethical conduct unfold over time." Perhaps, in the secular-liberal polity, in order to thrive, pious subjects have to be actively "multilingual."

CHAPTER 5
INTERSECTIONS OF ISLAMOPHOBIA, RACISM AND SEXISM, AND COPING STRATEGIES

Racism is arguably simultaneously constant and fluid—it continues to operate in its old forms but also constantly shifts, filling new gaps and molds (Miles and Brown 2003). Islamophobia is one such new iteration of racism, or, as Allen argues, it's only the terminology that's new and not the phenomenon (2016: 152). The niqab has been discussed in the literature as both a target and vehicle of contemporary orientalization as well as Islamophobia (Fredette 2015), but its constructions within the framework of racialization of Islam have not, as yet, been studied. While those who espouse it often differentiate between "unacceptable" biological racism and "acceptable," "cultural" critique of Islam (since Islam as a religion is framed as a choice, "not a race") (Meer and Modood 2009; Soubani 2019), the scholarly literature concludes that Islamophobia has always had distinct racial undertones. In recognition of that, many activists and scholars resist the term "Islamophobia," preferring "anti-Muslim racism" (Islam 2018).

The definition provided by Garner and Selod (2014: 5) usefully clarifies the connections and distinctions between Islamophobia and racialization: "it is the relationship between people, culture and religious observance that constitutes Islamophobia, while racialization provides a concept that enables an understanding of the process of linking them." In the rest of this chapter, drawing from this definition, I trace how racialization of Islam and racism complement each other in different ways for niqabis of different ethnic backgrounds in the United Kingdom and the United States. Using Garner and Selod's conceptualization, I identify how exactly different groups of people and different cultures are connected with the niqab as a form of religious observance, how these connections are formed and contested, and what implications they have. Hussein (2019) aptly points out that in the United States, it is less clear where racialized Muslimness is situated within the racial order that is defined by the logic of the Black-White binary. She points out that religion is largely absent from American theory on racial positioning, despite it having played a role in placing Whiteness and Blackness historically. Similarly, she asserts, the Muslim racialization literature neglects the Black-White racial order. Where then, ask Hussin (2018) and Gallonier (2017), do Black and White Muslims fit in? They indicate that both groups are racialized as foreign and brown when they are decoded as Muslim, but they are perceived as simply White or Black when their Muslimness is not signified.

In the United States, experiences and histories of Arab American and South Asian American Muslims are commonly perceived to be typical, obscuring experiences of

Muslims of other backgrounds, particularly Black Muslims (Islam 2018). This is particularly striking given that in the United States, most Arabs are Christian, and Muslims are a diverse group in ethnic/racial terms (Bagby 2012; Mohamed 2016). Furthermore, Arab Americans are still classified by the US census as "White," despite extensive advocacy by this group to be recognized as a separate category of people of Middle Eastern and North African background (Bayoumi 2019).

Taking the niqab as a focal point for this exploration, I trace how anti-Muslim prejudice is variously mobilized in the United States against different groups of American Muslim women who have adopted this dress. Based on interviews with "born" Muslim women, African American converts, and White converts to Islam, I examine their experiences in the American context that is powered by perceptions and constructions of both religion and race, and where assuming additional Otherized identities may have a host of different consequences. Finally, I identify ways in which women upon the adoption of the niqab resist and negotiate their new position in the matrix of exclusion.

Most of my UK interviews were with Muslim women of Pakistani and Indian origin in the North of England, and the Midlands, where the overwhelming majority of Muslims have a South Asian background; this was consistent with the ethnic composition of British Muslims, 73 percent of whom are South Asian. I also interviewed two White British converts. They all told me that they had experienced some form of racist abuse based on their background or perceived racial transgression. Unfortunately, I did not manage to recruit any Black British women wearing the niqab. In order to provide a comparative point of reference, I draw from two works where Black British Muslim experience is explicitly mentioned in relation to niqab-wearing women in the United Kingdom: Annabel Inge's *The Making of a Salafi Woman* (2016) which indicates that Salafism, a literalist and quietist variation of Islam that also advocates the wearing of the niqab, is particularly attractive to Black Muslims, and *Behind the Veil: Why 122 Women Choose to Wear the Full Face Veil in Britain*, a report commissioned by Open Society Foundations (Bouteldja 2015) that came amid the media excitement about a potential ban, proposed shortly before by right-wing Members of Parliament. I also refer to the report on Black British Muslims' experiences of anti-Black racism published by the Black Muslim Forum (2020) and digital media interviews with a prominent Black British writer who wears the niqab, Na'ima B. Robert.

While Inge (2016) focused mainly on Salafi-leaning Somali Muslims in London, the Open Society Foundations report (Bouteldja 2015) reached niqabis of different backgrounds, including UK-born, non-UK-born, South Asians, Arabs, African Muslims, as well as Black and White converts. Suleiman (2013) and Inge (2016) point out that the bulk of the UK literature addresses experiences of South Asian Muslims, and there is a paucity of scholarship about the lives of Black British Muslims despite Islam becoming more and more popular in Black British communities (Hooper 2013). Consequently, coupled with the scarcity of literature on the actual lives and views of niqab-wearing women, it appears that the niqab has not been studied before through the lens of racialization of religion in the British context. Neither has it been in the United States, despite the increasing focus on the study of race in all social contexts including religion, and the eventual recognition by the mainstream academia of the significance and long history of African American Islam.

Intersectionality and the Niqab

Scholars have highlighted the fact that the frequent collapse in the policy and media discourse of the "Arab," "immigrant," and "Muslim" categories has obscured the experiences of African American, Latinx, and White Muslims, bolstering the misperception that Islam is a religion without much history in the United States (Morales 2018; Evans 2015; Yazbeck Haddad 2011; Moxley-Rouse 2006). The myth of national unity that perpetuates White, Anglo-Saxon, and Christian privilege in both the United Kingdom and the United States excludes those who challenge this structure of inequality in a myriad of ways. Muslims are seen as a group that threatens established social norms. Chan-Malik writes: "Ways of being Muslim and practising Islam have consistently been forged against common sense notions of racial, gendered, and religious belonging and citizenship and require constant attention to, and cultivation of, embodied practices that are articulated against accepted social and cultural norms" (2018). This observation applies to many diverse Islamic groups in the United States, including Nation of Islam (NOI), Warith Deen Mohammad's (WDM) movement, now known as the American Society of Muslims, and various African American Sunni movements (Smith 1999). The neglect of racial and ethnic diversity of American Islam, including its indigenous variations, in the national American narrative (Chan-Malik 2018) has resulted in the construction of Islam as essentially foreign/Other. This, in turn, has led to symbolic bracketing out of all American Muslims from the national community *imagined as* unified by shared history, language, and values.

Black Femininities and the Niqab

For African American women, aggravating their racial marginality by adopting the niqab may seem counterproductive in relation to cultivating one's sense of belonging in the United States. It was definitely true for some participants. Jameela stated that "to be Black and a woman and wear a niqab and a Muslim, well . . . it's a quadruple . . . [vulnerability]." To make decisions that prevent one from flying under the radar of state and society, especially in the United States, can have dire consequences for individuals. Black Muslims are at an identity intersection doubly fraught with over-policing, mass-incarceration, mass-surveillance, and racial profiling (Mauleon 2018). Being a woman of color compounds the risk of gendered abuse and sexual harassment (Brunson and Miller 2006) including by the police (Weizer and Brunson 2015; Ritchie 2017; Capeheart 2018), while the niqab heightens one's visibility, putting one in the crosshairs of interconnected racist and anti-Muslim prejudice of not just passersby, but the law enforcement as well (Ahmad 2019; Edwards 2016, Zempi and Chakraborti 2014).

The idea of intersecting Black and female identities, and resultant risks, was put forward by the American civil rights activist Frances Beal (1969) who wrote a pamphlet *Double Jeopardy*, but it was not until 1989 that Kimberlé Crenshaw proposed the metaphor of intersectionality to illustrate the consequences of interwoven identities (and risks) that do not stack neatly on top of each other, but, rather, complicate each other in unexpected and paradoxical ways. Sadiqa (25, Somali American) implied she was well aware of this imbrication. Very euphemistically, she said, "Oftentimes, minorities, even in the justice system, don't exactly have a favourable position." For her, anti-Black racism was persistent enough on its own so that the adoption of the niqab, and the resultant Islamophobia, did not make much difference in terms of her overall social vulnerability, unavoidable one way or another: "even if we were to take off the niqab or take off hijab, we're still Black. Like, we're still, you know, African Americans, we're still have dark skin complexion. So even if they weren't judging on this [niqab] they could be judging us on our skin color . . . we're going to get something from somewhere, you know. So it's like, it's, I guess, in a way, so it's already been something very ingrained in us, not just as Muslim but as African Americans."

Sadiqa's case shows very clearly how prejudice and discrimination are anticipated; they sometimes shift between anti-Black racism and Islamophobia, but she expects at least one to play out against her in public spaces. Somewhat resignedly she said that she could probably survive the exposure to Islamophobia, having been socialized to deal with racism all her life. Her observation that even if she tried to downplay her Muslim identity by taking off the niqab, she was still Black which makes her a target, is key to understanding that Islam and race are closely interpolated. When I asked her what she would do if the niqab was banned in the United States, she said she simply could not imagine taking the niqab off, and perhaps she would still wear it in spite of the ban. Demonstrating an acute awareness of the intersecting vulnerabilities in relation to the justice system, she observed:

> I do know that it would probably cause a lot more trouble just because it wouldn't only be a woman wearing niqab, *it'd be a Black woman wearing it* [emphasis added]. So, it's a difference when you're also African American, because they already villainize us African Americans let alone Muslims.
>
> (Sadiqa, 25, Somali American)

Building on Mauleon's idea (2018: 1332) that Black Muslims are "Black twice," because their religion is considered antithetical to Christianity and hence to Whiteness, I argue that Black niqabis are "triply Black." The predominantly black niqab multiplies challenges, including the hegemonic resentment of the niqab's challenge to the predominantly White, sexually active, and secular model of femininity (Yoder Wesselhoeft 2011). The niqab also complicates hegemonic views of Black femininities which are often hypersexualized and stereotyped as promiscuous "Jezebels" (Givens and Monahan 2005; Durham 2012). Razack (2018: 178) argues that "niqab [is] the site of an enduring colonial fantasy, the place where discourses of sexual and colonial difference are powerfully mapped on to each other." Yet here, a niqab worn by Black Muslim women contradicts this host of misrepresentations in no uncertain terms; as a symbol of Islamic modesty and literally as a concealing item of clothing it blocks the male/female Western gaze.

Unexpected Shifts in Perception

This "niqab effect" was uneven across the entire sample of women I interviewed—while some were able to enjoy the desexualized status the niqab affords them, others, regardless of background or location, still experienced sexual harassment. Sadiqa disclosed that her friends get hit on by men on the streets, even though they are fully covered. In our conversations, many women commented that they were aware of the "gross kick," or a "mystery thing" some men were enjoying of engaging with a niqab-clad woman. This substantiates Shirazi's claims (2001) in her now classic book *The Veil Unveiled* where she has shown the veil's erotic appeal by tracing how images of Muslim covered women have been fetishized by pornographic magazines such as *Playboy* and *Penthouse*. Strikingly, she demonstrates how veiled models in these materials embody both Orientalist mystery/submission and Western dominance, which is echoed by the conflicted perceptions of niqab by men encountered by my respondents. Razack's argument (2018) that sexualization intersects with mechanisms that underpin more "conventional" racist and Islamophobic incidents that involve abuse, stigmatization, and exertion of privilege dovetails with Sadiqa's account. In fact, some authors argue that a common type of attack on niqabi and hijabi women that involves tearing off their niqabs, hijabs, and other pieces of clothing in the street (Zempi and Chakraborti 2014) is a particular racialized variety of sexual harassment; women who have experienced it, often perceive it in identical ways to "conventional" sexual harassment they experienced at other times. For example, Iffat, interviewed by Stahl (2018: np), said of having her hijab ripped off and being forced to witness a man expose himself to her: "Those two moments, I didn't feel a difference in the way that I felt about my body. I felt disgusted in myself."

The niqab, however, works in paradoxical ways, as the next two examples illustrate. Although I have encountered only a handful of such accounts, it appears that the adoption of the niqab for some women, thanks to its obscuring properties, had a protective effect as far as racist harassment was concerned. A 29-year-old respondent of mixed-race descent from the London area said: "It [the niqab] gave me confidence, my skin is quite dark, I had a lot of racism, I was always called "crocodile skin," "Your skin is very dark and it's tough." I was called "darky," "blacky," "n***** this, n****** that." . . . When I wore the niqab I wasn't seen as a "Black" sister [any more]. They judged me according to how I treated them. They saw me as a person" (Bouteldja 2015: 179). In that extract, the respondent did not specify who subjected her to racist harassment or who treated her kindly after she adopted the niqab; neither did she share whether she experienced Islamophobic abuse subsequently.

In a parallel example, Malika (30, White British convert) reported that her interactions with non-Muslims were much more negative before she replaced her hijab with a niqab.

She was called a "race traitor" by White British people who resented her fair complexion juxtaposed with a visible symbol of Islam. Her niqab covered her phenotypical features and passersby ascribed to her a different ethnic category. Racialized constructions of Islam become clear here—White converts "cross the boundary of Whiteness" (Franks 2000) and become non-normatively White (Galonnier 2015a and b), but when they adopt the niqab, they are constructed as non-White altogether. These two cases show how the niqab may change the type of racialization by either obscuring phenotypically dark skin or concealing the racialized religious transgression "out of" normative Whiteness. This effect of protection through concealment was certainly an exception in the data, rather than a rule.

Dynamic Belonging, Foreignness, and the Niqab

For some, the niqab may help them escape racialized stereotypes and thrive in their community. Others cease to be recognized as residents or citizens of their home country upon adoption of the niqab and are actively excluded from their community. This theme is profound in both my data and the literature and requires careful unpacking. Islam, to borrow Grewal's book title (2014), is, indeed, a foreign country; adoption and communication of it through its signifiers makes you a foreigner. "Go back to your country" is a phrase that rings again and again in narratives of first-, second-, and third-generation immigrants as well as those who had their Whiteness symbolically confiscated. Yasmeena (33, German American convert), told me that she had frequently been ordered on the streets to "go back to the Middle East" after adopting the niqab, even though she has an American accent. She says she usually waits "until people finish their rant to tell them I'm from here." She seemed stoical about it, and overall, she thought she did not receive "too much hate," although being told on a regular basis to leave the country one considers one's own would leave many people shaken up. This example illustrates aptly the way racialization operates: it singles out all members of the group, constructs them into a unified entity, and ascribes characteristics based on the imagined origins of the members or their beliefs. In that way diverse populations are essentialized and made homogeneous. Here Yasmeena, despite being White, American, and never even having visited the Middle East was told to go back there, as it was imagined that this is where she came from. Her experience dovetails with Grewal's observation (2014: 4) that "[i]n Dearborn [a city in Michigan with a large concentration of Arab Americans], everyone understands that citizenship is more than a legal status, that national belonging is fragile and that it can be withheld from those who are deemed foreign and different even if they are technically legal citizens."

Nabila (43, UK, British Pakistani) challenged the construct of "her kind," often bandied about by people who tell her and other Muslims to "go back." In this quote (also used in Chapter 4), she explained that the terms on which such ideas operated were phantasmatic for obvious reasons—her children not speaking Urdu, and her having lived her whole life in the United Kingdom, as well as the more abstract sense of belonging to the United Kingdom, despite continuous harassment.

> [T]hey're trying, [to make us] feel uncomfortable so that we go back and . . . live in lands where we would feel comfortable "around our own kind." If that's the case, it's not as simple as that. I've lived here my whole life. My home's here, our work is here. I haven't been to Pakistan for over twenty years, my children have never been to Pakistan, my children cannot even speak Urdu, they can only speak English . . . so why would we go there. I don't like Pakistan, I feel more English and British then I feel Pakistani, to be honest. Yeah, I might like the [Pakistani] clothes and food, but I feel more British and more English.
>
> (Nabila, 43, British Pakistani and Salafi Muslim)

What is striking here is that Nabila said twice that she felt not only British, which is considered a more neutral label and accepted by more than half of UK Muslims (Sherwood 2018), but English as well. The English identity is more racialized than Britishness, and often set at odds with Islam, especially as right-wing White supremacist movements (such as the English Defence League) are on the rise (Hellyer 2016). And yet, since in the United Kingdom there is no similar apparent clash between Scottish and Muslim, or Welsh and Muslim, the extract shows that the English identity may be seen as racially porous too.

The policing of racial boundaries in connection with Islam exists at many levels, and it appears, not only among the majority White society. Although I did not have a chance to interview a niqab-wearing Latina American myself, I chanced upon a "niqab testimony" written by Wendy Diaz (2019). The case of Latina Muslim identity is poignant, because Latino converts, unlike White converts (and similarly to Black converts) are faced with negotiating two stigmatized identities, all the while being racialized as Arabs or South Asians (Galonnier 2017). Diaz, a former niqabi, described a typical incident in the public space where she, or to be more precise, her veiled persona, would be debated condescendingly by Latino Americans in Spanish. As a result, she felt alienated from her community who assumed she would not speak Spanish herself. In that sense, she was no longer recognized as Latina herself, but racialized as "foreign"/Muslim brown. Diaz describes that she would then usually reclaim her Latina identity by loudly speaking Spanish to her kids and therefore make it known to others that she not only understands what they are saying, but she is one of them as well. When she moved away from her "community of niqabi sisters" (Diaz 2019: np), Diaz subsequently took off her niqab out of fear for herself and her children. She noted that in addition to the usual challenges related to niqab-wearing, it had taken away something else that she was glad to reclaim: a perception among Latinos that in her hijab, she bore a similarity to Virgin Mary (Diaz 2019) which made her interactions with them easier. Morales reports that Latinos often accuse Latino Muslims of "betraying their ethnicity" (2018: 100), so even such tenuous actions as having Catholic symbolism attached to the hijab may be helpful at times. This is corroborated by Galonnier's research with American Mexican and Puerto Rican respondents (2017) who report often being taken for Catholic nuns. Galonnier observes that it is their skin color, coupled with their phenotypical features and fluency in Spanish, that transforms the signification of the hijab (2017: 211). However, Diaz's example shows that the niqab may negate that effect. While the hijab is clearly polyvalent, the niqab leaves little scope for hesitation.

The next extract illustrates how the decision to wear the niqab, let alone embrace Islam, by Black British women resulted in the ire of some members of the Black community in the United Kingdom.[1] Here, a Black Caribbean British niqabi interviewed for the Open Society Foundations report (Bouteldja 2015: 97) described an incident where she was threatened and verbally abused by a man who accused her of "betraying" her Jamaican roots by embracing Islam:

> I was with my sister and my younger sister, and my two children as well. This guy could see my sisters were Black Caribbean and one of my sisters had a Jamaican flag on her. And he was Jamaican. And he was really, really angry at the fact that we had Jamaican in us and I was covered like this. He was livid. He was swearing. . . . He was saying stuff like, "You're lost. You're going down the wrong path," "You're a sell-out!" "How can you be a Muslim? That's not your ting! It's for Asians." My sister [said something] back to him and he said, "I'll beat you lot up!"

There were other similar incidents described in the report, among others by French Senegalese women living in Britain who were called "wannabe Arabs" (Bouteldja 2015: 98). This indicates that racialization of Islam may take many forms, not only a construction of it as a non-White, but also a non-Black, religion by members of different ethnic communities. This, however, shows that some women of color in the United Kingdom are subject to having their identities policed by males. This may be explained by the concept of bipolar masculinity which "seeks to seduce heterosexual Black men into accepting the right to subordinate others as compensation for our own subordination" (Cooper 2006: 853). Simultaneously, the idea that women are primary sites for fostering, protecting, and transmitting cultural identity (Lutz in Chamberlain 1998; Reynolds 2005) may lead some to the conclusion that Black Caribbean women who convert to Islam are cultural traitors. This perception of religious conversion as cultural and racial transgression has been described widely in the literature about White converts (Franks 2000; Galonnier 2015a and b), but not in connection to Black converts to Islam. While Islam is usually racialized as a "brown" religion (Galonnier 2015a: 570) that is also "antithetical to Whitcness" (Mauleon 2018: 1332), its relationship with Blackness appears to operate in a much more ambiguous way.

As a result, some Black niqabis may be in the crossfire of prejudice from within their faith community (for adopting the niqab, seen as extreme), ethnic community

---

[1] My interviews with African American niqab-wearing women did not indicate a similar problem. While there is not much published research on racial differences in the perception of Islam in the United States, Zainiddinov (2013) asserts that Islam is seen much more favorably by African Americans than Whites.

(for embracing Islam, and more to the point, leaving Christianity or other religions that have been racialized in connection with their ethnic community), as well as the majority White population (for both these reasons as well as for being Black). This could explain, at least in part, the appeal of Salafism for Black Caribbean and African women in Britain—as Salafism is focused on a literalist following of religious practice, and at least in the West, it appears to be ethnically and culturally inclusive insofar as women's groups are concerned (Inge 2016). In fact, adoption of Salafi Islam and particular Islamic practices, such as the niqab, may be a way to adapt to the environment and its challenges, a reaction to structural and individual challenges.

Sometimes the ostensible tension between race and Islam may have productive outcomes. For Na'ima Robert, a Black British writer who wears the niqab, her African heritage eventually became a helpful tool with which to build a Muslim identity. In a YouTube video (Robert 2017) produced by likeMEDIA.tv, a UK-based media production company which creates conversations around faith and identity among Muslims, she explained how eventually she came to understand that Islam had deep roots in Africa, and one did not need to be Arab or Asian in order to be Muslim:

> I came to England and became Muslim in England. One of the reasons I didn't become Muslim straightaway, was identity. But when it came time for Shahada, I was like, no way. And my friend who was Jamaican, I just converted, and she was like, you know, why don't you just take the plunge? And I said, Look, I'm African. Okay, I'm Black. So she said to me, I said, Look, Islam seems to me to be about Asians and Arab culture. And I'm African, I don't want to be an Arab and I don't want to be an Asian. So where does that leave me? And she said, very simply, well, there are African Muslims, you know, like, why don't you check that out?

Robert then reflected on her experience of the intersection of Islam and race:

> A lot of people don't know that I'm Black, because I could be kind of anything, like Pakistani or whatever. So until I actually say, I'm from Zimbabwe, or speak in African language or something, then people are not really sure where to place me. All my other identities aside, the fact that I wear the niqab, it just makes it slap, bang, Muslim woman, clearly!

In an interview for *The Black Muslim Times UK* website (Shode 2018: np), she commented: "I was no longer identifiable as African when I started wearing the niqab and it continues to be difficult. I get the Muslim privilege but don't get the Black privilege as they don't see themselves when they see me." Taking to heart her friend's advice, Robert tells how she realized that an African Muslim identity, and, by extension, a Black British Muslim identity is historically well founded and valid:

> So Islam has deep roots in Africa, there's no it's no small thing . . . . the so-called Caliphate, research "African, Muslim, and Islam in Africa." And you will see that

there's a long, rich and varied history there. So in a way, even if you're going to go back to Africa, there's no reason for us to have to adopt anything Islamic from anybody else's culture, we have our own traditional African Islamic culture.

Robert's early dilemmas regarding her established African and newly emerging Muslim identities echo perceptions of Islam in America as a foreign faith with not much history, and as a result, little cultural legitimization. This was, perhaps, influenced by the predominance of Christianity, and only a nominal presence of Islam in Zimbabwe, the country where she grew up. However, her research into African history revealed that Islam had been a part of the religious and social fabric in the medieval era, especially in Western African kingdoms such as Mali and Songhay (for an excellent analysis of this relationship, see Gomez [2019]). It was only once Robert became assured by her research that adopting Islam did not require disowning her African identity that she felt comfortable to say the *shahada*. This was potentially important as now the niqab literally covers up her skin and obscures the phenotypical markers of her racial identity, while emphasizing her religious identity as a Muslim. The realization that "people are not really sure where to place me" may play a role in her careful emphasis on her African background in interviews (Robert 2010), books (Robert 2005), and online literary spaces where she is celebrated as a children's, and young adult, fiction writer.

Language as a Tool of Racialization

One key way in which these women are cast as the "Other" in both countries is the assumption that they do not speak English fluently or at all. Interlocutors benevolently praise the women (who are British- and American-born) for their "good English," or enunciate their words particularly slowly at them, assuming that otherwise they would not be understood. The participants often told me of their shocked amusement at this experience. They were alarmed that suddenly, they were no longer "read" as local, or native. Henceforth, they would have to explain themselves and make constant claims to their national and cultural identities in conversations with total strangers. This constant need for self-justification has been described as a burden and a heavy mental drain. Noor (39, African American convert) noted with some defiance, however, that her very existence "kind of dispels this like, myth that all the women who are choosing to cover their faces are from somewhere you know, it's this perceived idea that you have you cant have grown up in this country and find it [being fully covered] as an acceptable way to be." This loss of cultural legibility means that by adopting the niqab, Black women may lose an important coping strategy that helps them escape racialized stereotypes, as Sadiqa describes her experience of trying to fit in at high school and college, before wearing the niqab:

I learned how to, I guess, in a way, speak White, because I went to high school, that was predominantly White, whereas my middle school was very, very diverse. . . . ,

I very much picked up on how they spoke in my high school class. . . . it was a very much a defense mechanism, because if I spoke like them, like, I wouldn't automatically come off, as you know, your ignorant, Black girl, and the fact that I was already also wearing a scarf and have a Muslim name. And I'm African American, you kind of have to, like, close yourself . . . there'll be people who say: "Oh, you speak so well, Oh, you don't sound black." And I've had that before. The funny thing is, the reason I don't sound Black is because I purposely did it. So you guys won't start thinking I'm ignorant or stupid, or, you know, ghetto or something like that, you know, and like, start being, all defensive.

(Noor, 39, African American convert)

In her narrative, Sadiqa was well aware of the stereotypes attached to her identity: "ghetto," "ignorant Black girl," compounded by a "scarf and a . . . Muslim name." Such negative coding of both Black and Muslim femininities (in many ways overlapping) has a long history in the United States. McCloud (1995) argues that African American women who wear the hijab are treated with more hostility than "immigrant Muslims," as non-Muslim Americans are jarred by the act of covering by women who were born and raised in America. Simultaneously, a wide range of negative qualities such as intellectual inferiority, rage, and promiscuity have been projected on individual Black women or Black women as a social group (Hill Collins 2000; Essed 1991; Guy-Sheftall 1990 and 1995). Women of color have always been under pressure to assimilate through adopting dominant communication styles (Essed 1991). And to some extent, adopting "White talk" in interactions with White peers mitigated the consequences of anti-Black stereotyping.

Once she is wearing the niqab, however, "White talk" may not be enough to make Sadiqa legible or included; at best, she may be read as an Other with "good" English/"White talk" skills who can still be told to "go back home." The social and cultural capital afforded by "white talk" is "confiscated" (Moosavi 2015: 45) by the associations inherent in the niqab. In fact, it appears that prejudices faced by niqab wearers compound the already difficult process of class mobility in the case of African American women. This was suggested by Sadiqa's further narration of her job hunt following her college graduation. She had been told by her professors that with an engineering degree, she would be swept off the labor market immediately, but, instead, she waited for a whole year before she managed to find employment. Even then, the job she was offered was outside her profession. The unsuccessful application experiences that she described were brutally humiliating, with HR departments in companies simply dropping her halfway through the hiring process with no further explanation. Therefore, one may question the value of such contingent social and cultural capital; it may be temporary and fractured; but after all, it affords only false inclusion because it promotes those [who] are "phenotypically Black, but culturally White" (Cooper 2006: 896).

In this stigmatizing process, niqab wearers (of all racial and ethnic backgrounds) are denied their national identity (Selod 2015) which in both the United States and the United Kingdom also depends, at least culturally, on possession of English language skills and recognizable (preferably dominant native) accents (Milroy 2000; Jones 2001; Lippi-Green 2012). Therefore, despite the partial invisibility of niqabi women's phenotypical features, they are immediately assessed as belonging to a race that is in some way "foreign" and which is operationalized through the use of infantilizing language toward them. This example demonstrates how conflations of national identity, language, and race may be variously valorized and attached to religious affiliation. It appears that racialization of the niqab may serve as an easy means of placing women who wear the niqab lower down in the social hierarchy.

Racialization and Resentment toward Women Who Wear the Niqab in Muslim Communities

By adopting the niqab, the women embrace a non-normative Islamic identity in the context of the American and British Muslim communities. Some members of the community distance themselves from niqab wearers. Niqab wearers are seen to tarnish the image of moderate, post-9/11 American Islam—and, therefore, are not acknowledged in public by returning their Islamic greetings. Shirazi and Mishra (2010) conducted a study aimed at examining young American Muslim women's attitudes toward the niqab; they interviewed only non-veiled and hijabi women. While these respondents expressed a variety of views on the niqab, the fact that no niqab wearers were included in this study (or, indeed, other studies) suggests that they are not considered sufficiently authoritative to define or comment on their own experience. The negative views of the niqab in Shirazi and Mishra's study (2010) conducted in the United States suggest that the participants attempted to resist the stigma commonly attached in the West to Islam, by disassociating themselves from the "deviant" others (Ryan 2011). It appears that negative perceptions of the niqab among some American Muslims inform subsequent interactions between them and niqab wearers:

> When we're at the mall, I'll see Muslim sisters and nine times out of ten, they don't reply to me [when I greet them with *salaams*]. And I think a part of it is because I wear niqab and You know, in the West, there's this idea that women who wear niqab are extremists it's connected with terrorism you know, so there's a lot of pushback against niqab so it's not that I don't want to feel close with these sisters who don't wear niqab, they don't want to associate with me. Unfortunately, I suffered it a lot.

(Sajida, 26, Jewish American convert)

Many African American women who wear the niqab report being shunned due to their racial background. When interviewed for this project, African American niqabis expressed disappointment that Arab and South Asian American Muslims often appeared to expel them from the Islamic fold (this is what ignoring one's *salaam aleikum* amounts to), and tentatively indicated that the reason for that could equally be dislike of the niqab, perceived as a symbol of Islamist ideology, or racism, or both. Sadiqa surmised: "some

Muslims are, like, are against it and don't like the idea of me wearing it, they might see the, the color first . . . there's always race, everywhere. [That's the] Reality, regardless of where you are, for the most part. So I feel like for some people, they will see this, see my color, who, some people, Muslim, even non-Muslims, you know, they might be of like, ethnic background, that they're seeing the black first." Sadiqa's point echoes a statement by Shantesa, an African American participant in Karim's (2008) study of American Muslim women's lives. She said:

> I welcome sisterhood, especially African American, because my experience as an African American will always be distinct from yours, though I know Islam does not say that it should be. My reality is that I will always be viewed differently from you. You will always be seen in some way as a Muslim first, as an Eritrean Muslim, as an Asian Muslim. On the other hand, I will be viewed first as an African American in this country, and in whichever masjid we go, and in a way filled with negative connotations and looked down and shunned.
>
> (in Karim 2008: 2)

Karim (2008) argues that the American *ummah* is blighted by inequalities, in particular those connected to race and class, often expressed spatially. She makes her case by quoting a study which showed that African American and South Asian Muslims (as well as Arabs) attend different mosques. Further, she asserts that South Asian Muslim immigrants have managed to attain the image of a "model minority" (2008: 10) composed of educated, usually financially comfortable, professionals. The label of a model minority comes with its own tensions pertaining to expectations of social mobility and negotiating racism, and it is the immigrant experience that, perhaps, contributes to anti-Black racism among some South Asian Muslims, argues Karim (2008: 29)—"why associate with the native underclass when one's immigrant status already threatens one's assimilation?" White supremacy creates hierarchies, and once it is internalized, it is "possible for those who experience one form of racism to discriminate against others" (Karim 2008: 29). This is particularly hurtful when South Asian success is celebrated at the expense of African Americans; without any regard for structural inequalities, the former group have been essentialized as diligent, middle-class, and smart, and the latter as incompetent and lazy (Karim 2008).

The manner in which these inequalities work at macro- and microlevels has been noted by Asma (46, African American), who surmises that other Muslims avoid associations not only with African American Muslims, but also with Islam at large:

> I'm talking about Muslims who I give salaams and sometimes they give me that "deer caught in the headlights" stare, like they're almost afraid to say it. Hmm, and when they do . . . they kind of like turn the corner quickly, and I just think: "It's so weird." This happened before I was wearing the niqab as well, so . . . I think that because I don't live in a predominantly Muslim area, I think that when Muslims

[get] here, they are trying to assimilate and fit in, and sometimes I think that that is the reason why their reaction is that way, it's almost like they don't want people to know they're Muslim. It really breaks my heart.

Karim notes that for Asian immigrants, distancing themselves from African Americans is a condition of assimilating into White communities and acquiring "cultural citizenship." She calls this process "the tragedy and centrality of race in America" (2008: 32).

Research conducted by the British Muslim Forum (2020) indicates that this phenomenon is by no means limited to the United States. Having surveyed a hundred Black British Muslims on their experiences of anti-Black racism within and outside the Muslim community, the organization found that speaking out on issues of rampant anti-Black discrimination within the *ummah* often results in accusations of discord sowing. One respondent described a visit to a store where she was harassed due to her race:

Once upon a time I went to a hair shop to buy shampoo for my hair. Obvs the shop was owned by Asian Pakistanis. I was wearing niqab these times. Not only were they blatantly following me around the shop (and other the other black people who were in that shop) they had the audacity to ask me if I was Muslim, when they saw me—a Black woman in niqab.

(in The British Muslim Forum Report 2020: np)

Respondents observed that discrimination against them was particularly jarring in mosques and madrassahs, as well as in the process of matchmaking.

This process of shunning women who wear the niqab by their (religious) communities does not necessarily always occur in public. Sometimes it is experienced within families. Some participants spoke of the painful consequences of going against the wishes of their husbands or families who are critical of the niqab:

You'll find that especially the niqab, the sisters that chose to wear it, have some negative reaction from their family, and their communities when they decide to wear it. It's their choice, nobody's telling them to do it. And there's instances, I heard, of . . . and I know, because I spoke to them. Sisters who wear a hijab, and a husband tells them not to. "Don't wear it, I don't want you to wear it."

(Soraya, 52, Scottish convert)

In contrast to common perceptions of sacrifice in the context of family, where (especially women) self-sacrifice for the sake of familial relationships (Dollahite, Layton, Bahr, Walker and Thatcher 2009), niqab adoption sometimes appears to be a source of family disputes. Many women who wear it refuse to give up their beliefs for the sake of the family's comfort. The reason for these disputes is related to the niqab's effect on external perceptions of the family as a unit. Such conflicts may have severe consequences for the wearers: Selina (29, British Pakistani) said that she had been disowned by a part of her family who "detested" her wearing the niqab, as they followed a liberal interpretation of Islam and were very middle-class and old-fashioned. She ascribed this dislike to (undefined) "cultural practices" that took precedence in their life. As a result, the decision to express her religious belonging in this particular way set her apart from the family; she understood the niqab as contradictory to her family's aspirations: liberal Islam, middle-classness, and traditional ways of being. She constructed the practice of niqab-wearing as a sacrifice; she chose to reject familial relationships in which she could participate only on her relatives' terms. Dollahite et al (2009: 693) argue that "the sacrifice changes the sacrifice in a religious direction. It affects one's identity."

Among British South Asian Muslim women, the adoption of the niqab is often a symbolic rejection of colorful saris and *shalwar kameez*,[2] seen as "too flashy in color, flimsy in texture, body hugging in style, too exposing of the neck and arms, too eye-catching and glaring, too Bollywood and Barbie-dollish, too ethnic, too Asian and, for some, too Hindu" (Tarlo 2013: 80). The niqab may be an Islamic alternative to not only the revealing "Western" but also the ethnic "Asian" clothing. (However, the women I interviewed were by no means clad universally in black—two of them wore sets consisting of long skirts, suit jackets, and high-necked tops, with niqabs placed on top of colorful hijabs, thus introducing a sartorial variety into their styles.) Mohammad (2013) similarly argues that for Muslims of South Asian background, such as Indian, Pakistani, or Bangladeshi, the "Other" in reference to whom they construct their identity is the Hindu. Therefore, in the recasting of their identity, second- and third-generation Muslims often forgo the traditions and sartorial styles of their parents, seen as too close to the South Asian culture.

Indeed, the distinction between religion and culture appeared frequently in the narratives. "Culture" is framed negatively, as a bundle of outdated, patriarchal customs from which Islam has liberated women. Among them, participants listed forced marriages, a de facto lack of legal personhood, and preventing girls from continuing their education. Sartorially, these customs are often associated with South Asian traditional dress. For women who adopt the niqab, with its loose-fitting form and understated colors, the rejection of *shalwar kameez* constitutes a challenge to South Asian "culture" and embrace of a global version of Islam, one that is devoid of cultural accretions. Wearing the niqab for women is "liberating" (a word used by many participants) precisely because they feel that they are free from these patriarchal and outdated constraints which they claim are superseded by Islam. They are now entitled to seek employment outside the home, or seek a husband on their own terms, as long as the modesty requirement is fulfilled. This process is then much more complex than Western opponents of the niqab are willing to accept; the assumption that Muslim women adopt the niqab in opposition to "Western values" may actually be mistaken as the discourse of choice and personal freedom they employ echoes the ideas of Islamic reformers of the early twentieth century who sought

---

[2]Traditional dress of South Asia consisting of loose trousers and a long tunic, worn by both men and women.

to identify the normative boundaries of Islam from "Muslim civilization characterized by *cultural decay, stagnation, or decline*" (Jouili 2019: 216).

Tarlo (2010) argues that controversies over the niqab in Muslim communities in the United Kingdom are caused by the iconic status the niqab has gained. As it is the most distinctive and visible type of Muslim dress, it has largely come to be perceived as representative of British Islam, causing irritation among those British Muslims who oppose it. Furthermore, Tarlo (2010) asserts that some women who do not wear it may resent the possible implication that by not wearing it they are less pious than niqab wearers (and this was corroborated by some of participants in this study based on their previous interactions), whereas some Muslim men may resent the implication that the niqab is necessary because they are incapable of controlling their sexual impulses and thoughts. Finally, some may fear that they may be attacked due to an association with a veiled woman; for example, Franks (2000) described a situation in which a husband requested his wife to abandon wearing her hijab, because he already felt vulnerable to harassment in public due to his darker complexion.

This section hinted at the dynamic nature of racially and religiously inflected symbolic group boundaries that affect many participants' experiences. Symbolic boundaries are "conceptual distinctions made by social actors . . . [that] separate people into groups and generate feelings of similarity and group membership." When symbolic boundaries become institutionalized, they evolve into "social boundaries [which] are objectified forms of social differences manifested in unequal access to an unequal distribution of resources . . . and social opportunities" (Lamont and Molnár 2002: 168). Bail (2008: 39) proposed that attention be directed to "configurations of multiple symbolic boundaries (e.g., race, religion, language, culture, or human capital)." The niqab may be harnessed all too easily for production of particular symbolic boundaries that may obscure other reasons for exclusion. For example, the niqab may be castigated as a symbol of religious extremism, but when African American (or other non-White) Muslim women wear it and are symbolically excluded (ostensibly on this basis), such exclusion may just be a refraction of "explicit." The manner in which symbolic boundaries that rest on mainstream perceptions of the niqab are policed reveals the strategic interests of majority groups (Bail 2008). Here, such groups could include Muslim proponents of "progressive" Islam who wish to maintain a positive image of the community, or Muslims who are able to "pass" and therefore avoid being connected with the negative notions that the niqab invokes in the West.

Coping Strategies

Building Bridges

Women's narratives reveal a host of social strategies that help them resist such othering formulas. Almost all participants described attempts to build bridges with their communities by being extra friendly, helpful, engaged, and sociable in public so as to erase the negative connotations. Sadiqa described how, before adopting her niqab, she used to smile a lot to appear non-threatening in her hijab and abaya. She worried that by adopting the niqab, she could no longer use that strategy and had fewer means to communicate that she was non-threatening. Shafeeqa commented that she was very active at her children's school and at parent-teacher conferences, so that she could be known as supportive of the school and "engaged," in an attempt to challenge the perception of niqab wearers as disconnected from society. Selina told me that she was always keen to help others when she saw someone struggling:

> I was in town and there was an old White man and he was in a wheelchair and he was using his feet to move along and I had loads of bags, and I was coming back from shopping. I had my niqab on and I'd seen this man and I was like, oh, God, he looks like he needs help, you know. So I went over to him and I was like, oh excuse me, like, do you want me to push you or something?

(Selina, 29, British Pakistani)

Selina said that the man whom she offered to help was genuinely curious, jokingly asking "what it was with them Muslims," as so many offers of help were coming to him from Muslim women. She explained that helping strangers simultaneously earned her a good deed and warmed up the public image of niqab wearers and Islam more widely. Other participants told me that they sometimes engaged with children in order to demystify their niqab, sometimes by lifting it to show their faces or chatting with them light-heartedly. Soraya (52, Scottish convert) described an encounter with young boys during which she was able to position herself as Scottish and a Muslim in a friendly manner:

> There was some young boys who were like "All right? Missus? How are you?" I said: "I'm fine, how are you?" . . . And they were being a little cheeky but they said "Yeah . . . why can't we see your face?" and I says "part of my religion." "You're Scottish!" "Yes" And then they said: "If you showed your face would you not get your hand chopped off or something?" I say "Naaa naa naa" I made some kind of joke with them . . . they might never have interacted with a Muslim woman, they had a positive experience and I've had a positive experience.

The boys were clearly fascinated with her dress, not in the least because they associated it with religious law that dealt out harsh punishment for transgressions. To them, Soraya was initially the ultimate foreigner figure so the fact that she responded to their questioning in a clear Scottish accent was surprising to them. It was also an educational moment; the boys realized that there are variations of what it means to be Scottish. For Soraya, it was a satisfying moment of asserting her identity as a Scottish Muslim woman who wears the niqab.

Simultaneous engagement in positive interactions and fashioning the modest body are, in fact, central to the cultivation of a pious disposition whose outward expression may act as an act of *da'wa*, "making this style of clothing more attractive to other Muslim women" and making "Islam more inviting to non-Muslims" (Bucar 2017: 187). *Da'wa* in this context is realized through the participant's attempt to carry out a good deed, which is also an Islamic duty, as enjoined in the Qur'an which urges the believers to "compete toward all that is good" (Shihab 2004: 72) in verse 2: 148: "Vie therefore, with one another in doing good works."

In another extract Soraya explained that she adapted her behavior according to the situation and people she encountered. Through language, she preemptively communicated her good intentions, but in gendered variations (friendly toward women, friendly but detached toward men) in order to conform to Islamic norms:

> I think I have to be more outwardly . . . chatty and friendly. If I'm standing at a bus stop and I say "hi," you can see I am smiling. But if my face is covered, you cannae see I'm smiling. So, I have to make extra effort especially with women. I mean men, I try to deal with politely, and sometimes a little cheeky, but not rude. If I'm speaking, like I do when I'm teaching, I speak very slowly and say "how are you?" "goodbye," like proper English, but if there's a [Muslim] brother or a man at the bus stop and he was being a bit . . . hmmm, I'd say "You're all right, mate?"

While one explanation for these efforts is framed by many women as wanting to be "ambassadors of Islam" (i.e., educating the public about the faith and being good role models), others often describe interactions where they keenly assert their "localness," or even "nativeness," and being a part of the social fabric of the local community as well as the nation. Similar to findings of other studies on American and British converts to Islam, they often downplay the stigmatizing social significance of the niqab, representing themselves and acting "as American as apple pie" (Evans 2015: np), or, in Britain, "as British as fish and chips" (Moosavi 2015: 169).

Reappropriation of Stigmatizing Labels

In the following extract, Lila considered four different labels, one of which, ninja, she reappropriated; she resignified it by claiming it. As a result, she transformed the negative connotative meanings intended by harassers into positive, empowering meanings.

> It happened several times in this area [locally], this old guy rides past me on a bicycle and when he's well out of reach, he shouts "ninja, ninja!" or "letterbox!" that's really popular recently. . . . I'm not feeling upset. I want to laugh. How can you get such an idea, to call someone a letterbox? It's so silly! [laughs] And my friend Saida says that she'd rather be called a ninja or a letterbox than a "nice piece of ass." That's offensive. I'm not offended if someone calls me ninja. I call myself a ninja, what's offensive in that? I look like a ninja, so what? I'm proud of that. Pointing to someone's backside is more of an invasion of privacy. If you put on a red coat, you should be prepared to be called Red Riding Hood, you're always going to look like something, aren't you.

(Lila, 29, Polish convert living in the UK)

She achieved it relationally by placing the label in the context of other labels. First, she distanced herself from the deviant connotations of the label "letterbox" using laughter and ridicule as a form of stigma management, similarly to Sofia in Chapter 3 who managed professional interactions with driving examiners.[3] The label she felt was truly offensive and invasive was a sexist reference that emphasized her sexual attributes. Humiliation experienced due to such name-calling is no doubt related to a compromised sense of privacy and dignity, as well as modesty, valued by many participants long before they adopted the niqab. As discussed in Chapter 4, on-street sexual harassment may expedite women's decision to start dressing in silhouette-concealing clothes (although in some cases, religious dress did not protect them from it). Finally, Lila mentioned an ostensibly neutral, "to be anticipated" label—"Red Riding Hood" as a harmless connotation that could be experienced by anyone. Such a hypothetical incident might not be detached, however; the act of labeling another is an exercise of power that is never neutral (McConnell-Ginnet 2003). Not all have the power to successfully define it; this is reserved for socially dominant individuals (Valentine 1998); yet, as seen in the case of Boris Johnson's offensive language and the ensuing spike in anti-Muslim hate crime, some of those placed lower in the social hierarchy keenly adopt dominant labeling practices (and other hostile behaviors), thus reenacting the spectacle of humiliating the Other. Yet, Lila was able to reclaim the obviously negatively intended "ninja" shouted by an old man riding the bicycle because while the figure of the ninja, a stealthy Japanese warrior, may symbolize Otherness, it is also imbued with the positive attributes of physical agility, stealth, street smarts, and determination (Kim 2018). In this context, Lila reappropriation of the label "ninja" is a successful coping strategy, as she takes away the harasser's weapon and turns it into her armor. Galinsky, Hugenberg, Groom, and Bodenhausen (2003: 231) write in their analysis of reappropriation of stigmatizing labels: "by the fact that it is used by the group to refer to itself, it comes to connote pride in the groups' unique characteristics. Where before it referred to despised distinctiveness, it now refers to celebrated distinctiveness. Reappropriation allows the label's seemingly stable meaning to be open to negotiation." By renegotiating the meaning of "ninja" in this context, Asma was able to reconfigure the entire social interaction in which the label is mobilized: it was an incident defined by her uniqueness, not humiliation.

Mapping Safe and Unsafe Spaces

Women have a fraught relationship with urban spaces. For niqab wearers, negotiation of towns and cities is likely much harder than for an average woman who does not

---

[3]It is worth noting that the label "letterbox" rose to UK-wide prominence following Boris Johnson's column (2018) in which he compared women who wear the niqab to letterboxes and bank robbers. In the week following the publication of the column, the number of anti-Muslim hate crime incidents increased fourfold (from eight to thirty-eight), with two-thirds of those (twenty-two) targeting women who wore face veils (Tell MAMA Report 2019). Fifty-six percent (thirty-seven) of all anti-Muslim attacks (fifty-seven) in the three-week period following the publication of the column were directed at visibly Muslim women; 42 percent (twenty-four) of the attacks "directly referenced Boris Johnson and/or the language used in his column" (Tell MAMA 2019: 7).

visually stand out. For niqab wearers, not only gender, but also religion and ethnicity define their spatial practices. Fear of violence in urban spaces is shared by women with different characteristics (Valentine 1989; Beall 1997; Pain 1997; Koskela 2010; Tiftik and Turan 2015), but niqab wearers enter public spaces with not just fear, but also expectations of some level of violence (Zempi and Chakraborti 2014). Islamophobic incidents become normalized, and, in Nabila's words, "you almost stop noticing them after a while."

Verbal and physical attacks on Muslim women are described with depressing regularity in reports and academic studies (Bouteldja 2011 and 2015; Zempi and Chakraborti 2014). In this section, I go beyond such discussions and address the mental mapping utilized by niqab wearers to categorize different spaces as safe/unsafe, and coping strategies akin to those identified by Valentine (1989) mobilized during the negotiation of unsafe spaces. Valentine (1989) argues that women's perceptions of risk associated with different environments have a bearing on their use of public space. While she focuses specifically on the risk of men's violence against women, I analyze intersecting risks of violence against women and anti-Muslim prejudice. These risks often overlap but may apply to divergent areas in terms of ethnic, class, and economic composition. As seen in the narratives in this section, women talk both about environments where they feel comfortable and safe, and those where they feel uncomfortable and unsafe with the niqab on. This grading, if applied to a physical map of different neighborhoods where the participants live and move about, would illustrate the extent to which niqab wearers are socially excluded.

Creating such a mental map, according to Valentine (1989), is based on personal experience of particular spaces, others' narratives, and media reporting. Violent incidents become associated with spatial environment in the minds of women. In addition, media represent certain spaces as dangerous, reinforcing women's fear of male violence. Thus, both fear and dangerous spaces are socially produced (Koskela 2010). This process serves to push women out of public space and limit their opportunities therein, amplifying the consequences of patriarchy. Mohammad (2013: 1819), in her study of youthful British Muslim femininities in urban areas, similarly found that transition through such spaces involves complex mental calculations of a multitude of factors which constantly shift: "Women's mental maps of the city classify city spaces according to social/'racial'/gender difference, forms of risk (in particular, 'racial', sexual, physical violence), utility, level of attachment, safety, comfort, and trust. While feelings of fear and comfort that guide women's personal geographies center on perceptions of social differences, where the lines of difference get drawn, where or what is the inside and outside, the same and other, shift across 'race', gender, and generation. With respect to 'race', informants overwhelmingly but not exclusively foreground the White/non-White dualism."

For Muslim women, and niqab wearers in particular, two kinds of risks intersect. They are vulnerable to abuse both as women and as Muslims. Moving between "Muslim/ Asian" and mainstream areas means being interchangeably faced with different kinds of trouble; they associate sexual harassment with the former and anti-Muslim abuse with the latter. Iman (29, British Pakistani), who used to be a pharmacy employee, had to flee her workplace because of unwanted male attention: "But they [Asian men] only do it just to see and stare at me and I've had somebody, I'm not even gonna say it, but an incident happened where, you know, I had to just completely go out the back of the shop and tell the other assistant, you know, if he comes in, don't call me out. I'm inside, you take over, I'm not dealing with him."

These narratives reveal a double bind that Muslim women face and that speaks to what Zine (2006: 239) described as "dual oppressions, confronting racism and Islamophobia in society at large and at the same time contending with patriarchal forms of religious oppression and sexism in their communities." While some participants expressed a sense of relief related to adopting the niqab in order to fend off sexual harassment from Asian men, it made them vulnerable to anti-Muslim abuse by the mainstream population. This suggests that they have to be very perceptive, indeed, to recognize where one type of threat is superseded by another. As these boundaries are porous, there are areas of intersecting risks where they may be subject to either type of abuse. The participants were acutely aware of the boundaries between different kinds of areas that carried associated risks. Risk assessment becomes second nature outside the home not just for the women, but for their children as well, as this example demonstrates:

[w]e went to this, on one occasion we went to IKEA with my son and it was late at night, and I asked him—"do you want me to keep it on or shall I take it off? How do you feel with it, 'cos . . . in this area, everyone's aware of people in niqab, but when I go to IKEA . . . um, a lot of the shoppers are not from this area, they haven't seen people in niqab," so I was like, should I keep it on, or should I take it off, and he said, "oh, whatever you want to do, yeah, take it off," and I took it off, but when we were going back to the bus stop he said "oh, put it on now!" so I put it back on again.

(Sadiyah, 37, British Pakistani)

This memory shared by the participant documents the existence of a boundary between the safe area where the participant lives, and IKEA which, although technically located within the administrative boundaries of the participant's hometown, represents the mainstream public space's overlap with the "Asian area," because it is frequented by people unfamiliar with the sight of the niqab. This particular local IKEA is a popular leisure space among both Muslim and non-Muslim families and so constitutes a space where different ethnic groups meet. This extract demonstrates that mental maps may be symbolic rather than strictly geographic, because they are socially constructed. Sadiyah explained how she classified "safe zones" and "unsafe zones":

And [town name] and [town name] are completely, completely safe. It's when I go to locations where I know that they haven't seen people in niqab before . . . and it's not people even when they make comments, it's just that uncomfortable feeling of . . . they are going to be judging me, by what I'm wearing.

Her reasoning is that in the case of the niqab, contrary to the popular saying, it is unfamiliarity rather than familiarity that breeds contempt. This contempt, sometimes subtle and barely perceptible to a bystander, may cause a niqab wearer to feel like she does not belong, and seek to employ a coping strategy. For the visit to IKEA, she took the niqab off. For some participants the issue of the reception of the niqab was, indeed, a cause of anxiety, as they felt they were forced to take it off in an unwelcoming or even hostile atmosphere. They felt they were a target for abuse and preferred to remove the niqab in some situations, often for the sake of their children. Her conversation with her child reveals two other things: the act of wearing the niqab is relational, and the risks associated with it are internalized by niqab wearers' children from an early age. The impact of anti-Muslim abuse on young children of visibly Muslim women who frequently witness their mothers' victimization has not been thoroughly studied, but the limited extant literature indicates that they "experience a sense of cultural inferiority, losing confidence both in themselves and in their parents" (Sporton, Valentine and Nielsen 2006: 210).

The dynamic management of risks related to niqab-wearing can also be based on a creative approach to the style of the garment. Sadiyah made a reference to female tourists practicing the niqab in France, where it has been criminalized. What she describes constitutes an interesting example of "guerilla veiling" whereby, instead of wearing the typical combination of the abaya or the jilbab with the headscarf and face covering which immediately draws attention, women use non-suspect accessories to achieve a level of coverage as close to the niqab as possible: "I have talked to people that have been to France. And they managed to get by by covering their face in different ways and I think that they said that it's not tourist that are the main thing that [inaudible] people have done it in a different way where they are covered but it's not the . . . you know, the whole black thing. So they use their shawls to cover their faces, or they use sunglasses . . . shades, you know, to cover as much as they could."

In the American context, taking the niqab off was also a coping strategy practiced in places perceived as unsafe: "There was a time when I actually did take it off to go into a convenience store, and forgive me, but the area is a predominantly White area, a minimum African American [presence]. . . . Hmm, so I just [thought] 'Okay, this is a double negative.' Hmm, and I actually took the niqab off [but] I left my khimar on and hijab on" (Asma, 46, African American). Such constant scrutiny of urban spaces, with a particular focus on the ethnic composition and perceived risks this carries becomes second nature for women who, like Asma, are highly mobile. Asma is a healthcare worker and visits clients in different neighborhoods, so she is highly attuned to her surroundings. These accounts resonate with Tarlo's findings (2007) about areas of London frequented or avoided by Muslim women who assessed whether they felt sartorially conspicuous in a given neighborhood. They also dovetail with Dwyer's analyses of women wearing the hijab strategically, depending on the social setting (1999).

However, not wearing the niqab in certain spaces may equally indicate a sense of belonging and security. It may be a coping strategy used for "domesticating" them. In the next presented extract, a participant talked about not putting it on while moving about in the immediate neighborhood.

> I gave her [a White neighbor] the food in a big massive dish, erm, and I think I took some pakoras and stuff with me, and I was a bit nervous, carrying like this, across the road, thinking this time I'm not wearing the niqab. So I wasn't wearing the niqab, erm, with my neighbors I don't, so I don't make them to feel that I'm so extreme that I have to wear it everywhere I go, to go to the garden, to throw something in the bin, it's ridiculous, do you know what I mean?
>
> (Sofia, 39, British Pakistani)

Typically, niqab wearers would put it on once they transition from the religiously defined private space into the public space. Through appearing unveiled outdoors, Sofia symbolically extended the boundaries of the home to include the surrounding area. Projecting an ostensibly "moderate," rather than an "extreme" image, that is, of a woman who does not insist on wearing the niqab all the time is a result of the emotional labor of maintaining good neighborly relationships across racial lines. Once again, boundaries between safe and unsafe spaces for "doing Muslimness" turn out to be flexible and socially constructed. Here they were based not just on previous experience or secondary knowledge of what is "safe," but on careful negotiation of local relationships and perceptions of the boundaries between the "local" and "beyond." In northern British post-industrial towns, Muslims and non-Muslim communities live side by side. With the capacity for positive interactions, as in the example above, some participants told me that in their local towns, they were able to take verbal harassment in their stride. This indicates that even places defined as "safe areas" are not entirely risk-free. Wafa (25, British Pakistani), along with several others, ascribed harassment she received from the local White residents to deprivation and lack of education:

> The . . . English community, I think of it as a deprived area where . . . they're from a background where they've not been educated, or you know, maybe it's assumptions that we make . . . they come from a council estate,[4] they've had a certain upbringing . . . maybe they see us as "oh, you're taking all the things," and it's like, it's OK . . . you know, I can handle them, they might be nasty in other ways, this is one way of them being nasty to people and don't fear that.

This suggests that participants feel more empowered in areas where they have a sense of belonging and security, and the reaction to harassment is less traumatic than in less familiar neighborhoods. This further explains the frequently limited mobility of those niqab wearers who rarely venture outside the "safe" areas into other neighborhoods.

---

[4]In Britain, the term "council estate" denotes public housing areas. While the intention behind creating council estates was to supply affordable, spacious and good-quality housing to socioeconomically disadvantaged people, in modern day they often suffer from urban decay.

However, participants' narratives also reveal the existence of "safe islands" in the largely unsafe areas, and for this woman from West Yorkshire, it was her university campus where she did not feel threatened but accepted with her niqab on. The difficulty in this case was that she had to negotiate travel to campus, and public transportation, with associated amenities such as bus stops emerging in the data uniformly as one of the riskiest spaces as far as Islamophobic abuse was concerned. She described an incident at a bus stop that was typical of harassment that niqab wearers faced in city centers:

> I was on my way back from university or on my way to university, and there was a drunk, and he was quite aggressive, and he was like, take it off, take it off and I think adrenaline just kicked in, 'cos at the time . . . I was on my own and, erm, I was like no I'm not going to take it off, how dare you tell me to take it off, you know, it's my choice, if I want to take it off I'll take it off on my terms, not anybody's, and I think after that, it was so funny 'cos I think once I'd said no, I'm not going to take it off, he was like ok then, that's fine, he toddled off and, you know, and I think after I was like, no, I'm not going to take it off.

(Selina, 29, British Indian)

By standing up to her harasser, Selina defended herself, but she also risked retaliation. While this incident did not involve physical violence described in the literature (in the study by Zempi and Chakraborti (2014), these included being slapped in the face, elbowed in the stomach while pregnant, and being beaten up), it caused a long-lasting anxiety. This is consistent with the findings of Abu Ras and Suarez (2009) who found a strong correlation between posttraumatic stress disorders symptoms and experiences of anti-Muslim hate crime post-9/11. Women in particular expressed the fear of being alone in public spaces in that study. Poignantly, the incident strengthened the participant's conviction to keep her niqab on. Confrontation with a harasser may have a positive effect as it has been found to increase the feeling of self-efficacy in women who regain control over the situation of harassment (Kaiser and Miller, 2004). It does come with the risk of aggravating an already threatening situation. Therefore, many women who described experiences of harassment tend to ignore it, but it does have an impact on their psychological well-being, as told by this participant who was targeted in a city center: "You know they mumble and they say . . . in a racist way . . . [something] that's really hurtful. You try and show you're not bothered but you are."

The idea of "safe space" emerges as temporally dynamic. The characteristic of safeness changes as a function of the moment in time when it is assessed. This is emphasized by Nabila, who explained that terrorist incidents as well as certain political developments palpably give rise to aggression against those visibly Muslim but after some time passes, and the incident disappears from news reports, things calm down:

> There's periods of time when you go out, for example into the city centre and the people are more or less okay, because Birmingham is like really, really multicultural,

and there's lots of Muslims and lots of women with their versions of hijab and there's lots of people wearing niqab in Birmingham, but I notice that every time something happens, for example Lee Rigby who was decapitated in Woolwich round about that time, every time something like that happens I'm like, "oh God" of course yeah you feel bad for the person who's you know, the victim but then we get the brunt of it. It's just like the backlash, it's like "right now things are going to be really bad for a while." And then it calms down, and then when you go out, it's like people have kind of forgotten. You know, it's faded and they're okay again.

(Nabila, 43, British Pakistani and Salafi Muslim)

In this extract, Nabila discursively constructed the Birmingham city center as, generally speaking, a safe, multicultural space, where, importantly, non-Muslims are used to seeing women wearing hijabs and niqabs. That familiarity is superseded by Islamophobic sentiment stirred by the media following terrorist incidents and the resulting abuse. For a period of time, those visibly Muslim are not welcome in public spaces anymore. This dynamic is sometimes recognized by the majority population and challenged by grassroots activism mobilized with hashtags such as #illridewithyou in Australia in 2014, or #VoyageAvecMoi in France in 2015. However, kind-hearted offers of public transport travel companionship and solidarity can only deal with some of the consequences of Islamophobia, but not its causes. They also peter out as the publicity dies down, and do not address day-to-day Islamophobic abuse. Such fluctuations are typical of (un)safe space dynamics experienced by niqabi women. Similar to Valentine's argument for a "spatial expression of patriarchy" (1989), there is a case for a socially constructed "spatial expression of Islamophobia," as illustrated by Nabila's narrative.

Four categories of spaces in relation to niqab-wearing have emerged from the UK-based interviews. For the British participants, they included *the places where it is safe to wear the niqab*, and these included the "local" area, or "Muslim/Asian" areas of other cities, and London; university campuses (but not schools); mosques; and Saudi Arabia where many participants went on Hajj. Second, *public places where it is safe to take the niqab off*: local areas (close to home), and the city center. Third, *places where it is unsafe/ uncomfortable to wear the niqab*: the city center, public transport, "White" areas of London, IKEA, and roads. Finally, *places where it is unsafe to remove the niqab*: the local areas, and "back home" in Pakistan.

Inevitably, some of these categories overlap. The "local area" is a complex place, as some participants enjoy wearing the niqab there but feel free to sometimes take it off. Others feel they have to wear it there to minimize the risk of harassment which tends to be verbal rather than physical there. Some locations, like the city center, were identified as both safe and unsafe to wear the niqab: given the wide range of attitudes toward the niqab, the classification was possibly dictated by individual experiences, different times of day, and, as Nabila explained, current political events involving Muslims.

For the American participants, the safe areas for wearing the niqab included "[Ethnically] diverse areas," "African American neighborhoods," community colleges, workplace (the participants who mentioned the workplace as safe worked in a candy store, an IT company, and a restaurant), Dearborn, MI, and mosques. Places safe to remove the niqab identified by the American participants were the workplace and the hospital. They did not feel safe to enter "predominantly White areas," empty roads, or high traffic areas like gas stations while wearing the niqab. No places were identified as unsafe to remove the niqab. These categories suggest that safety for niqab wearers is largely correlated with ethnic diversity, "localness," and public spaces which are likely to be regulated and monitored. In contrast, "White" areas and non-regulated public areas are perceived as unsafe.

Zempi and Chakraborti (2014) who interviewed veiled women of Leicester, United Kingdom, also point to the same mechanism among women who fear anti-Muslim-inspired attacks. According to them, women see areas with a higher concentration of Muslims as safer, and by contrast, areas with low concentrations of Muslims as riskier. Only withdrawing to the former are women able to lower the chances of experiencing anti-Muslim hostilities, but that comes at a price of forgoing services and interactions that are available mostly outside of the "safe zones." Women interviewed by Zempi and Chakraborti (2014) describe deep-cutting lifestyle changes resulting from this fear of hostilities. With time, potential and actual victimization leads to production of boundaries and segregation of communities.

This finding highlights the ambivalence between accounts of the niqab as socially liberating and limiting. This echoes the contradiction addressed in Chapter 3 that hinges on a particular interpretation of religious choice and requirements regarding the niqab. Here, on the one hand, interviewees embrace liberation from the sexual gaze of men (as discussed in Chapter 4), while on the other, they are aware that this comes at the cost of Islamophobic harassment. The lived religion framework explains these apparent paradoxes, as it embraces religious accounts that may initially seem mutually exclusive; understanding how they operate together requires several shifts in perspective. McGuire (2008: 16) contends that "we must grapple with the complexities, apparent inconsistencies, heterogeneity, and untidiness of the range of religious practices that people in any given culture and period find meaningful and useful." In the case of niqab wearers, I argue that structuring their social lives according to the mental maps, as well as applying other coping strategies, constitutes active management of challenges inherent in their intersecting identities. Goffman's work on stigma management and self-presentation (1961, 1963) illuminates the fragility of interactions between niqab wearers and others. Interaction participants resist the view of themselves as abnormal (Goffman 1961), and this explains Sadiyah's fears of being judged by people who had not seen the niqab before in a context where she faces ostensibly much more serious risks of verbal and physical harassment. Her use of coping strategies can be explained by the fact that, according to Goffman (1961: 104), "an individual does not remain passive in the face of potential meanings generated regarding him, but, so far as he can, actively participates in sustaining a definition of the situation that is stable and consistent with his image of himself." Ryan (2011) examined ways in which Muslim women strive to mobilize association with "normality" in order to manage the stigma they face, noting that notions of what are "normal" and "abnormal" are situationally, dynamically defined; in Ryan's study, respondents defined "normality" as conforming to the concept of a "good Muslim" produced through their behavior, including modest clothing; this may have rendered their attempts to resist stigmatization futile, and actually reinforce it. Collective stigmatization, as noted by Ryan, meant that even those participants who did not feel stigmatized, expressed empathy for other Muslims who did. This was certainly the case in this study, because the women I interviewed were acutely aware of stigmatizing perceptions of them as Muslims and Muslim women and actively preempted situations where they could inadvertently aggravate their vulnerable position. Visiting neighbors and offering them food, friendly chatter at the bus stop, or, indeed, adjusting the level of body coverage by taking the niqab off temporarily are examples of such preemptive action. Thus, they engineer interactions where they produce the notion of self as "normal." The symbolic interactionist framework may help us understand this effort; since "the meanings that things have for human beings are central in their own right," (Blumer 1969: 7) and result from a process of interaction between individuals and groups and the context under which this interaction takes place, by producing "normality" of self, and by extension, of the interaction in which they are legitimate partners, they are able to define and enjoy particular locations as "normal," and thus safe.

Concluding Remarks

How then do we explain the experiences of Muslim women who wear the niqab, and who are ethnically, nationally, racially, and phenotypically diverse, in terms of racism as well as Islamophobia? Zopf (2015) argues that in order to understand holistically how the exclusion of Muslims operates, three theoretical frameworks have to be integrated: Orientalism (to make sense of how perceptions of the [Middle] East dictate constructions of Islam and Arabs [Said 1978]); Islamophobia (to make sense of the struggles of Muslims living in the West [Kumar 2012]); and racialization of Islam (Joshi 2006; Selod and Embrick 2013; Selod 2015; Galonnier 2015a and b).

Racialization of Islam is possible through construction of a visible archetype of "Muslim" utilizing symbolic markers such as name, dress, phenotype, and language (Naber 2008). In the case of niqab wearers I interviewed, and the interactions they narrated, symbolic markers of the archetype were mostly limited to dress, while their phenotype was largely obscured by dress and face veil. The immediate consequence of it is that it is no longer easy to designate them as Black or White, Arab or Asian. However, the concealment of phenotypical features does not mean that racialization ceases; it is still inscribed on the women in a myriad of other, socially constructed ways as noted by critical race theory scholars (Crenshaw 1995 and 2002; Mutua 2006). "To be Muslim in America . . . means to claim a faith tradition marked by both African American and immigrant struggles," asserts Karim (2008: 4). The adoption of the niqab by Black Muslim women in the United States, whether intended or not, appears to be a part of an identity trajectory that is opposite to respectability politics and related ideas of social uplift in African American communities. Instead of trying to assimilate within the majority society by following ready scripts that exist separately for people of color, Muslims, and women, they negotiate their own identity that is founded on their relationship with God, independence, and the self-respect they derive from opposing conventional ways of expressing their Blackness, Muslimness, and femininities. This examination of niqab wearers' experiences indicates how constructions of race, gender, and religion are dynamically upheld, reproduced, and resisted.

In my analysis, I illustrated how racism works in configurations with religion, gender, and class at the microlevel of society, in both institutional and individual forms. I suggested that it may have unconscious, as well as conscious elements, discussed its impact on participants' lives, and their coping strategies. Such discussions are necessary to highlight and contest the continued impact dominant ideologies of race and culture, inflected by the colonial baggage, have on structuring of modern-day Western societies. The stories such as those told by participants in this study constitute experiential knowledge which is critical to understanding our social reality and its inequalities (Solorzano 1997). The impact of racism, Islamophobia, and sexism on women is serious and long-lasting—in addition to public humiliation and a short-term disruption of the sense of personal safety, they experience a sense of isolation, a fear of living in a given area, and a wish to move away. In light of such experiences, it is clear that integration, so often discussed in the context of Muslim women's choices to cover their faces, should not be seen as one-sided, but a two-way process. It ought to begin with changing the majority society's attitudes and behaviors through education, promoting safe spaces for positive interactions, and more effective prosecution of hate crime.

CONCLUSIONS

Women who choose to wear the niqab make up a "new form of Islam" (Vallely and Brown 1995: np). This new form of Islam involves a degree of individualism that is often based on women's rejection of historically embedded *cultural* norms. It is difficult to pigeonhole niqabis, as usually they are politically and theologically separate from groups that have recently come to symbolically "represent" Islam. This has been a problem for politicians, community leaders, and journalists who attempt to pin their own agendas on women who wear the niqab, with little understanding of how the niqab may be interpreted at theological and social levels by its wearers. The controversy over the niqab poignantly illustrates the cultural reality in which women's bodies are conceptualized as ideological battlefields (Zine 2012).

The long-standing emphasis on traditionalist Islam as a perspective that advocates Islam has obfuscated the possibility that the niqab may be individually interpreted as a purely religious artefact by women who choose to wear it. Yet, almost all the niqab wearers I interviewed were indifferent to interpretations of Islam produced by traditionalist male scholars, and radical or militant revivalists who dominate the theological debates about whether the niqab is mandatory or optional in Islam (Afshar, Aitken, and Franks 2007). Instead, they constructed their own explanations that highlight personal piety, self-reflection, and often mystical religious experiences.

My analysis shows that women who wear the niqab test the secular-liberal polity's ability to transcend its own privileged position. This vast, invisible privilege limits its willingness to understand unfamiliar or radical religious practices such as wearing the niqab. By dismissing religious frames of reference, it condemns itself to a flattened worldview in which we inevitably become uniform and driven by similar motivations. In contrast, the women interviewed for this study have shown an astute ability to shift discursive registers by employing narratives intelligible for different audiences.

By engaging in deeply theological discussions of lived religion, they emerge as agential makers of meaning. Moxley Rouse's observation (2004: 212) that "[w]hile Islam articulates a body of laws and definitions of moral excellence, the ways in which individuals use Islam to frame meaning and purpose are entirely indigenous" illuminates the logic of orienting toward the niqab articulated by the women I interviewed. The universal goal of pious Muslims, submission to God, is best achieved by them as individuals while clothed in the niqab, but they do not see the niqab as normative because they recognize that for others, other paths may be more suitable. They exert authority by challenging interpretations of Islam that attempt to limit this religious practice. Importantly, this approach reveals the degree to which Christian-centric reasoning that underpins international human rights legislation such as the European Convention of Human Rights is insufficient in addressing religious questions whose parameters, such as hierarchy of authority, texts, and spaces, are not consistent with Christianity.

Simultaneously, niqab wearers' mobilization of the secular language of rights demonstrates a high degree of participation in the public life, more than they would achieve by unveiling. This rhetorical versatility is "emblematic of the West in that they foreground at an ideological level the sovereignty of the individual as a rational agent and prioritize individual freedom" (Mohammad 2013: 1805). The niqab is a source of secular-liberal (and illiberal) frustrations which manifest themselves in established ways. Under the guise of feminism, progress, and common sense, the desire to control Muslim femininities, femininities of color, immigrant, Asian, and non-normative femininities takes the form of narrow cultural prescriptions. This book shows that there is a palpable sense of offense at niqab wearers' refusal to enact such "liberation scripts" on secular-liberal terms, such as acceptance of the male gaze or performance of the "good Muslim" role.

The data collected for this book suggests that rather than being a political protest or a separation of oneself from society, the niqab is first and foremost a religious practice of piety as well as a critique of gender relations in Western societies, in both Muslim and non-Muslim communities. Based on the analysis of popular discourses about the niqab in Chapter 1, this book reveals that the niqab is misinterpreted, often intentionally, in the West. It deals with several of these misinterpretations by framing them with the existing literature and juxtaposing them with narratives of women who wear the niqab in the West, in the subsequent chapters. This enables me to illuminate discontinuities in the hegemonic discourse about the niqab that shape current policy and practice affecting niqab wearers in the West.

The reduction of the niqab to merely "Saudi" or "Arab" culture lays the groundwork for the first misinterpretation of the niqab: the niqab is commonly misread as inherently conservative but in my study, women's explanations for it are not related to "Saudi" or "Arab" cultures; rather, they refer to the early Islamic culture which absorbed traditions of many peoples that inhabited Arabia and neighboring regions at the time of the Prophet Muhammad's life. Although some women self-labeled as religiously conservative, it would be a mistake to read this category as directly equivalent to Christian religious conservatives. They clearly expressed support for social justice movements (sometimes explicitly mentioning LGBTQ+ groups), environment, science, and reproductive rights.

The second misconception dealt with here is that the niqab is an accessory of patriarchy. Niqabi women in the West are harassed for their dress which is often read as a tool of their oppression; it is seen as something that patriarchal relatives "made them wear." Neither the data I collected nor the extant literature evidences this. It does, however, identify sexual oppression in the web of dynamics that envelops women who wear the niqab but in a different form—that of sexual harassment in public. This experience is often intertwined with Islamophobic abuse. These two forms of oppression are managed dynamically through a variety of coping strategies in different spaces, and they reveal the extent to which Western anxieties about the niqab are often misplaced.

The third misconception is related to the perception that the niqab is meant to separate its wearer from the world. Not only do I demonstrate that the participants are deeply engaged in the community and public life, but I also show that they consider wearing the niqab to be a practice that enables them to be active members of their communities *through*, not despite, concealing the physical aspect of the body. Instead of inhibiting the wearers' agency in the public sphere, the niqab facilitates and even strengthens niqabis' agency in spaces they inhabit.

The fourth misconception, underpinning the first three, is that the niqab is seen as foreign, threatening, and anti-Western. I show in my discussion that this view is yet another iteration of the colonialist, Orientalist way of perceiving the world. The West makes a claim to be more tolerant and "civilized" by virtue of being more open to difference—but the case of the niqab demonstrates that this self-congratulatory view is misguided. The niqab represents Otherness that is not tolerated in the West because it constitutes a necessary counterpoint to the West's notion of itself as the bedrock of freedom and equality. It is constructed as a benchmark against which the West may be compared to the Orient, and inevitably emerge victorious. Yet, as I demonstrate in this book, the argument for the West's cultural superiority and the niqab's inferiority rings hollow when we consider how women interviewed for this project challenge recriminations against the niqab at various levels: sociological, theological, political, and cultural. In addition to giving religious justifications, women deftly mobilize the language of secular rights and freedoms that stems from the premises of liberalism to argue for their right to choose their attire, thus demonstrating their philosophical rootedness in the Enlightenment framework of Western liberalism.

Khiabany and Williamson (2011: 173) assert that "it has become impossible to talk about Islam without reference to women, and impossible to talk of Muslim women without reference to the veil." Paradoxically, it is this triad that enables the discursive production of the elusive European and American public spheres. By providing a negative reference point, imaginaries framed by progress, equality, and freedom, symbolically established in opposition to Islam, are mobilized in the construction of European and American identities (Göle 2002).

The multimodality of the niqab is encapsulated by Inglis's observation (2017: 289) that "both masks and veils have been thoroughly bound up with imaginings of what constitutes sound social order and chaotic disorder. Both have made possible and potentially undo bodily regimes of control in general and facial ones in particular." My study demonstrates that the niqab becomes the focal point for a wider conflict that affects both the British and American contexts: a disagreement over what constitutes a political community, social contract, and democracy at large (Marzouki 2017). The niqab controversies, as well as the pushback against "Shari'a law" in the United States, highlight the conflict between an understanding based on "the normative dimension of constitutional rights that guarantee the equality of citizens," and the opposing vision which draws from populist interpretations of foundational legal acts and a normativity of behaviors and affect (Marzouki 2017: 7).

By acknowledging hitherto neglected voices of niqab-wearing women, this book challenges the essentialist understanding of the niqab as resistance to "Western values." It shows how women's adoption of a religious practice often read as oppressive constitutes an assertion of their agency and identity. Therefore, it contributes to a decolonization of assumptions about what constitutes patriarchy, agency, as well as feminism itself (Salem 2013).

Furthermore, it illuminates the ways in which the niqab is experienced and interpreted by niqab wearers of different racial, linguistic, and economic backgrounds. By providing an analysis of different women's accounts, the book demonstrates the unfixed quality of the niqab as a religious artefact that is often used by its wearers for negotiating gender boundaries. The focus on the lived, socially situated experience of wearing the niqab demonstrates how discontinuities between political agenda-oriented and everyday gendered readings of Islam may facilitate women claiming authority over their religious experiences.

Updates, clarifications, responses, and reviews of this book will be shared at www.annapiela.com.

GLOSSARY

Abaya (Arabic) a loose cloak or robe.

Ayah (Arabic) a Qur'anic verse.

Ayatollah (Arabic) a high-ranking Shi'a Muslim cleric.

Burka, burqa (Arabic), chadaree (Pashto) an all-enveloping piece of fabric with a grille covering up the eyes, common in Afghanistan, some parts of Pakistan, and increasingly observed in Central Asian republics.

Chador (Persian) a (usually black) cloak worn over the head and the rest of the body, mostly worn by Shi'a women.

Deen (Arabic) the pious way of life or religion.

Fard or wajib (Arabic) religious duty.

Hadith (Arabic) the record of words and actions of Prophet Muhammad. It is considered second only to the Qur'an in rank of Islamic texts.

Hajj (Arabic) pilgrimage to Makkah during the month of Dhu al-Hijjah, one of the five pillars of Islam.

Hijab (Arabic) a curtain; it denotes a principle of modesty in behavior and dress, or, in common usage, a headscarf and modest attire. It is not explicitly mentioned in the Qur'an as a head or hair covering.

Hijabi (Arabic) a woman who wears a hijab.

Ijtihad (Arabic) in Islamic legal studies it means independent reasoning applied to religious texts.

Islam (Arabic) "voluntary submission to God." Other meanings include peace, wholeness, sincerity, and safety. Islam is the name of the second largest world religion with approximately 1.8 billion followers.

Jilbab (Arabic) a cloak or outer garment similar to abaya. Jilbab is explicitly mentioned in the Qur'an.

Khimar (Arabic) a shawl, the only garment except the jilbab mentioned in the Qur'an. It is not explicitly mentioned in the Qur'an as a head or hair covering.

Madhab (Arabic) a jurisprudential school of thought in Sunni Islam.

Madinah, Medina the city where the first Muslim community was founded by the Prophet Muhammad. His migration to Madinah (622 CE) marks the first year of the Islamic calendar (1 AH).

Makkah, Mecca the birthplace of the Prophet Muhammad and the site of revelation of most verses of the Qur'an. Situated in Saudi Arabia, it is considered the holiest city of Islam.

Masjid (Arabic) mosque, a place of Muslim worship.

Mustahhab (Arabic) recommended act.

Niqab (Arabic) a face veil or a face covering that leaves the eyes visible.

Niqabi (Arabic) a woman who wears the niqab.

Prophet Muhammad (570–632 CE) the religious and political leader who founded and led the Muslim community in Arabia. Muslims believe Muhammad was the last prophet sent by God to humanity and that the Qur'an was revealed to him through the Angel Jibril (Gabriel). In Islam, Abraham, Noah, Moses, Jesus and many others are revered as prophets.

Qur'an (Arabic) the holy book of Islam believed by Muslims to be revealed by God.

Salafi (Arabic) a revivalist branch within Sunni Islam. The name refers to salaf, the first three generations of Muslims whose practice of Islam is considered untainted by innovation. Many Salafi women wear the niqab, but not all women who do are Salafi.

Sari (Sanskrit) a women's traditional garment worn in South Asia, in particular India. It is worn by Muslim Indian women and also sometimes in Pakistan.

Shalwar kameez (Persian and Arabic) a traditional garment popular in Pakistan consisting of wide trousers and a long tunic. Women usually complement it with dupatta, a long shawl covering the neck and sometimes also the head.

Shari'a (Arabic) Islamic religious law.

Shi'i Islam, Shiism (Arabic) the second largest branch of Islam (after Sunni Islam). Shi'a Muslims form the majority of the population in Azerbaijan, Bahrain, Iraq, and Iran. The split between Sunni and Shi'a Muslims happened due to disagreements over the succession of leadership in Islam after the death of the Prophet Muhammad.

Sufi (from Arabic tasawwuf) a mystical branch of Islam that emphasizes a spiritual connection to God.

Sunnah (Arabic) a body of knowledge based on traditions and customs of the Islamic community; often based on the Hadith. It is sometimes used as an adjective to refer to actions or beliefs that are in accordance with the Sunnah.

Sunni Islam, Sunnism (Arabic) the largest branch of Islam. Sunni Muslims are called "the people of the sunnah and the community." The split between Sunni and Shi'a Muslims happened due to disagreements over the succession of leadership in Islam after the death of the Prophet Muhammad.

Ummah (Arabic) the global community of all Muslims.

Umrah (Arabic) pilgrimage to Makkah outside of the month of Dhu al-Hijjah.

REFERENCES

Aaronson, T. (2019), "Terrorism's Double Standard: Violent Far-Right Extremists Are Rarely Prosecuted as Terrorists," *The Intercept*, March 23. Available online: https://theintercept.com/2019/03/23/domestic-terrorism-fbi-prosecutions (accessed August 27, 2020).

Abu-Lughod, L. (2013), *Do Muslim Women Need Saving?* Cambridge, MA: Harvard University Press.

Abu-Ras, W. and Z. Suarez (2009), "Muslim Men and Women's Perception of Discrimination, Hate Crimes, and PTSD Symptoms Post 9/11," *Traumatology*, 15 (3): 48–63.

Abu-Shahba, J. (nd), "Is Niqab a Taboo for Islam and Muslim Women?" *Ijtihad Network*, June 20, 2018. Available online: http://ijtihadnet.com/is-niqab-a-taboo-for-islam-and-muslim-women (accessed March 30, 2020).

Afshar, H. (2008), "Can I See Your Hair? Choice, Agency and Attitudes: The Dilemma of Faith and Feminism for Muslim Women Who Cover," *Ethnic and Racial Studies*, 31 (2): 411–27.

Afshar, H. (2013), "The Politics of Fear: What Does It Mean to Those Who Are Otherized and Feared?" *Ethnic and Racial Studies*, 36 (1): 9–27.

Afshar, H., R. Aitken, and M. Franks (2007), "Feminisms, Islamophobia, and Identities," *Political Studies*, 53 (6): 262–83.

Ahmad, F. (2006), "British Muslim Perceptions and Opinions on News Coverage of September 11," *Journal of Ethnic and Migration Studies*, 32 (6): 961–82.

Ahmad, S. M. (2019), "Islamophobic Violence as a Form of Gender-based Violence: A Qualitative Study with Muslim Women in Canada," *Journal of Gender-Based Violence*, 3(1): 45–66.

Ahmed, S. (2014), *Cultural Politics of Emotion*, Edinburgh: Edinburgh University Press.

Ahmed, S. T. (2019), "Converging Identities, Emerging Discourses: Muslim Female Voices in British Media," *ESSACHESS- Journal for Communication Studies*, 12(2): 79–97. Available online: http://essachess.com/index.php/jcs/article/view/465 (accessed March 30, 2020).

Ahmed, S. T. and T. B. Roche (2018), "The Hijab and Niqab: Omani Women's Reflections on Law and Practice," *Journal of Intercultural Studies*, 39 (1): 50–66.

Ajrouch, K. J. (2007), "Global Contexts and the Veil: Muslim Integration in the United States and France," *Sociology of Religion*, 68 (3): 321–5.

Al-Faifi, S. (nd), "Sahar Al-Faifi." Available online: https://www.sahar-alfaifi.com (accessed March 30, 2020).

Al-Faifi, S. (2013), "I Wear the Niqab, Let me Speak on My Own Behalf," *The Independent*, September 2013. Available online: https://www.independent.co.uk/voices/comment/i-wear-the-niqab-let-me-speak-on-my-own-behalf-8824243.html (accessed September 30, 2019).

Alghadir A., F. Aly, and H. Zafar (2012), "Effect of Face Veil on Ventilatory Function among Saudi Adult Females," *Pakistan Journal of Medical Science*, 28 (1): 71–4.

Al-Lami, M. (2009) "Studies of Radicalization: State of the Field Report." London: Politics and International Relations Working Paper, Royal Holloway University. Available online: https://static1.squarespace.com/static/566d81c8d82d5ed309b2e935/t/567ab488b204d58613bf92aa/1450882184032/Studies_of_Radicalisation_State_of_the_F.pdf (accessed September 30, 2019).

Al-Mogbel, E. S. (2012), "Vitamin D status among Adult Saudi Females Visiting Primary Health Care Clinics," *International Journal of Health Sciences (Qassim)*, 6 (2): 116–26.

Ali, L. (2010), "Behind the Veil," *The New York Times*, June 11. Available online: https://www.nytimes.com/2010/06/13/fashion/13veil.html (accessed September 30, 2019).

Alibhai-Brown, Y. (2011), "Jack Straw Is Right to Ask Hard Questions about Asian Men," *The Independent*, January 10. Available online: https://www.independent.co.uk/voices/commenta tors/yasmin-alibhai-brown/yasmin-alibhai-brown-jack-straw-is-right-to-ask-hard-questi ons-about-asian-men-2180318.html (accessed September 30, 2019).

Alibhai-Brown, Y. (2015), "As a Muslim Woman, I See the Veil as a Rejection of Progressive Values," *The Guardian*, March 20. Available online: https://www.theguardian.com/comment isfree/2015/mar/20/muslim-woman-veil-hijab (accessed September 30, 2019).

All Sides (2019a), "The Daily Telegraph – UK," *All Sides*. Available online: https://www.allsides .com/news-source/telegraph-uk (accessed September 30, 2019).

All Sides (2019b), "The Hill," *All Sides*. Available online: https://www.allsides.com/news-source/ hill-media-bias (accessed September 30, 2019).

Allah.is.the.most.merciful.1 (2020), "People Suddenly Looking at Niqabi Sisters with a New Sense of Respect," April 6. Facebook post. Available online: https://www.facebook.com/Allah .is.the.Most.Merciful.1/photos/a.135299253152513/3401438996538506/?type=3&theater (accessed April 15, 2020).

Allen, A. L. (2014), "Veiled Women in the American Courtroom: Is the Niqab a Barrier to Justice?" Faculty Scholarship. Paper 1618. Available online: https://scholarship.law.upenn. edu/faculty_scholarship/1618 (accessed September 30, 2019).

Allen, C. (2016), *Islamophobia*, Farnham: Ashgate.

Alqahtani, A. S., M. Sheikh, K. Wiley, and A. E. Heywood (2015), "Australian Hajj Pilgrims' Infection Control Beliefs and Practices: Insight with Implications for Public Health Approaches," *Travel Medicine and Infectious Disease*, 13 (4): 329–34.

Alsultany, E. (2012), *Arabs and Muslims in the Media: Race and Representation after 9/11*. New York: New York University Press.

Amaria, K. (2011), "The 'Girl In The Blue Bra,'" *NPR WBEZ*, December 21. Available online: https://www.npr.org/sections/pictureshow/2011/12/21/144098384/the-girl-in-the-blue-bra (accessed April 15, 2020).

Amer, S. (2014), *What Is Veiling?* Edinburgh: Edinburgh University Press.

Ammerman, N. (2017), "On Things Seen and Unseen: Enlarging the Vision in Sociology of Religion," in L. Doggett and A. Arat (eds.), *Foundations and Futures in the Sociology of Religion*, 101–14, London: Routledge.

Andrews, J. and R. Johnes (2016), "Faith Schools, Pupil Performance, and Social Selection." London: Education Policy Institute. Available online: https://dera.ioe.ac.uk//27949 (accessed April 15, 2020).

Appiah, K. A. (2020), "The Case for Capitalizing the B in Black," *The Atlantic*, June 18. Available online: https://www.theatlantic.com/ideas/archive/2020/06/time-to-capitalize-blackand-whitc/613159 (accessed September 15, 2020).

Arato, A. and J. L. Cohen (2018), "Civil society, Populism, and Religion," in C. de la Torre (ed.), *Routledge Handbook of Global Populism*, 98–118, London: Routledge.

Asad, T. (1999), "Religion, Nation-State, Secularism," in P. van der Meer and H. Lehmann (eds.), *Nation and Religion: Perspectives on Europe and Asia*, 178–96, Princeton, NJ: Princeton University Press.

Asad, T. (2009a), *Genealogies of Religion: Discipline and Reasons of Power in Christianity and Islam*, Baltimore: JHU Press.

Asad, T. (2009b), "Free Speech, Blasphemy, and Secular Criticism," in T. Asad, J. Butler, S. Mahmood, and W. Brown (eds.), *Is Critique Secular? Blasphemy, Injury, and Free Speech* (The Townsend Papers in the Humanties), 20–63, Berkeley: The University of California Press.

Asad, T. (2009c), "The Idea of Anthropology of Islam," *Qui Parle*, 17 (2): 1–30.

Auestad, L. (2015), *Respect, Plurality, and Prejudice: A Psychoanalytical and Philosophical Enquiry into the Dynamics of Social Exclusion and Discrimination*, London: Karnac Books.

Avishai, O. (2008), "'Doing Religion' in a Secular World: Women in Conservative Religions and the Question of Agency," *Gender & Society*, 22 (4): 409–33.

Aziz, S. (2012), "From the Oppressed to the Terrorist: Muslim-American Women in the Crosshairs of Intersectionality," *Hastings Race and Poverty Law Journal*, 9 (2): 191–263. Available online: https://scholarship.law.tamu.edu/cgi/viewcontent.cgi?referer=https://www.google.com/&httpsredir=1&article=1099&context=facscholar (accessed April 15, 2020).

Badran, M. (2001), "Understanding Islam, Islamism, and Islamic Feminism," *Journal of Women's History*, 13 (1): 47–52.

Badran, M. (2005), "Between Secular and Islamic Feminism/s: Reflections on the Middle East and Beyond," *Journal of Middle East Women's Studies*, 1 (1): 6–28.

Badran, M. (2009), *Feminism in Islam: Religious and Secular Convergences*, Oxford: Oneworld.

Bagby, I. (2012), "The American Mosque 2011," The Islamic Society of North America. Available online: http://www.hartfordinstitute.org/The-American-Mosque-Report-2.pdf (accessed September 30, 2019).

Bail, C. A. (2008), "The Configuration of Symbolic Boundaries against Immigrants in Europe," *American Sociological Review*, 73 (1): 37–59.

Baker, P., C. Gabrielatos, and T. McEnery, (2013), *Discourse Analysis and Media Attitudes: The Representation of Islam in the British Press*, Cambridge: Cambridge University Press.

Bakht, N. (2009), "Objection, Your Honour! Accommodating Niqab-Wearing Women in Courtrooms," in R. Grillo, R. Ballard, A. Ferrari, A. J. Hoekema, M. Maussen, and P. Shah (eds.), *Legal Practice and Cultural Diversity*, 115–33, Surrey: Ashgate Publishing Ltd.

Bakht, N. (2012), "Veiled Objections: Facing Public Opposition to the Niqab," in L. G. Beaman (ed.), *Reasonable Accommodation: Managing Religious Diversity*, 70–108, Vancouver: UBC Press.

Bakht, N. (2015), "In Your Face: Piercing the Veil of Ignorance about Niqab-Wearing Women," *Social and Legal Studies*, 24 (3): 419–41.

Barford, V. (2010), "Should the UK Ban the Muslim Face Veil?" BBC News, January 27. Available online: http://news.bbc.co.uk/2/hi/8481617.stm (accessed April 15, 2020).

Barlas, A. (2002), *Unreading Patriarchal Interpretations of the Qur'an*, Austin: University of Texas Press.

Barnard, A. and A. Feuer (2010), "Outraged, and Outrageous," *The New York Times*, October 8. Available online: https://www.nytimes.com/2010/10/10/nyregion/10geller.html (accessed September 30, 2019).

Barrett, D. (2010), "British Schools Where Girls Must Wear the Islamic Veil," The Daily Telegraph, October 2. Available online: https://www.telegraph.co.uk/education/educationnews/8038820/British-schools-where-girls-must-wear-the-Islamic-veil.html (accessed September 30, 2019).

Bartkowski, J. P., and J. G. Read (2003), "Veiled Submission: Gender, Power, and Identity Among Evangelical and Muslim Women in the United States," *Qualitative Sociology*, 26 (1): 71–92.

Bautista, J., (2008), "The Meta-Theory of Piety: Reflections on the Work of Saba Mahmood," *Contemporary Islam*, 2 (1): 75–83.

Bayoumi, M. (2019), "I'm a Brown Arab-American, and the US Census Refuses to Recognize Me," *The Guardian*, February 14. Available online: https://www.theguardian.com/commentisfree/2019/feb/14/arab-american-census-america-racism (accessed April 15, 2020).

BBC News (2006a), "'Remove Full Veils' Urges Straw," BBC News, October 6. Available online: http://news.bbc.co.uk/2/hi/uk/5411954.stm (accessed September 21, 2019).

BBC News (2006b), "Prescott Backs Right to Wear Veil," BBC News, October 8. Available online: http://news.bbc.co.uk/2/hi/uk_news/politics/4801801.stm (accessed September 21, 2019).

BBC News (2016), "'Traditionally Submissive Muslim Women' Say Who Us?" BBC Trending, January 25. Available online: https://www.bbc.com/news/blogs-trending-35403106 (accessed April 15, 2020).

References

BBC News (2020), "Paris Fashion Week: Facemasks on Show Amid Coronavirus Concern." BBC News, February 28. Available online: https://www.bbc.com/news/entertainment-arts-516727 53 (accessed April 15, 2020).

Beal, F. (1969), "Double Jeopardy: To Be Black and Female," *CWLU Herstory Project*. Available online: https://www.cwluherstory.org/classic-feminist-writings-articles/double-jeopardy-to-be-black-and-female (accessed September 30, 2019).

Beall, J. (ed.) (1997), *A City for All: Valuing Difference and Working with Diversity*, London: Zed Books.

Beck, U. and E. Beck-Gernsheim (2002), *Individualization: Institutionalized Individualism and Its Social and Political Consequences*. London: Sage.

Beckett, L. (2019), "'Blood on Their Hands': The Intelligence Officer Whose Warning over White Supremacy Was Ignored," *The Guardian*, August 8. Available online: https://www.theguard ian.com/us-news/2019/aug/07/white-supremacist-terrorism-intelligence-analyst (accessed September 30, 2019).

Begum vs Headteacher and Governors of Denbigh High School case (2006), UKHL 15. Available online: https://publications.parliament.uk/pa/ld200506/ldjudgmt/jd060322/begum.pdf (accessed September 30, 2019).

Beirich, H. (2013), "Hate Across the Waters: The Role of American Extremists in Fostering an International White Consciousness," in R. Wodak, M. KhosraviNik, and B. Mral Right-Wing (eds.), *Right-Wing Populism in Europe: Politics and Discourse*, 89–103, London: Bloomsbury.

Benedictus, L. (2017), "Blowing in the Wind: Why Do so Many Cities Have Poor East Ends?" *The Guardian*, May 12. Available online: https://www.theguardian.com/cities/2017/may/12/blo wing-wind-cities-poor-east-ends (accessed September 30, 2019).

Bennoune, K. (2007) "Secularism and Human Rights: A Contextual Analysis of Headscarves, Religious Expression, and Women's Equality under International Law," *Columbia Journal of Transnational Law*, 45 (2): 367–426.

Ben-Zur, H., S. Gil, and Y. Shamshins (2012), "The Relationship between Exposure to Terror through the Media, Coping Strategies and Resources, and Distress and Secondary Traumatization," *International Journal of Stress Management*, 19 (2): 132–50.

Berenstein Rojas, L. and Y. Nouh (2011), "'The right to choose how we dress:'American Muslim Women Speak out on French Burqa Ban," KPCC Radio, April 13. Available online: https://ww w.scpr.org/blogs/multiamerican/2011/04/13/7347/the-french-burqa-ban-american-muslim-w omen-speak-o (accessed April 15, 2020).

Bergen, P. and D. Sterman (2018), "The Real Terrorist Threat in America: It's No Longer Jihadist Groups," *Foreign Affairs*, October 30. Available online: https://www.foreignaffairs.com/arti cles/united-states/2018-10-30/real-terrorist-threat-america (accessed September 30, 2019).

Bergengruen, V. and W. J. Hennigan (2019), "'We Are Being Eaten from Within.' Why America Is Losing the Battle Against White Nationalist Terrorism," *Time*, August 8. Available online: https ://time.com/5647304/white-nationalist-terrorism-united-states/ (accessed September 30, 2019).

Berlant, L. G. (1997), *The Queen of America Goes to Washington City: Essays on Sex and Citizenship*, Durham, NC: Duke University Press.

Bever, L. (2016), "After Outcry, Georgia Lawmaker Abandons Bill That Would Have Banned Muslims from Wearing Veils," *The Washington Post*, November 18. Available online: https ://www.washingtonpost.com/news/acts-of-faith/wp/2016/11/18/after-outcry-georgia-lawmaker-abandons-bill-that-would-have-banned-muslims-from-wearing-veils (accessed September 30, 2019).

Bhimji, F. (2012), *British Asian Muslim Women, Multiple Spatialities and Cosmopolitanism*, Basingstoke: Palgrave Macmillan.

Biker Niqabi (2020), "Did they . . . did they just make niqab fardh ??" April 2, 11: 17 am. Tweet. Available online: https://twitter.com/bikerniqabi/status/1245732171719094274.

Bilge, S. (2010), "Beyond Subordination vs. Resistance: An Intersectional Approach to the Agency of Veiled Muslim Women," *Journal of Intercultural Studies*, 31 (1): 9–28.

Bindel, J. (2013), "Why Are My Fellow Feminists Shamefully Silent over the Tyranny of the Veil, asks JULIE BINDEL," *The Daily Mail*, September 17. Available online: https://www.dailymail.co.uk/debate/article-2424073/Why-fellow-feminists-shamefully-silent-tyranny-veil-asks-JULIE-BINDEL.html (accessed September 30, 2019).

Bindel, J. (2018), "Why Are so Many Left-wing Progressives Silent about Islam's Totalitarian Tendencies?" *Unherd.com*. Available online: https://unherd.com/2018/04/many-left-wing-progressives-protest-pope-silent-islams-totalitarian-tendencies-victims-cowardice-overwhelmingly-women (accessed September 30, 2019).

Black Muslim Forum (2020), "Report on the Experiences of Black British Muslims," Black Muslim Forum, April 5. Available online: https://blackmuslimforum.org/2020/04/05/they-had-the-audacity-to-ask-me-if-i-was-muslim-when-they-saw-me-a-black-woman-in-niqab-experiences-of-black-british-muslims/ (accessed April 15, 2020).

Boaz, D. (2019), "Practices 'Odious Among the Northern and Western Nations of Europe': Whiteness and Religious Freedom in the United States," in P. Essed, K. Farquharson, K. Pillay, and E. J. White (eds.), *Relating Worlds of Racism: Dehumanisation, Belonging, and the Normativity of European Whiteness*, 39–62, Basingstoke: Palgrave Macmillan.

Bonazzo, J. (2017), "Getty Is Combating Negative Images of Muslim Women With This Powerful Photo Project," *The Observer*, March 9. Available online: https://observer.com/2017/03/getty-images-muslim-girl-partnership (accessed January 21, 2020).

Blumer, H. (1969), *Symbolic Interactionism: Perspective and Method*, Englewood Cliffs, NJ: Prentice-Hall, Inc.

Boaz, D. (2019), "Practices 'Odious Among the Northern and Western Nations of Europe': Whiteness and Religious Freedom in the United States," in P. Essed, K. Farquharson, K. Pillay, and E. J. White (eds.), *Relating Worlds of Racism: Dehumanisation, Belonging, and the Normativity of European Whiteness*, 39–62, Basingstoke: Palgrave Macmillan.

Bolognani, M. and J. Mellor (2012), "British Pakistani Women's Use of the 'Religion versus Culture' Contrast: A Critical Analysis," *Culture and Religion*, 13 (2): 211–26.

Bonazzo, J. (2017), "Getty Is Combating Negative Images of Muslim Women with This Powerful Photo Project," *The Observer*, March 9. Available online: https://observer.com/2017/03/getty-images-muslim-girl-partnership/ (accessed September 30, 2019).

Bonnett, A. (2017), *The Idea of the West: Culture, Politics and History*, Basingstoke: Palgrave Macmillan.

Booth, R. (2019), "Racism Rising Since Brexit Vote, Nationwide Study Reveals," *The Guardian*, May 20. Available online: https://www.theguardian.com/world/2019/may/20/racism-on-the-rise-since-brexit-vote-nationwide-study-reveals (accessed September 30, 2019).

Bourdieu, P. (1991), *Language and Symbolic Power*, Cambridge, MA: Harvard University Press.

Bouteldja, N. (2011), "Unveiling the Truth: Why 32 Muslim Women Wear the Full-face Veil in France," The Open Society Foundations. Available online: https://www.opensocietyfoundations.org/sites/default/files/a-unveiling-the-truth-20100510_0.pdf (accessed September 30, 2019).

Bouteldja, N. (2014), "France vs England," in E. Brems (ed.), *The Experiences of Face Veil Wearers in Europe and the Law*, 115–60, Cambridge: Cambridge University Press.

Bouteldja, N. (2015), "Behind the Veil: Why 122 Women Choose to Wear the Full Facial Veil in the UK," The Open Society Foundations. Available online: https://www.opensocietyfoundations.org/sites/default/files/behind-veil-20150401.pdf (accessed September 30, 2019).

Bosankić, N. (2014) *Psychosocial Aspects of Niqab Wearing: Religion, Nationalism and Identity in Bosnia and Herzegovina*, Basingstoke: Palgrave Macmillan.

Bottici, C. and B. Challand (2013), *The Myth of the Clash of Civilizations*, London: Routledge.

Bowe, B. J., S. Fahmy, and W. Wanta (2013), "Missing Religion: Second Level Agenda Setting and Islam in American Newspapers," *International Communication Gazette*, 75 (7): 636–52.

References

Braasch, S. (2010), "See the Veil, See the Light," *The Humanist*, 70 (5): 8–12.

Brems, E., Y. Janssens, K. Lecoyer, S. Ould Chaib, and V. Vanderstaan (2012), "Wearing the Face Veil in Belgium," Human Rights Centre: University of Ghent. Available online: https://biblio.ugent.be/publication/8635340/file/8635351.pdf (accessed August 27, 2020).

Bribosia, E. and I. Rorive (2014), "Insider Perspectives and the Human Rights Debate on Face Veil Bans," in E. Brems (ed.), *The Experiences of Face Veil Wearers in Europe and the Law*, 163–83, Cambridge: Cambridge University Press.

Brighenti, A. (2007), "Visibility: A Category for the Social Sciences," *Current Sociology*, 55 (3): 323–42.

Brown, A. (2017), "Sweden Is Often Misunderstood, But Trump's Views Subvert the Truth," *The Guardian*, February 20. Available online: https://www.theguardian.com/commentisfree/2017/feb/20/sweden-donald-trump-crime-muslim-immigrants (accessed September 30, 2019).

Brown Givens, S. M. and J. L. Monahan (2005), "Priming Mammies, Jezebels, and Other Controlling Images: An Examination of the Influence of Mediated Stereotypes on Perceptions of an African American Woman," *Media Psychology*, 7 (1): 87–106.

Brunson, R. K. and J. Miller (2006), "Gender, Race, and Urban Policing: The Experience of African American Youths," *Gender & Society*, 20 (4): 531–52.

Bucar, E. (2017), *Pious Fashion: How Muslim Women Dress*, Cambridge, MA: Harvard University Press.

Butler, J. (1993), *Bodies that Matter: On the Discursive Limits of Sex*, New York: Routledge.

Butler, J. (1997), *Excitable Speech: A Politics of the Performative*, New York: Routledge.

Butler, J. (2003), *Kritik der ethischen Gewalt* (Adorno Lectures, 2002), Frankfurt am Main: Institut fur Sozialforschung an der Johann Wolfgang Goethe-Universitat.

Byman, D. (2019), "Right-Wingers Are America's Deadliest Terrorists," *Slate*, August 5. Available online: https://slate.com/news-and-politics/2019/08/right-wing-terrorist-killings-government-focus-jihadis-islamic-radicalism.html (accessed September 30, 2019).

Caetano, K. (2006), "The Women of Islam: The Role of Journalistic Photography in the (Re) production of Character-type," *Brazilian Journalism Research*, 2 (1): 141–56.

Cantwell v. Connecticut (1940), 310 U.S. 296. Available online: https://supreme.justia.com/cases/federal/us/310/296/ (accessed September 30, 2019).

Capeheart, J. (2018), "Police Violence Affects Women of Color Just as Much as Men. Why Don't We Hear about It?" *The Washington Post*, March 27. Available online: https://www.washingtonpost.com/blogs/post-partisan/wp/2018/03/27/police-violence-affects-women-of-color-just-as-much-as-men-why-dont-we-hear-about-it/ (accessed September 30, 2019).

Center for American Progress (2011), "Fear, Inc.: The Roots of the Islamophobia Network in America," Center for American Progress. Available online: https://cdn.americanprogress.org/wp-content/uploads/issues/2011/08/pdf/islamophobia.pdf (accessed September 30, 2019).

Cesari, J. (2013), *Why the West Fears Islam: An Exploration of Muslims in Liberal Democracies*, New York: Springer.

Chakraborti, N. and I. Zempi (2012), "The Veil under Attack: Gendered Dimensions of Islamophobic Victimization," *International Review of Victimology*, 18 (3): 269–84.

Chan-Malik, S. (2011), "Chadors, Feminists, Terror," *The Annals of the American Academy of Political And Social Science*, 637 (1): 112–40.

Chan-Malik, S. (2018), *Being Muslim: A Cultural History of Women of Color in American Islam*, New York: New York University Press.

Channel 4 (2013), "Debate: Should British Women Wear the Niqab?" October 24. Available online: https://www.channel4.com/news/debate-should-british-women-wear-the-niqab-video (accessed September 30, 2019).

Channel 4 (2017), "Fact Check: Is the Burqa Really a Terror Threat?" April 27. Available online: https://www.channel4.com/news/factcheck/is-the-burqa-really-a-terror-threat (accessed September 30, 2019).

Cherti, M. and L. Bradley (2011), "Inside Madrassas: Understanding and Engaging with British-Muslim Faith Supplementary Schools," London: Institute for Public Policy Research. Available online: https://www.ippr.org/files/images/media/files/publication/2011/11/inside-madrass as_Nov2011_8301.pdf (accessed August 21, 2019).

Cheruiyot, D. (2019), "Criticising Journalism: Popular Media Criticism in the Digital Age," PhD Dissertation, Karlstad University. Available online: http://www.diva-portal.org/smash/get/div a2:1353724/FULLTEXT02.pdf (accessed April 15, 2020).

Chesler, P. (2010), "Ban the Burqa? The Argument in Favor," *Middle East Quarterly*, Fall issue, 33–45. Available online: https://www.meforum.org/middle-east-quarterly/pdfs/2777.pdf (accessed September 30, 2019).

Choudhry, A. J., K. S. Al Mudaimegh, A. M. Turkistani, and N. A. Al Hamdan (2006), "Hajj-Associated Acute Respiratory Infection among Hajjis from Riyadh," *Eastern Mediterranean Health Journal*, 12 (3–4): 300–9.

Clarke, L. (2013), "Women in Niqab Speak: A Study of the Niqab in Canada." Canadian Council of Muslim Women. Available online: http://ccmw.com/women-in-niqab-speak-a-study-of-th e-niqab-in-canada (accessed September 30, 2019).

Clerget, S. (2011), "Timing Is of the Essence: Reviving the Neutral Law of General Applicability Standard and Applying It to Restrictions against Religious Face Coverings Worn While Testifying in Court," *George Mason Law Review* 18 (4): 1013–43.

Cochrane, K. (2013), "The Niqab Debate: 'Is the Veil the Biggest Issue We Face in the UK?'" *The Guardian*, September 16. Available online: https://www.theguardian.com/world/2013/sep/16/veil-biggest-issue-uk-niqab-debate (accessed September 30, 2019).

cooke, m. (2008), "Deploying the Muslimwoman," *Journal of Feminist Studies in Religion*, 24 (1): 91–9.

Cooper, F. R. (2006), "Against Bipolar Black Masculinity: Intersectionality, Assimilation, Identity Performance, and Hierarchy," *U.C. Davis Law Review*, 39 (3): 853–904.

Cornell, V. (2007), "Introduction: Voices of the Spirit," in V. Cornell (ed.), *Voices of the Spirit* (Voices of Islam series), xii–xxvi, Westport, CT: Praeger.

Coughlan, S. (2016), "Should There Be More Muslim State Schools?" *BBC News*, October 6. Avalable online: https://www.bbc.com/news/education-37484358 (accessed April 15, 2020).

Council of Europe (1950), "European Convention for the Protection of Human Rights and Fundamental Freedoms, as Amended by Protocols Nos. 11 and 14," November 4. Available online: https://www.refworld.org/docid/3ae6b3b04.html (accessed September 30, 2019)

Cox, J. (2010), *An Introduction to the Phenomenology of Religion*, London: Bloomsbury.

Crawford, R. (2000), "The Ritual of Health Promotion," in Michael Calnan, Jonathan Gabe, and Simon J. Williams (eds.), *Health, Medicine and Society: Key Theories, Future Agendas*, 219–35, London: Routledge.

Crenshaw, K. W. (1995), "Mapping the Margins: Intersectionality, Identity Politics, and Violence against Women of Color," in K. Crenshaw, N. Gotanda, G. Peller, and K. Thomas (eds.), *Critical Race Theory: The Key Writings That Formed the Movement*, 357–83, New York: New Press.

Crenshaw, K. W. (2002), The First Decade: Critical Reflections, or "a Foot in the Closing Door," *UCLA Law Review*, 49: 1343–72.

Crosby, E. (2014), "Faux Feminism: France's Veil Ban as Orientalism," *Journal of International Women's Studies*, 15 (2): 46–60.

Dar, Jehanzeb (2008), "Female, Muslim and Mutant: Muslim Women in Comic Books," *Muslimah Media Watch*, July 8. Available online: https://www.patheos.com/blogs/mmw/2

008/07/female-muslim-and-mutant-a-critique-of-muslim-women-in-comic-books-part-1-of-2/ (accessed September 30, 2019).

Davie, G. (2017), "Sociological Approaches to Religion in Britain," in L. Doggett, A. Arat (eds.), *Foundations and Futures in the Sociology of Religion*, 13–26, London: Routledge.

Davis, J. and R. Westerfelhaus (2013), "Finding a Place for a Muslimah Heroine in the Post-9/11 Marvel Universe: New X-Men's Dust," *Feminist Media Studies*, 13 (5): 800–9.

Diaz, W. (2019), "What the Niqab Taught Me About Myself as A Muslim Convert and a Latina," Muslim Matters, February 4. Available online: https://muslimmatters.org/2019/02/04/what-the-niqab-taught-me-about-myself-as-a-muslim-convert-and-a-latina/ (accessed September 30, 2019).

Doggett, L. and A. Arat (2017), "Introduction: Foundations and Futures," in L. Doggett and A. Arat (eds.), *Foundations and Futures in the Sociology of Religion*, 1–10, London: Routledge.

Dollahite, D. C., E. Layton, H. M. Bahr, A. B. Walker, and J. Y. Thatcher (2009), "Giving Up Something Good for Something Better: Sacred Sacrifices Made by Religious Youth," *Journal of Adolescent Research*, 24 (6): 691–725.

Dowler, L. (2002), "The Uncomfortable Classroom: Incorporating Feminist Pedagogy and Political Practice into World Regional Geography," *Journal of Geography*, 101 (2): 68–72.

Downey, J. and N. Fenton (2002), "New Media, Counter Publicity and the Public Sphere," *New Media & Society* 5 (2): 185–202.

Duits, L. and L. van Zoonen (2006), "Headscarves and Porno-Chic: Disciplining Girls' Bodies in the European Multicultural Society," *European Journal of Women's Studies*, 13 (2): 103–17.

Dunkel, T., D. Davidson, and S. Qurashi (2010), "Body Satisfaction and Pressure to Be Thin in Younger and Older Muslim and Non-Muslim Women: The Role of Western and Non-Western Dress Preferences," *Body Image*, 7 (1): 56–65.

Durham, A. (2012), "'Check On It' Beyoncé, Southern Booty, and Black Femininities in Music Video," *Feminist Media Studies*, 12 (1): 35–49.

Dwyer, C. (1999), "Veiled Meanings: Young British Muslim Women and the Negotiation of Differences," *Gender, Place & Culture*, 6 (1): 5–26.

Eck, D. (2001), *A New Religious America: How a "Christian Country" Has Become the World's Most Religiously Diverse Nation*, New York: HarperCollins.

Eck, D. (2007), "Prospects for Pluralism: *Voice and Vision in the Study of Religion*," *Journal of the American Academy of Religion*, 75 (4): 743–76.

Eddo-Lodge, R. (2017), "Why I'm No Longer Talking to White People about Race," *The Guardian*, May 30. Available online: https://www.theguardian.com/world/2017/may/30/why-im-no-longer-talking-to-white-people-about-race (accessed August 21, 2019).

Edwards, S. S. M. (2016), "Targeting Muslims Through Women's Dress: The Niqab and the Psychological War against Muslims," in J. A. Scutt (ed.), *Women, Law and Culture: Conformity, Contradiction, and Conflict*, 51–68, London: Palgrave Macmillan.

Eltahawy, M. (2009), "Ban the Burqa," *The New York Times*, July 2. Available online: https://www.nytimes.com/2009/07/03/opinion/03iht-edeltahawy.html (accessed September 30, 2019).

Eltahawy, M. (2018), "#MosqueMeToo: What Happened When I Was Sexually Assaulted during The Hajj," *Chicago Tribune*, February 19. https://www.chicagotribune.com/lifestyles/ct-muslim-sexual-assault-20180215-story.html (accessed August 21, 2019).

El-Kaissi S. and S. Sherbeeni (2010), "Vitamin D Deficiency in the Middle East and Its Health Consequences for Adults," in M. Holick (ed.), *Vitamin D: Physiology, Molecular Biology, and Clinical Applications*, 495–504, Totowa, NJ: Humana Press.

El Rashidi, Y. (2013), "Mona Eltahawy," *Bidoun*, 28. Available online: https://bidoun.org/articles/mona-eltahawy (accessed August 21, 2019).

Engeland, A. Van (2019), "What If? An Experiment to Include a Religious Narrative in the Approach of the European Court of Human Rights," *Journal of Law, Religion and State*, 7 (2): 213–41.

Esposito, J. (2010), *The Future of Islam*, New York: Oxford University Press.

Essed, P. (1991), *Understanding Everyday Racism: An Interdisciplinary Theory*, Newbury Park, CA: Sage.

Evans, C. (2001), *Freedom of Religion under the European Convention on Human Rights*, Oxford: Oxford University Press.

Evans, K. N. (2015), "As American as Apple Pie: US Female Converts to Islam", *British Association for American Studies*, July 22. Available online: http://www.baas.ac.uk/usso/as-american-as-apple-pie-u-s-female-converts-to-islam (accessed September 30, 2019).

Evolvi, G. (2018), *Blogging My Religion: Secular, Muslim, and Catholic Media Spaces in Europe*, London: Routledge.

Evolvi, G. (2019), "The Veil and Its Materiality: Muslim Women's Digital Narratives About the Burkini Ban," *Journal of Contemporary Religion*, 34 (3): 469–87.

Faizal, H. (nd), "Hafsah Faizal," https://www.hafsahfaizal.com (accessed March 21, 2019).

Fernando M., (2010), "Reconfiguring Freedom: Muslim Piety and the Limits of Secular Law and Public Discourse in France," *American Ethnologist*, 37 (1): 19–35.

Ferrari, A. and S. Pastorelli (eds.) (2013), *The Burqa Affair Across Europe: Between Public and Private Space*, London: Routledge.

Flores, L. A. (1996), "Creating Discursive Space through a Rhetoric of Difference: Chicana Feminists Craft a Homeland," *Quarterly Journal of Speech*, 82 (2): 142–56.

Foucault, M. (1980), "Two Lectures," in C. Gordon (ed.), *Power/Knowledge: Selected Interviews and Other Writings by Michel Foucault, 1972–1977*, 78–108, New York: Pantheon Books.

Foucault, M. (1981), "The Order of Discourse," in R. Young (ed.), *Untying the Text: A Post-structural Anthology*, 48–78, Boston: Routledge & Kegan Paul.

Foucault, M. (1988), "Technologies of the Self," in *Technologies of the Self*, 16–49, Amherst, MA: University of Massachusetts Press.

Franks, M. (2000), "Crossing the Borders of Whiteness? White Muslim Women Who Wear The Hijab in Britain Today," *Ethnic and Racial Studies*, 23 (5): 917–29.

Fredette, J. (2015), "Becoming a Threat: The Burqa and the Contestation over Public Morality Law in France," *Law & Social Inquiry*, 40 (3): 585–610.

Frieden, T. (2004), "U.S. to Defend Muslim Girl Wearing Scarf in School: Federal Position Will Oppose Oklahoma School District Policy," *CNN News*, March 31. Available online: https://www.cnn.com/2004/LAW/03/30/us.school.headscarves/ (accessed August 29, 2020).

Fuleihan, G. E.-H. (2010), "Vitamin D Deficiency in the Middle East and Its Health Consequences," in M. Holick (ed.), *Vitamin D: Physiology, Molecular Biology, and Clinical Applications*, 469–94, Totowa, NJ: Humana Press.

Furedi, A. (2016), *The Moral Case for Abortion*, Basingstoke: Palgrave MacMillan.

Galinsky, A., K. Hugenberg, C. Groom, and G. Bodenhausen (2003), "The Reappropriation of Stigmatizing Labels: Implications for Social Identity," *Research on Managing Groups and Teams*, 5: 221–56.

Galonnier, J. (2015a), "The Racialization of Muslims in France and the United States: Some Insights from White Converts to Islam," *Social Compass*, 62 (4): 570–83.

Galonnier, J. (2015b), "When 'White Devils' Join the Deen: White American Converts to Islam and the Experience of Non-Normative Whiteness," *HAL Archives-Ouvertes*, hal-01422847. Available online: https://hal.archives-ouvertes.fr/hal-01422847/document (accessed September 30, 2019).

Galonnier, J. (2017), "Choosing Faith and Facing Race: Converting to Islam in France and the United States," PhD dissertation, Northwestern University and Institut d'Études Politiques, Paris. https://search.proquest.com/openview/4a79913c10d18723fff3e7600052fc76/1?pq-origsite=gscholar&cbl=18750&diss=y (accessed September 30, 2019).

Garner, S., and S. Selod (2014), "The Racialization of Muslims: Empirical Studies of Islamophobia," *Critical Sociology*, 41 (1): 9–19.

References

Geller, P. (2016) "Yes, Ban The Burqa, It Is a National Security Necessity," The Hill, November 23. Available online: https://thehill.com/blogs/pundits-blog/civil-rights/307399-yes-ban-the -burqa-it-is-a-national-security-necessity (accessed September 30, 2019).

Getty Images (2017), "Getty Images and MuslimGirl.com Partner to Promote Positive Images of Modern Muslim Women," Getty Images, March 8. Available online: http://press.gettyimages. com/getty-images-and-muslimgirl-com-partner-to-promote-positive-images-of-modern -muslim-women/ (accessed September 30, 2019).

Getty Images (2019), "Niqab." Available online: https://www.gettyimages.com/photos/niqab?lice nse=rf&fa . . . (accessed September 30, 2019).

Giddens, A. (1999), *Modernity and Self-Identity: Self and Society in the Late Modern Age*, Cambridge: Polity Press.

Giordan, G. (2009), "The Body between Religion and Spirituality," *Social Compass*, 56 (2): 226–36

Goffman, E. (1961), *Encounters: Two Studies in the Sociology of Interaction*, London: Penguin Books.

Goffman, E. (1963), *Stigma: Notes on the Management of Spoiled Identity*, Upper Saddle River, NJ: Prentice-Hall.

Gomez, M. (2019), *African Dominion: A New History of Empire in Early and Medieval West Africa*, Princeton, NJ: Princeton University Press.

Gov.uk (2019), "All Schools and Colleges in England," *Gov.uk*. Available online: https://www.com pare-school-performance.service.gov.uk/schools-by-type?step=default&table=schools&reg ion=all-england&for=secondary (accessed April 15, 2020).

Göle, N. (2002), "Islam in Public: New Visibilities and New Imaginaries," *Public Culture*, 14 (1): 173–90.

Göle, N. (2011), "The Public Visibility of Islam and European Politics of Resentment: The Minarets-mosques Debate," *Philosophy & Social Criticism*, 37 (4): 383–92.

Goyanes, M. (2019), "Antecedents of Incidental News Exposure: The Role of Media Preference, Use and Trust," *Journalism Practice*, https://doi.org/10.1080/17512786.2019.1631710.

Gramsci, A. (1971), *Selections from the Prison Notebooks*, New York: International Publishers.

Grewal, Z. (2014), *Islam Is a Foreign Country: American Muslims and the Global Crisis of Authority*, New York: New York University Press.

Grierson, J. (2013), "Wearing Niqab Should Be Woman's Choice, Says Theresa May," *The Independent*, September 17. https://www.independent.co.uk/news/uk/home-news/wearing -niqab-should-be-womans-choice-says-theresa-may-8822449.html (accessed April 15, 2020).

Griffin, J. (1961), *Black Like Me*, Chicago, IL: Houghton Mifflin.

Grosfoguel, R. and E. Mielants (2006), "The Long-Durée Entanglement Between Islamophobia and Racism in the Modern/Colonial Capitalist/Patriarchal World-System: An Introduction," *Human Architecture: Journal of the Sociology of SelfKnowledge*, 5 (2). Available online: https ://scholarworks.umb.edu/cgi/viewcontent.cgi?article=1151&context=humanarchitecture (accessed September 30, 2019).

Gu, R. (2020), "From Apathy to Action: A Muslim Activist Standing Up against Islamophobia," *InterCardiff*, March 12. Available online: https://www.jomec.co.uk/intercardiff/global-city/f rom-apathy-to-action-a-muslim-activist-standing-up-against-islamophobia (accessed April 15, 2020).

Guimond, A. M. (2017), *Converting to Islam: Understanding the Experiences of White American Females*, Basingstoke: Palgrave Macmillan.

Gulamhussein, Q. and N. R. Eaton (2015), "Hijab, Religiosity, and Psychological Wellbeing of Muslim Women in the United States," *Journal of Muslim Mental Health*, 9 (2): 25–40.

Guy-Sheftall, B. (1990), *Daughters of Sorrow: Attitudes toward Black Women, 1880–1920*, New York: Carlson.

Guy-Sheftall, B. (1995), "Introduction," in B. Guy-Sheftall (ed.), *Words of Fire: An Anthology of African-American Feminist Thought*, 1–22, New York: The New Press.

Habermas, J. (1992), "Further Reflections on the Public Sphere," in C. Calhoun (ed.), *Habermas and the Public Sphere*, 421–461, Cambridge, MA: The MIT Press.

Hall, S. (2007), "The West and the Rest: Discourse and Power," in T. D. Gupta, C. James, R. Maaka, G. E. Galabuzi, and C. Andersen (eds.), *Race and Racialization: Essential Readings*, 56–60, Toronto: Canadian Scholar Press.

Halley, J. (2006), *Split Decisions: How and Why to Take a Break from Feminism*, Princeton, NJ: Princeton University Press.

Hanes, E. and S. Machin (2014), "Hate Crime in the Wake of Terror Attacks: Evidence From 7/7 and 9/11," *Journal of Contemporary Criminal Justice*, 30 (3): 247–67.

Harris, A. and Hussein, S. (2018), "Conscripts or Volunteers? Young Muslims as Everyday Explainers," *Journal of Ethnic and Migration Studies*, Online First, 1–18.

Hassouneh-Phillips, D. (2001), "'Marriage Is Half of Faith and the Rest is Fear Allah': Marriage and Spousal Abuse among American Muslims," *Violence Against Women*, 7 (8): 927–946.i

Heath, B. (2020), "Starting at Midnight, People in Laredo, Texas, Will Be Required to 'wear some form of covering over their nose and mouth, such as a homemade mask, scarf, bandana, or handkerchief, when entering into or inside of any building open to the public.' Not Having One Is a Crime." April 1, 10:29 pm. Available online: https://twitter.com/bradheath/status/124 5538889068134401 (accessed April 15, 2020).

Hegarty S. (2017), "Burkas Are Political Symbols Not Islamic Ones, Muslim Scholar Says," *ABC News Australia*. September 10. Available online: https://www.abc.net.au/news/2017-08-28/b urkas-are-political-symbols-not-islamic-says-muslim-scholar/8843916 (accessed September 30, 2019).

Hellyer, H. A. (2016), "Observance of Islam Is a Way to Defeat Extremism," *The National*, February 25. Available online: https://www.thenational.ae/opinion/observance-of-islam-is-a-way-to-defeat-extremism-1.205220 (accessed September 30, 2019).

Hendrix, S. (2011), "The few U.S. Muslim Women Who Choose Full Veil Face Mix of Harassment, Sympathy," *The Washington Post*, April 13. Available online: https://www.was hingtonpost.com/local/the-few-us-muslim-women-who-choose-full-veil-face-mix-of-harass ment-sympathy/2011/04/13/AFLrwzYD_story.html (accessed September 30, 2019).

Hill, M. (2013), "Legal and Social Issues Concerning the Wearing of the Burqa and Other Head Coverings in the United Kingdom," in A. Ferrari and S. Pastorelli (eds.), *The Burqa Affair Across Europe: Between Public and Private Space*, 77–100, London: Ashgate.

Hill, M. and R. Sandberg (2007), "Is Nothing Sacred? Clashing Symbols in a Secular World," *Public Law*, 3: 488–506.

Hill Collins, P. (2000), "Gender, Black Feminism, and Black Political Economy," *Annals of the American Academy of Political and Social Science*, 568 (1): 41–53.

Hitlin, S. and G. H. Elder, Jr. (2007), "Time, Self, and the Curiously Abstract Concept of Agency," *Sociological Theory*, 25 (2): 170–91.

Hollywood, A. (2002), "Performativity, Citationality, Ritualization," *History of Religions* 42 (2): 93–115.

Hollywood, A. (2004), "Gender, Agency, and the Divine in Religious Historiography," *Journal of Religion*, 84 (4): 514–28.

Hooper, S. (2013), "Black Britons Confront 'radical Islam,'" *Al-Jazeera*, December 19. Available online: https://www.aljazeera.com/indepth/features/2013/12/black-britons-confront-radica l-islam-2013121871456382764.html (accessed September 30, 2019).

Hopkins, P. (2014), "Managing Strangerhood: Young Sikh Men's Strategies," *Environment and Planning*, 46 (7): 1572–85.

Howarth, C. (2006), "Race as Stigma: Positioning the Stigmatized as Agents, Not Objects," *Journal of Community and Applied Social Psychology*, 16 (6): 442–51.

Hunter, J. D. and C. D. Bowman (2016), "The Vanishing Center of the American Democracy: The 2016 Survey of American Political Culture," Institute for Advanced Studies in Culture at the University of Virginia, https://s3.amazonaws.com/iasc-prod/uploads/pdf/2dc83bd6050a7 5f3fe9a.pdf (accessed March 29, 2020).

Hussein, A. (2019), "Moving Beyond (and Back to) the Black–White Binary: A Study of Black and White Muslims' Racial Positioning in the United States," *Ethnic and Racial Studies*, 42 (4): 589–606.

Hustad, K. (2018), "'Now It's a Sign of Protest:' Muslim Women in Denmark Defy the Face Veil Ban," *Time*, August 2. Available online: https://time.com/5356136/denmark-burqa-ban-pr otest/ (accessed September 30, 2019).

Inge, A. (2016), *The Making of a Salafi Muslim Woman: Paths to Conversion*, Oxford: Oxford University Press.

Iqbal, N. (2010), "Beyond the Veil: London's Burka Wearers Go on the Defensive," *Evening Standard*, November 5. Available online: https://www.standard.co.uk/lifestyle/beyond-the-ve il-londons-burka-wearers-go-on-the-defensive-6532864.html (accessed September 30, 2019).

Imtoual, A. (2011), "Religious Racism and the Media: Representations of Muslim Women in the Australian Print Media," *Outskirts Online Journal*, 13. Available online: https://www.outskirt s.arts.uwa.edu.au/volumes/volume-13/imtoual (accessed August 27, 2020).

Inglis, D. (2017), "Cover Their Face: Masks, Masking, and Masquerades in Historical-Anthropological Context," in A. Almila, and D. Inglis (eds.), *The Routledge International Handbook to Veils and Veiling*, 278–91, London: Routledge.

Isaacs, J. (2018), "The Real Founders of Fake News? American Islamophobes," *The Nation*, July 31. Available online: https://www.thenation.com/article/real-founders-fake-news-america n-islamophobes/ (accessed September 30, 2019).

Islam, N. (2018), "Soft Islamophobia," *Religions*, 9 (9): 280–96.

Islam Anani, N. (2020), "And Here I Was Told Covering Your Face Was Objectively Offensive and a Security Threat," March 8, 04:09 pm. Tweet. Available online: https://twitter.com/namir ari/status/1236761054753030149?lang=en (accessed April 15, 2020).

Jacobsen, C. M. (2011), "Troublesome Threesome: Feminism, Anthropology and Muslim Women's Piety," *Feminist Review*, 98 (1): 65–82.

Jan, T. (2020), "Two Black Men Say They Were Kicked Out of Walmart for Wearing Protective Masks. Others Worry It Will Happen to Them," *The Washington Post*, April 9, www.washin gtonpost.com/business/2020/04/09/masks-racial-profiling-walmart-coronavirus (accessed April 15, 2020).

Jardina, A. (2019), *White Identity Politics*, New York: Cambridge University Press.

Jawhar, S. (2011), "Why I Hate the Burqa — And Yes, I Wear One," *HuffPost*, May 25. Available online: https://www.huffingtonpost.com/sabria-jawhar/why-i-hate-the-burqa----a_b_669953. html (accessed September 30, 2019).

Jeldtoft, N. (2011), "Lived Islam: Religious Identity with 'Non-organized' Muslim Minorities," *Ethnic and Racial Studies*, 34 (7): 1134–51.

Johnson, A. (2017), "Getting Comfortable to Feel at Home: Clothing Practices of Black Muslim Women in Britain," *Gender, Place & Culture*, 24 (2): 274–87.

Johnson, B. (2018), "Denmark Has Got It Wrong. Yes, the Burka is Oppressive and Ridiculous – but That's Still No Reason to Ban It," *The Daily Telegraph*, August 5. Available online: https:// www.telegraph.co.uk/news/2018/08/05/denmark-has-got-wrong-yes-burka-oppressive-ridiculous-still (accessed September 15, 2020).

Johnson, D. (2005), *The Popular and the Canonical: Debating Twentieth-century Literature 1940–2000*, London: Psychology Press.

Jones, K. W. (2001), *Accent on Privilege: English Identities and Anglophilia in the U.S*, Philadelphia, PA: Temple University Press.

Jones, L. (2009), "My Week Wearing a Burka: Just a Few Yards of Black Fabric, But It Felt Like a Prison," *Daily Mail*, August 10. Available online: https://www.dailymail.co.uk/debate/article-

1205208/LIZ-JONES-My-week-wearing-burka--Just-yards-black-fabric-felt-like-prison.html (accessed September 30, 2019).

Joshi, K. Y. (2006), "The Racialization of Hinduism, Islam, and Sikhism in the United States," *Equity & Excellence in Education*, 39 (3): 211–26.

Jouili, J. S. (2019), "Islam and Culture: Dis/junctures in a Modern Conceptual Terrain," *Comparative Studies in Society and History*, 61 (1): 207–37.

Kabir, N. A. (2010), *Young British Muslims: Identity, Culture, Politics and the Media*, Edinburgh: Edinburgh University Press.

Kahf, M. (1999), *Western Representations of the Muslim Woman from Termagant to Odalisque*, Austin: University of Texas Press.

Kaiser, Cheryl R. and Miller, Carol T. (2004). "A Stress and Coping Perspective on Confronting Sexism," *Psychology of Women Quarterly*, 28 (2): 168–78.

Karim, J. (2008), *American Muslim Women: Negotiating Race, Class, and Gender within the Ummah*, New York: NYU Press.

Karim K. H. (1998), "From Ethnic Media to Global Media: Transnational Communication Networks Among Diasporic Communities," Working Papers, http://www.transcomm.ox.a c.uk/working%20papers/karim.pdf (accessed January 29, 2020).

Karim K. H. (2002), "Diasporas and Their Communication Networks: Exploring the Broader Context of Transnational Narrowcasting," Virtual Diasporas and Global Problem Solving Project Papers. Available online: http://oldsite.nautilus.org/gps/virtual-diasporas/paper/Kari m.html (accessed January 29, 2020).

Kearns, E. M., A. E. Betus, and A. F. Lemieux (2019), "Why Do Some Terrorist Attacks Receive More Media Attention Than Others?" *Justice Quarterly*, 36 (6): 985–1022.

Kearns, M. (2017), "Gender, Visuality and Violence: Visual Securitization and the 2001 War in Afghanistan," *International Feminist Journal of Politics*, 19 (4): 491–505.

Khamal, R. (2019), "What It's Like to Wear the Niqab in (Not So Tolerant) Canada," *The Globe and Mail*, July 3. Available online: https://www.theglobeandmail.com/life/first-person/artic le-what-its-like-to-wear-the-niqab-in-not-so-tolerant-canada (accessed January 29, 2020).

Khamis, S. et al. (2016), "Self-branding, 'Micro-celebrity' and the Rise of Social Media Influencers," *Celebrity Studies*, 8 (2): 191–208.

Khiabany, G., and M. Williamson (2008), "Veiled Bodies, Naked Racism: Culture, Politics and Race in the Sun," *Race and Class*, 50 (2): 69–88.

Khiabany, G. and M. Williamson (2011), "Muslim Women and Veiled Threats: From Civilizing Mission to Clash of Civilizations," in J. Petley and R. Richardson (eds.), *Pointing the Finger: Islam and Muslims in the British Media*, 173–200, London: One World Publications.

Killian, C. (2007), "From a Community of Believers to an Islam of the Heart: 'Conspicuous' Symbols, Muslim Practices, and the Privatization of Religion in France," in Monahan, S. C., W. Mirola, and M. O. Emerson (eds.), *Sociology of Religion: A Reader*, 36–44, London: Routledge.

Kiliç, S. (2008), "The British Veil Wars," *Social Politics: International Studies in Gender, State & Society*, 15 (4): 433–54.

Kim, A. (2018), *Secrets of the Ninja*, Lake Alfred, FL: Dojo Press.

Kirk, D. (2013), "Appearance in Court – Veiled Threats," *The Journal of Criminal Law*, 77 (6): 459–61.

Koskela, H. (2010), "Fear and Its Others," in S. Smith, R. Pain, S. A. Marston, and J. P. Jones (eds.), *The SAGE Handbook of Social Geographies*, 389–407, London: Sage Publications

Kosut, M. (2000), "Tattoo Narratives: The Intersection of the Body, Self-identity and Society," *Visual Sociology*, 15 (1): 79–100.

Krugman, P. (2017), "The Bad, The Worse, and the Ugly," *The New York Times*, April 7. Available online: https://www.nytimes.com/2017/04/07/opinion/the-bad-the-worse-and-the-ugly.html (accessed September 30, 2019).

References

Kugle, S. A. (2014), *Living Out Islam: Voices of Gay, Lesbian, and Transgender Muslims*, New York: New York University Press.

Kumar, D. (2012), *Islamophobia and the Politics of Empire*, Chicago, IL: Haymarket Press.

Kundnani, A. (2009), "Spooked! How Not to Prevent Violent Extremism," Institute of Race Relations. Available online: http://www.kundnani.org/wp-content/uploads/spooked.pdf (accessed September 30, 2019).

Kundnani, A. (2014), *The Muslims Are Coming! Islamophobia, Extremism, and the Domestic War on Terror*, London: Verso Books.

Kuruvilla, C. (2018), "Trump's New Ambassador Finally Tells Dutch He Was Wrong About Muslim 'No-Go' Zones," *HuffPost.com*, November 1. https://www.huffpost.com/entry/pete -hoekstra-anti-muslim-comments-dutch-media_n_5a577124e4b03bc4d03e97bc (accessed September 30, 2019).

Laird, K. (2014) "Confronting Religion: Veiled Witnesses, the Right to a Fair Trial and the Supreme Court of Canada's Judgment in R v N.S.," *Modern Law Review*, 77 (1): 123–38.

Lalonde, J. S. (2020) "If You're Gonna Fight with Others about Masks and Face Coverings in Canada, Please Situate It in Context. We're a Country That Outlawed Face Coverings at Protests and Is Constantly Targeting Muslim Women Who Wear Hijab or Niqab," April 6, 07: 39 am. Tweet. Available online: https://twitter.com/JulieSLalonde/status/12471719893553 31584 (accessed April 15, 2020).

Lamont, M. and V. Molnár (2002), "The Study of Boundaries in the Social Sciences," *Annual Review of Sociology*, 28: 167–95.

Lamothe-Ramos, A. (2012), "I Walked Around in a Burqa All Day (And I'm Not Muslim)," *Vice*, August 7. Available online: https://www.vice.com/en_us/article/dp4wpa/i-walked-around-in -a-burqa-all-day-and-im-not-muslim (accessed September 30, 2019).

Lamptey, J. T. (2018) *Divine Words, Female Voices: Muslima Explorations in Comparative Feminist Theology*, New York: Oxford University Press.

Langlaude, S. (2006), "Indoctrination, Secularism, Religious Liberty, and the ECHR," *International and Comparative Law Quarterly*, 55 (4): 929–44.

Lewis, R. (2013), *Gendering Orientalism: Race, Femininity and Representation*, London: Routledge.

Lewis, R. (2015), *Muslim Fashion: Contemporary Style Cultures*, Durham, NC: Duke University Press.

Lewis, R. (2017), "Futures in Fashions: Modest Fashion Practices and Influence," in L. Doggett and A. Arat (eds.), *Foundations and Futures in the Sociology of Religion*, 115–32, London: Routledge.

Levine, D. N. (1977), "Simmel at a Distance: On the History and Systematics of the Sociology of the Stranger," *Sociological Focus*, 10 (1): 15–29.

Lippi-Green, R. (2012), *English with an Accent Language, Ideology and Discrimination in the United States*, New York: Routledge.

Losh, E. (2014), "Hashtag Feminism and Twitter Activism in India," *Social Epistemology Review and Reply Collective*, 3 (3): 11–22.

Lövheim, M. (2017), "Media and Religion: Bridging Incompatible Agendas," in L. Doggett and A. Arat (eds.), *Foundations and Futures in the Sociology of Religion*, 39–52, London: Routledge.

Lutz, H. (1998), "The Legacy of Migration: Immigrant Mothers and Daughters and the Process of Intergenerational Transmission," in M. Chamberlain (ed.), *Caribbean Migration: Globalized Identities*, 96–110, London: Routledge.

Lynch, G. (2017), "Researching the Religious Dimensions of Social Life: The Sacred and the Social Uses of Moral Meaning in Contemporary Society," in L. Doggett and A. Arat (eds.), *Foundations and Futures in the Sociology of Religion*, 151–64, London: Routledge.

MacConnell-Ginet, S. (2003), "What's in a Name? Social Labeling and Gender Practices," in J. Holmes and M. Meyerhoff (eds.), *The Handbook of Language and Gender*, 69–97, London: Blackwell Publishing.

Macdonald, M. (2006), "Muslim Women and the Veil Problems of Image and Voice in Media Representations," *Feminist Media Studies*, 6 (1): 7–23.

Mack, P. (2003), "Religion, Feminism, and the Problem of Agency: Reflections on Eighteenth-Century Quakerism," *Signs*, 29 (1): 149–77.

Magnus, K. D. (2006), "The Unaccountable Subject: Judith Butler and the Social Conditions of Intersubjective Agency," *Hypatia*, 21 (2): 81–103.

Magsi, M. (2012), "The Day I Wore a Niqab," *The Express Tribune*, April 17. Available online: https://blogs.tribune.com.pk/story/11136/the-day-i-wore-a-niqab/comment-page-2/ (accessed September 30, 2019).

Mahmood, S. (2005), *The Politics of Piety: The Islamic Revival and the Feminist Subject*, Princeton, NJ: Princeton University Press.

Mandaville, P. (2010), *Global Political Islam*, London: Routledge.

Malik, Z. (2006), "Zaiba Malik Wears a Niqab for a Day and Is Shocked by the Reaction of Strangers," The Guardian, October 17. Available online: https://www.theguardian.com/world/2006/oct/17/gender.religion (accessed September 30, 2019).

Marcus, G. (2013), "Foreword," in E. Lott (ed.), *Love and Theft: Blackface Minstrelsy and the American Working Class*, New York: Oxford University Press.

Marranci, G. (2013), "Introduction: Studying Islam in Practice," in G. Marranci (ed.), *Studying Islam in Practice*, London: Routledge. Available online: https://www.taylorfrancis.com/books/e/9781315850955/chapters/10.4324/9781315850955-7 (accessed September 30, 2019).

Martin, J. (1993), "The Notion of Difference for Emerging Womanist Ethics: The Writings of Audre Lorde and bell hooks," *Journal of Feminist Studies in Religion* 9 (1–2): 39–51.

Martin, R. and A. Barzegar (2010), *Islamism: Contested Perspectives on Political Islam*, Berkeley, CA: Stanford University Press.

Marvasti, A. (2005), "Being Middle Eastern American: Identity Negotiation in the Context of the War on Terror," *Symbolic Interaction*, 28 (4): 525–47.

Mauleón, E. (2018), "Black Twice: Policing Black Muslim Identities," *UCLA Law Review*, 65(5): 1326–90.

Mazrouki, N. (2017), *Islam: An American Religion*, New York: Columbia University Press.

McCarthy, N. (2019), "Report: Hate Crime Is Rising In 30 Major American Cities," *Forbes*, August 1. Available online: https://www.forbes.com/sites/niallmccarthy/2019/08/01/report-hate-crime-is-rising-in-30-major-american-cities-infographic/#4ee2a2bdb8d0 (accessed September 30, 2019).

McClay, W. M. (2001), "Two Concepts of Secularism," *Journal of Policy History*, 13 (1): 47–72.

McCloud, A. B. (1995), *African American Islam*, New York: Routledge.

McCombs, M. (1997), "Building Consensus: The News Media's Agenda-Setting Roles," *Political Communication*, 14 (4): 433–43.

McCombs, M. and D. L. Shaw (1972), "The Agenda-Setting Function of Mass Media," *Public Opinion Quarterly*, 36 (2): 176–87.

McGhee, D. (2008), *The End of Multiculturalism? Terrorism, Integration and Human Rights*, Maidenhead: McGraw-Hill Education.

McGovern, C. (2006), *Sold American: Consumption and Citizenship, 1890–1945*, Chapel Hill, NC: University of North Carolina Press.

McGuire, M. (2006), "Embodied Practices: Negotiation and Resistance," in N. T. Ammerman (ed.), *Everyday Religion: Observing Modern Religious Lives*, 187–200, New York: Oxford University Press.

McGuire, M. (2008), *Lived Religion: Faith and Practice in Everyday Life*, Oxford: Oxford University Press.

References

McRobbie, A. (2004), "Notes on 'What Not to Wear' and Post-Feminist Symbolic Violence," *The Sociological Review*, 52 (2): 99–109.

Meer, N. and T. Modood (2009), "Refutations of Racism in the 'Muslim Question,'" *Patterns of Prejudice*, 43 (3–4): 335–54.

Meer, N., C. Dwyer, and T. Modood (2010), "Embodying Nationhood? Conceptions of British National Identity, Citizenship, and Gender in the 'Veil Affair,'" *The Sociological Review*, 58 (1): 84–111.

Middle East Forum (2019), "About the Middle East Forum," Available online: https://www.meforum.org/about/ (accessed September 30, 2019).

Miles, R. and M. Brown (2003), *Racism*, London: Routledge.

Mills, C. W. (1949), "Situated Actions and Vocabularies of Motive," *American Sociological Review*, 5 (6): 904–9.

Milroy, L. (2000), "Britain and the United States: Two Nations Divided by the Same Language (and Different Language Ideologies," *Journal of Linguistic Anthropology*, 10 (1): 56–89.

Modood, T. (2006), "British Muslims and the Politics of Multiculturalism," in T. Modood, A. Triandafyllidou, and R. Zapata-Barrero (eds.), *Multiculturalism, Muslims and Citizenship: A European Approach*, 37–56, London: Routledge.

Moghadam, V. M. (2003), *Modernizing Women: Gender and Social Change in the Middle East*, Boulder, CO: L. Rienner.

Mohamed, B. (2016), "A New Estimate of the U.S. Muslim Population." Pew Research Center. Available online: http://www.pewresearch.org/fact-tank/2016/01/06/a-new-estimate-of-the-u-s-muslim-population (accessed August 27, 2020).

Mohamed, B., G. A. Smith, A. Cooperman, and A. Schiller (2017), "U.S. Muslims Concerned About Their Place in Society, but Continue to Believe in the American Dream," Pew Research Center, July 26. Available online: https://www.pewresearch.org/wp-content/uploads/sites/7/2017/07/U.S.-MUSLIMS-FULL-REPORT.pdf (accessed September 30, 2019).

Mohammad, R. (2013), "Making Gender Ma(r)king Place: Youthful British Pakistani Muslim Women's Narratives of Urban Space," *Environment and Planning A: Economy and Space*, 45 (8): 1802–22.

Mohanty, C. T. (1991), "Under Western Eyes: Feminist Scholarship and Colonial Discourses," in C. T. Mohanty, A. Russo, and L. Torres (eds.), *Third World Women and the Politics of Feminism*, 51–80, Indianapolis: Indiana University Press.

Mojab, S. (1998), "'Muslim' Women and 'Western' Feminists: The Debate on Particulars and Universals," *Monthly Review*, 50 (7): 19–30.

Moors, A. (2011), "Niqabitch and Princess Hijab: Niqab Activism, Satire and Street Art," *Feminist Review*, 98 (1): 128–35.

Moosavi, L. (2015), "The Racialization of Muslim Converts in Britain and Their Experiences of Islamophobia," *Critical Sociology*, 41 (1): 41–56.

Moore, K. M. (2007), "Visible through the Veil: The Regulation of Islam in American Law," *Sociology of Religion*, 68 (3): 237–51.

Moore, P. (2016), "Most Americans Oppose a European-style Burqa Ban," *YouGov*, August 30. Available online: https://today.yougov.com/topics/politics/articles-reports/2016/08/30/most-americans-oppose-european-style-burqa-ban (accessed September 30, 2019).

Moors, A. (2014), "Face Veiling in the Netherlands: Public Debates and Women's Narratives," in E. Brems (ed.), *The Experiences of Face Veil Wearers in Europe and the Law*, 19–41, Cambridge: Cambridge University Press.

Morales, H. D. (2018), *Latino and Muslim in America: Race, Religion, and the Making of a New Minority*, New York: Oxford University Press.

Morris, C. (2018), "Re-Placing the Term 'British Muslim': Discourse, Difference and the Frontiers of Muslim Agency in Britain," *Journal of Muslim Minority Affairs*, 38 (3): 409–27.

Moxley Rouse, C. (2004), *Engaged Surrender: African American Women and Islam*, Berkeley, CA: University of California Press.

Munnik, M. (2017), "A Field Theory Perspective on Journalist–Source Relations: A Study of 'New Entrants' and 'Authorised Knowers' among Scottish Muslims," *Sociology*, 52 (6): 1169–84.

Murray, T. (2013), "Why Feminists Should Oppose the Burqa," *The New Humanist*, June 26. Available online: https://newhumanist.org.uk/articles/4199/why-feminists-should-oppose-the-burqa (accessed September 30, 2019).

Muslim Council of Britain (2015), "British Muslims in Numbers," Available online: https://www.mcb.org.uk/wp-content/uploads/2015/02/MCBCensusReport_2015.pdf (accessed September 30, 2019).

Muslim Women's Council (2014), *Shared Heritage of Daughters of Eve: Headcoverings – Reflections from Women of Faith*, Wakefield: Route Publishing.

Mutua, A. D. (2006), "The Rise, Development and Future Directions of Critical Race Theory and Related Scholarship," *Denver University Law Review*, 84 (2): 329–94.

Naber, N. (2008), "'Look, Mohammed the Terrorist is Coming!': Cultural Racism, Nation-Based Racism, and Intersectionality of Oppressions after 9/11," in A. Jamal and N. Naber (eds.), *Race and Arab Americans Before and After 9/11: From Invisible Citizens to Visible Subjects*, 276–304, Syracuse. NY: Syracuse University Press.

Nadal, K. L., K. E. Griffin, S. Hamit, J. Leon, M. Tobio, and D. P. Rivera (2012), "Subtle and Overt Forms of Islamophobia: Microaggressions toward Muslim Americans," CUNY Academic Works. Available online: https://academicworks.cuny.edu/gc_pubs/289 (accessed September 30, 2019).

Nasr, V. (2006), *The Shia Revival: How Conflicts Within Islam Will Shape the Future*, New York: W.W. Norton and Company.

Newsom, V. A. and Lengel, L. (2012) "Arab Women, Social Media, and the Arab Spring: Applying the Framework of Digital Reflexivity to Analyze Gender and Online Activism," *Journal of International Women's Studies*, 13 (5): 31–45.

Nieuwkerk, K. van (2006), *Women Embracing Islam: Gender and Conversion in the West*, Austin: University of Texas Press.

Nisa, E. F. (2013), "The Internet Subculture of Indonesian Face-Veiled Women," *International Journal of Cultural Studies*, 16 (3): 241–55.

Nyhagen Predelli, L. (2008), "Religion, Citizenship and Participation: A Case Study of Immigrant Muslim Women in Norwegian Mosques," *European Journal of Women's Studies*, 15 (3): 241–60.

Ogilvie, M. H. (2013), "Niqabs in Canadian Courts: R v NS," *Ecclesiastical Law Review*, 15 (3): 334–43.

O'Neill, B., E. Gidengil, C. Côté, and L. Young (2015), "Freedom of Religion, Women's Agency and Banning the Face Veil: The Role of Feminist Beliefs in Shaping Women's Opinion," *Ethnic and Racial Studies*, 38 (11): 1886–901.

Orsi, R. (2005), *Between Heaven and Earth: The Religious Worlds People Make and the Scholars Who Study Them*, Princeton, NJ: Princeton University Press.

Osborn, M. (1967), "Archetypal Metaphor in Rhetoric: The Light-Dark Family," *Quarterly Journal of Speech*, 53 (2): 115–26.

Østergaard, K., M. Warburg, and B. Johansen (2014), "Niqabis in Denmark: When Politicians Ask for a Qualitative and Quantitative Profile of a Very Small and Elusive Subculture," in E. Brems (ed.), *The Experiences of Face Veil Wearers in Europe and the Law*, 42–76, Cambridge: Cambridge University Press.

Pace, E. (2011), "Spirituality and Systems of Belief," in G. Giordan and W. H. Swatos (eds.), *Religion, Spirituality and Everyday Practice*, 23–32, Dordrecht: Springer.

Pain, R. H. (1997), "Geographies of Women's Fear of Crime," *Transactions of the Institute of British Geographers*, 22 (2): 231–44.

Pakulski, J. (1997), "Cultural Citizenship," *Citizenship Studies*, 1 (1): 73–86.

References

Patel, S. (2009), "The Anti-terrorism Act and National Security: Safeguarding the Nation against Uncivilized Muslims," in J. Zine (ed.), *Islam in the Hinterlands: Muslim Cultural Politics in Canada*, 272–92, Vancouver: UBC Press.

Pearson, A. (2011), "We Too Should Ban the Burka," *The Daily Telegraph*, April 13. Available online: https://www.telegraph.co.uk/comment/columnists/allison-pearson/8449101/We-too-should-ban-the-burka.html (accessed September 30, 2019).

Pearson, A. (2014), "Banning the Burka Is Not Racist – It's a Kindness," *The Daily Telegraph*, July 2. Available online: https://www.telegraph.co.uk/news/religion/10940882/Banning-the-bu rka-is-not-racist-its-a-kindness.html (accessed September 30, 2019).

Pearson, A. (2017), "For the Sake of National Security, We Must Ban the Burka," *The Daily Telegraph*, May 2. Available online: https://www.telegraph.co.uk/women/politics/sake-nationa l-securitywe-must-ban-burka/ (accessed September 30, 2019).

Pearson, A. (2018), "Don't Ban Boris . . . Ban the Burka!" *The Daily Telegraph*, August 7. Available online: https://www.telegraph.co.uk/women/life/dont-ban-boris-ban-burka/ (accessed September 30, 2019).

Pennington, R. (2018), "Making Space in Social Media: #MuslimWomensDay in Twitter," *Journal of Communication Inquiry*, 42 (3): 199–217.

Perry, B. (2015), "'All of a Sudden, There Are Muslims': Visibilities and Islamophobic Violence in Canada," *International Journal for Crime, Justice and Social Democracy*, 4 (3): 4–15.

Peterson, K. (2016), "Voiceless Icons No More: the Self-Representations of Muslim American Lives in Digital Media," PhD Dissertation, University of Colorado Boulder. https://pdfs.semanticscho lar.org/c4f6/b17e12e386a81da95dc83ca091def6d82f5c.pdf (accessed April 15, 2020).

Peterson, K. M. (2020), "Hybrid Styles, Interstitial Spaces, and the DigitalAdvocacy of the Salafi Feminist," *Critical Studies in Media Communication*, 37 (3): 254–66.

Picheta, R. (2018), "France's Niqab Ban Violates Human Rights, UN Committee Says," *CNN World*, October 23. Available online: https://www.cnn.com/2018/10/23/europe/france-niqab -ban-un-intl/index.html (accessed September 30, 2019).

Pidd, H. (2010), "Niqab-ban Tory MP Told He Is Breaking the Law," *The Guardian*, July 25. Available online: https://www.theguardian.com/global/2010/jul/25/niqab-ban-mp-philip-hol lobone (accessed September 30, 2019).

Piela, A. (2012), *Muslim Women Online: Faith and Identity in Virtual Space*, London: Routledge.

Piela, A. (2013), "I Am Just Doing My Bit to Promote Modesty": Niqabis' Self-portraits on Photo-sharing Websites," *Feminist Media Studies*, 13 (5): 781–90.

Piela, A. (2015), "Online Islamic Spaces as Communities of Practice for Female Muslim Converts Who Wear the Niqab," *Hawwa: Journal of Women of the Middle East and the Islamic World*, 13 (3): 363–82.

Piela, A. (2018), "The Niqab-wearers Bracing Themselves for Abuse: 'It's Open Season on the Muslims Now,'" *New Statesman*, August 10. Available online: https://www.newstatesman.com/ politics/uk/2018/08/niqab-boris-johnson-muslim-women-burka-burqa (accessed September 30, 2019).

Piela, A. (2020), "Muslim Women Who Cover Their Faces Find Greater Acceptance Among Coronavirus Masks – 'Nobody is giving me dirty looks,'" *The Conversation*, April 10. https://th econversation.com/muslim-women-who-cover-their-faces-find-greater-acceptance-among-coronavirus-masks-nobody-is-giving-me-dirty-looks-136021 (accessed September 30, 2020).

Piela, A. (forthcoming), "The Digital Niqabosphere as a Hypermediated Third Space," in R. Rozehnal (ed.), *Cyber Muslims: Mapping Islamic Networks in the Digital Age*, New York: Bloomsbury Academic.

Pierpoint, G. (2018), "'Sexualised' Niqab Hero Gets Makeover after Costume Criticism," *BBC News*, August 29. https://www.bbc.com/news/blogs-trending-45331730 (accessed April 15, 2020).

Poole, E. (2002), *Reporting Islam: Media Representations of British Muslims*, I.B. Tauris: London.

Poole, E. (2011), "Change and Continuity in the Representation of British Muslims Before and After 9/11: The UK Context," *Global Media Journal – Canadian Edition*, 4 (2): 49–62. http://eprints.keele.ac.uk/1750/1/GlobalMedia_poole.pdf (accessed April 15, 2020).

Puar, J. (2007), *Terrorist Assemblages: Homonationalism in Queer Times*, Durham, NC: Duke University Press.

Qutb, S. ([1964] 1990), *Milestones*, revised and trans. A. Zaki Hammad, Indianapolis: American Trust.

Razack, S. H. (2018), "A Site/Sight We Cannot Bear: The Racial/Spatial Politics of Banning the Muslim Woman's Niqab," *Canadian Journal of Women and the Law*, 30 (1): 169–89.

Reddit (2011), "I Am A," Reddit, August 26. Available online: https://www.reddit.com/r/IAmA/comments/jvtnw/iama_woman_who_wears_niqab_the_full_face_veil (accessed April 15, 2020).

Reid, W. (2018), "Black Twitter 101: What Is It? Where Did It Originate? Where Is It Headed??" *UVA Today*, November 28. https://news.virginia.edu/content/black-twitter-101-what-it-where -did-it-originate-where-it-headed (accessed April 15, 2020).

Reuters (2013), "France Stands By Veil Ban after Riots," *Reuters World News*, July 22, https://www.reuters.com/article/us-france-riots/france-stands-by-veil-ban-after-riots-idUSBRE96L09A2 0130722 (accessed April 15, 2020).

Reynolds v. United States (1878), 98 U.S. 145. Available online: https://supreme.justia.com/cases/federal/us/98/145 (accessed September 30, 2019).

Reynolds, T. (2005), *Caribbean Mothers: Identity and Experience in the U.K.*, London: Tufnell Press.

Ritchie, A. J. (2017), *Invisible No More: Police Violence Against Black Women and Women of Color*, Boston, MA: Beacon Press.

Rivka Sajida (2016), "Chai and Chocolate." Available online: http://hijabininjette.blogspot.com/2016/09/ (accessed September 30, 2019).

Robert, N. (2005), *From My Sisters' Lips*, London: Bantam Press.

Robert, N. (2010), "Being Na'ima B. Robert: An Interview with Award Winning Muslim Woman Author," *Muslim Matters*, July 19. Available online: https://muslimmatters.org/2010/07/19/being-naima/ (accessed September 30, 2019).

Robert, N. (nd), "Na'ima Robert." Available online: https://www.naimarobert.com (accessed April 15, 2020).

Robert, N. B. (2017), "Black, British, Muslim," likeMEDIA.tv, *YouTube*, October 19. Available online: https://www.youtube.com/watch?v=GSgZT9UUvS4 (accessed September 30, 2019).

Rosemarine, A. M. (2010), "Sheikh Mohamed Sayyid Tantawi: Controversial Imam Who Preached Tolerance," *The Independent*, March 19. Available online: https://www.independent.co.uk/news/obituaries/sheikh-mohamed-sayyid-tantawi-controversial-imam-who-preach ed-tolerance-1923670.html (accessed September 30, 2019).

Rubin, R. (2019), "NIH Director Takes Stand Against 'Manels,'" *Journal of American Medical Association*, 322 (4): 295. Available online: https://jamanetwork.com/journals/jama/article -abstract/2738532 (accessed April 15, 2020).

Rupar, V. (2017), "Inclusive Journalism: How to Shed Light on Voices Traditionally Left Out in News Coverage," *Journal of Applied Journalism & Media Studies*, 6 (3): 417–23.

Rush, J. A. (2005), *Spiritual Tattoo: A Cultural History of Tattooing, Piercing, Scarification, Branding, and Implants*, Berkeley, CA: Frog Publications.

Ryan, L. (2011), "Muslim Women Negotiating Collective Stigmatization: 'We're Just Normal People,'" *Sociology*, 45 (6): 1045–60.

Ryan, L. and E. Vacchelli (2013), "Mothering Through Islam: Narratives of Religious Identity in London," *Religion and Gender*, 3 (1): 90–107.

Ryder, A. R., L. Rostas, and M. Taba (2014), "Nothing about Us without Us": The Role of Inclusive Community Development in School Desegregation for Roma Communities, *Race, Ethnicity and Education*, 17 (4): 518–39.

References

Said, E. (1978), *Orientalism*, London: Routledge and Kegan Paul Ltd.

Said, E. (2001), *Reflections on Exile and Other Essays*, Cambridge, MA: Harvard University Press.

Salem, S. (2013), "Feminist Critique and Islamic Feminism: The Question of Intersectionality," *The Postcolonialist*, 1 (1). Available online: http://postcolonialist.com/civil-discourse/fe minist-critique-and-islamic-feminism-the-question-of-intersectionality (accessed April 15, 2020).

Sandberg, R. (2009), "The Changing Position of Religious Minorities in English Law: The Legacy of Begum," in R. Grillo, R. Ballard, A. Ferrari, A. J. Hoekema, M. Maussen, and P. Shah (eds.), *Legal Practice and Cultural Diversity*, 267–82, London: Ashgate.

Sapphire (2020), "This Is a Typical Message from Patriarchal Muslim Men. That Somehow #hijab and #niqab Protect Us. If That Is the Case, Then Why Do Fully Covered Women Still Get Sexually Assaulted? Why Does This Happen even on #Hajj?" February 2, 03:28 pm. Tweet. Available online: https://twitter.com/Khaybari628/status/1224067021043793920 (accessed April 15, 2020).

Sarrasin, O. (2016), "Attitudes Toward Gender Equality and Opposition to Muslim Full-Face Veils," *Swiss Journal of Psychology*, 75: 153–160.

Sayeed, A. (2013), *Women and the Transmission of Religious Knowledge in Islam*, Cambridge: Cambridge University Press.

Särmä, S. (nd), "All Male Panels." Available online: allmalepanels.tumblr.com (accessed April 15, 2020).

Schwartzbaum, A. (2011), "The 'Niqab' in the Courtroom: Protecting Free Exercise of Religion in a Post-Smith World," *University of Pennsylvania Law Review*, 159 (5): 1533–76.

Scotch, R. K. (2009), "'Nothing About Us Without Us': Disability Rights in America," *OAH Magazine of History*, 23 (3): 17–22.

Sedgwick, M. (2013), "Islam and Popular Culture," in J. T. Kenney and E. Moosa (eds..), *Islam in the Modern World*, 279–98, London: Routledge.

Selby, J. A. (2011), "French Secularism as a 'Guarantor' of Women's Rights? Muslim Women and Gender Politics in a Parisian *Banlieue*," *Culture and Religion*, 12 (4): 441–62.

Selod, S. (2015), "Citizenship Denied: The Racialization of Muslim American Men and Women post-9/11," *Critical Sociology*, 41 (1): 77–95.

Selod, S. and D. G. Embrick (2013), "Racialization and Muslims: Situating the Muslim Experience in Race Scholarship," *Sociology Compass*, 7 (8): 644–55.

Sherwood, H. (2018), "Muslims Place Greater Importance on National Identity, Finds UK Study," *The Guardian*, March 20. Available online: https://www.theguardian.com/world/2018/mar/21 /muslims-british-national-identity-uk-report (accessed September 30, 2019).

Shihab, A. (2004), "Christian-Muslim Relations into the Twenty-first Century," *Islam and Christian-Muslim Relations*, 15 (1): 65–77.

Shirazi, F. (2001), *The Veil Unveiled: The Hijab in Modern Culture*, Gainesville, FL: University Press of Florida.

Shirazi, F. and S. Mishra (2010), "Young Muslim Women on the Face Veil (niqab): A Tool of Resistance in Europe But Rejected in the United States," *International Journal of Cultural Studies*, 13 (1): 42–62.

Shode, H. (2018), "Empowering Muslim Women in Literature: In Conversation with Na'ima B. Robert," *The Black Muslim Times* UK, March 7. Available online: https://bmtimesuk.wixsite .com/mysite/single-post/2018/03/07/Empowering-Muslim-Women-in-Literature-In-conv ersation-with-Naima-B-Robert (accessed September 30, 2019).

Shoemaker, P. (1991), *Gatekeeping*, Newbury Park, CA: Sage.

Simmel, G. (1950) [1908], "The Stranger," in *The Sociology of Georg Simmel*, trans. K. H. Wolff, 402–8, New York: Free Press.

Smith, J. I. (1999), *Islam in America*, New York: Columbia University Press.

Smith, M. (2017), "About Half of Brits Support a Burqa Ban," *YouGov*, April 27. Available online: https://yougov.co.uk/topics/politics/articles-reports/2017/04/27/about-half-brits-support-burqa-ban (accessed September 30, 2019).

Solorzano, D. G. (1997), "Images and Words That Wound: Critical Race Theory, Racial Stereotyping, and Teacher Education," *Teacher Education Quarterly*, 24 (3): 5–19.

Soubani, N. (2019), "What Is Islamophobia? The Politics of Anti-Muslim Racism," Yaqeen Research Institute, March 20. Available online: https://yaqeeninstitute.org/nour-soubani/what-is-islamophobia-the-politics-of-anti-muslim-racism/#.XY5_bChKiUl (accessed September 30, 2019).

Southern Poverty Law Center (2018), "Anti-Sharia Law Bills in the United States," February 5. Available online: https://www.splcenter.org/hatewatch/2018/02/05/anti-sharia-law-bills-united-states (accessed September 30, 2019).

Southern Poverty Law Center (2019), "About Pamela Geller." Available online: https://www.splcenter.org/fighting-hate/extremist-files/individual/pamela-geller (accessed September 30, 2019).

Spivak, G. C. (1988), "Can the Subaltern Speak?" in C. Nelson and L. Grossberg (eds.), *Marxism and the Interpretation of Culture*, 271–313, Chicago: University of Illinois Press.

Sporton, D., G. Valentine, and K. Bang Nielsen (2006), "Post Conflict Identities: Affiliations and Practices of Somali Asylum Seeker Children," *Children's Geographies*, 4 (2): 203–17.

Stahl, A. (2018), "The Sexual Assault Epidemic That No One Is Talking About," *Village Voice*, July 25. Available online: https://www.villagevoice.com/2018/07/25/the-sexual-assault-epidemic-that-no-one-is-talking-about (accessed September 30, 2019).

State of Georgia (2015), "Georgia Disaster Facts." Georgia Emergency Department and Homeland Security Agency. Available online: http://gema.georgia.gov/document/publication/georgia-disasters-facts/download (accessed September 14, 2020).

Stevenson, L. (2003), "Opinion, Belief or Faith, and Knowledge," *Kantian Review*, 7 (1): 72–101.

Suleiman, Y. (2013), *Narratives of Conversion to Islam: Female Perspectives*, Cambridge: University of Cambridge Press.

Swatos, W. H. and G. Giordan (2011), "Introduction: The Spiritual 'Turn' in Religion as Process and Outcome," in G. Giordan and W. H. Swatos (eds.), *Religion, Spirituality and Everyday Practice*, xi–xv, Dordrecht: Springer.

Targoff, R. (1997), "The Performance of Prayer: Sincerity and Theatricality in Early Modern England," *Representations*, (60): 49–69.

Tarlo, E. (2007), "Hijab in London: Metamorphosis, Resonance and Effects," *Journal of Material Culture*, 12 (2): 131–56.

Tarlo, E. (2010), *Visibly Muslim: Fashion, Politics, Faith*, Oxford: Berg.

Tarlo, E. (2013), "Landscapes of Attraction and Rejection: South Asian Aesthetics in Islamic Fashion in London," in E. Tarlo and A. Moors (eds.), *Islamic Fashion and Anti-Fashion: New Perspectives from Europe and North America*, 73–92, London: Bloomsbury Academic.

Tarlo, E. and A. Moors (eds.) (2013), *Islamic Fashion and Anti-Fashion: New Perspectives from Europe and North America*, London: Bloomsbury Academic.

Tell MAMA (2019), "Normalising Hatred: Tell MAMA Annual Report 2018)," London: Faith Matters, Available online: https://www.tellmamauk.org/wp-content/uploads/2019/09/Tell%20MAMA%20Annual%20Report%202018%20_%20Normalising%20Hate.pdf (accessed September 30, 2019).

Thamin, D. (2016), "#DressCodePM & Re-Framing The Niqab: News Sources, Hashtag Activism, and Media Representation," MA Thesis, Queens University, Kingston. Available online: https://qspace.library.queensu.ca/handle/1974/14612 (accessed April 15, 2020).

The Globe and Mail (2019), "I Wear a Niqab: 'It Is My Choice, That's the Point of Being a Feminist,'" *The Globe and Mail*, October 27. Available online: https://www.theglobeandmail.com/canada/i-wear-a-niqab-it-is-my-choice-thats-the/video45e41ef8-9032-4520-868b-4677b1024c0f-2/ (accessed April 15, 2020).

References

The Guardian (2011), "What I'm Really Thinking: The Veiled Woman," *The Guardian*, April 30. https://www.theguardian.com/lifeandstyle/2011/apr/30/what-really-thinking-veiled-woman (accessed April 15, 2020).

Tiftik, C. and İ. Turan (2015), "Women, Social Housing and Urban Spaces: Places to Dwell and Places Where Women Are Being Attacked On Their Way Home," *ITU AZ*, 12 (1): 243–55.

Tiryakian, E. A. (1973), "Sociological Perspectives on the Stranger," *Soundings: An Interdisciplinary Journal*, 56 (1): 45–58.

Tissot, S. (2011), "Excluding Muslim Women: From Hijab to Niqab, from School to Public Space," *Public Culture*, 23 (1): 39–46.

Toledo Bastos, M., R. L. Galdini Raimundo, and R. Travitzki (2013), "Gatekeeping Twitter: Message Diffusion in Political Hashtags," *Media, Culture and Society*, 35 (2): 260–70.

TRC Leiden (nd), "Afghan Dress." Available online: https://www.trc-leiden.nl/trc-digital-exhibit ion/index.php/afghan-dress (accessed April 15, 2020).

Trust for London (2019), "Tower Hamlets: Poverty and Inequality Data." Available online: https ://www.trustforlondon.org.uk/data/boroughs/tower-hamlets-poverty-and-inequality-indic ators/ (accessed September 30, 2019).

Vakulenko, A. (2012), *Islamic Veiling in Legal Discourse*, London: Routledge.

Valentine, G. (1989), "The Geography of Women's Fear," *Area*, 21 (4): 385–90.

Valentine, J. (1998), "Naming the Other: Power, Politeness and the Inflation of Euphemisms" *Sociological Research Online*, 3 (4). Available online: https://journals.sagepub.com/doi/pdf/10. 5153/sro.184 (accessed September 30, 2019).

Vallely, P. and A. Brown (1995), "The Best Place to Be a Muslim," *The Independent*, December 6. Available online: http://www.independent.co.uk/news/the-best-place-to-be-a-muslim-152426 7.html (accessed September 30, 2019).

Van Dijk, T. A. (1993), "Principles of Critical Discourse Analysis," *Discourse Analysis*, 4 (2): 249–83.

Van Gilder, B. J. and Z. B. Massey (2016), "Islamophobic Discourse and Interethnic Conflict: The Influence of News Media Coverage of the ISIS Beheadings on Identity Processes and Intergroup Attitudes," in S. Gibson and A. L. Lando (eds.), *Impact of Communication and the Media on Ethnic Conflict*, 147–61, Hershey, PA: IGI Global.

Vice (2012), "A Response to the Detractors of Our Burqa-for-a-Day Article," *Vice*, August 9. Available online: https://www.vice.com/en_us/article/bny5av/a-response-to-the-detractors -of-our-burqa-for-a-day-article (accessed September 30, 2019).

Vidali, D. S. (2010), "Millennial Encounters with Mainstream Television News: Excess, Void, and Points of Engagement," *Journal of Linguistic Anthropology*, 20 (2): 372–88.

Wade, W. C. (1998), *The Fiery Cross: The Ku Klux Klan in America*, New York: Oxford University Press.

Wadhia, S. S. (2018), "National Security, Immigration and the Muslim Ban," *Washington and Lee Law Review*, 75 (3): 1475–506.

Wadud, A. (2006), *Inside the Gender Jihad: Women's Reform in Islam*, Oxford: Oneworld.

Walford, G. (2008), "Faith-based Schools in England After Ten Years of Tony Blair," *Oxford Review of Education*, 34 (6): 689–99.

Waltorp, K. (2013), "Public/Private Negotiations in the Media Uses of Young Muslim Women in Copenhagen: Gendered Social Control and the Technology-enabled Moral Laboratories of a Multicultural City," *International Communication Gazette*, 75 (5–6): 555–72.

Waltorp, K. (2015), "Keeping Cool, Staying Virtuous: Social Media and the Composite Habitus of Young Muslim Women in Copenhagen," *MedieKultur: Journal of Media and Communication Research*, 31 (58) Available online: https://tidsskrift.dk/mediekultur/article/ view/19373/18332 (accessed September 30, 2019).

Warner, S. and J. G. Wittner (1998), *Gatherings in Diaspora: Religious Communities and the New Immigration*, Philadelphia, PA: Temple University Press.

Waterhouse, R. (2010), "Universities Must Take Action on Muslim Extremism," *The Independent: Education*, March 18. Available online: https://www.independent.co.uk/news/education/higher/rosie-waterhouse-universities-must-take-action-on-muslim-extremism-1922730.html (accessed September 30, 2019).

Weinstock, D. (2002), "Citizenship and Pluralism," in R. Simon (ed.), *The Blackwell Guide to Social and Political Philosophy*, 239–70, London: Blackwell.

Weizer, R. and R. K. Brunson (2015), "Policing Different Racial Groups in the United States," *Cahiers Politiestudies* 35: 129–45. Available online: http://skat.ihmc.us/rid=12271878668 19_1140452997_15052/communities%20of%20practice_wenger.doc (accessed September 30, 2019).

Werbner, P. (2007), "Veiled Interventions in Pure Space: Honour, Shame and Embodied Struggles among Muslims in Britain and France," *Theory, Culture and Society*, 24 (2): 161–86.

Williams, A. (2008), "The Veiled Truth: Can the Credibility of Testimony Given By a Niqab-wearing Witness Be Judged Without the Assistance of Facial Expressions?" *University of Detroit Mercy Law Review*, 85(2): 273–91.

Wilson, H. (2017), "Senate Bill 97: Are Foreign Law Bans Helpful or Harmful for Montana?" *Montana Law Review Online*, 78. Available online: https://scholarship.law.umt.edu/cgi/view content.cgi?article=1082&context=mlr_online (accessed January 29, 2018).

Witworth, D. (2018), "Taj Hargey Interview: 'The Burka Is a Fifth Column . . . We Will Wake in the Islamic Republic of Britain,'" *The Times*, August 11. Available online: https://www.the times.co.uk/article/taj-hargey-interview-the-burka-is-a-fifth-column-we-will-wake-in-the-i slamic-republic-of-britain-5wqhk0q8m (accessed January 29, 2018).

Woodhead L. (2011), "Spirituality and Christianity: The Unfolding of a Tangled Relationship," in G. Giordan and W. Swatos, Jr. (eds.), *Religion, Spirituality and Everyday Practice*, 3–21, Springer: Dordrecht.

Wuthnow, R. (2001), *Creative Spirituality: The Way of the Artist*, Berkeley, CA: University of California Press.

Yakushko, O. (2018), "Witches, Charlatans, and Old Wives: Critical Perspectives on History of Women's Indigenous Knowledge," *Women and Therapy*, 41 (1–2): 18–29.

Yazbeck Haddad, Y. (2011), *Becoming American? The Forging of Arab and Muslim Identity in Pluralist America*, Waco, TX: Baylor University Press.

Yaqzan, H. (2019), "Islamophobia in 'Academic' Garb," *Crescent International* 47 (12). Available online: https://www.icit-digital.org/articles/islamophobia-in-academic-garb (accessed August 27, 2020).

Yazdiha, H. (2019), "Law as Movement Strategy: How the Islamophobia Movement Institutionalizes Fear Through Legislation," *Social Movement Studies*, 13 (2): 267–74.

Yildirim, S. (2010), "Freeman v. Dep't of Highway Safety & Motor Vehicles and Webb v. City of Philadelphia - Accommodation Tangles in the Laws Over Hair," in Leslie C. Griffin (ed.), *Law and Religion: Cases in Context*, 293–309, New York: Aspen Publishers.

Yoder Wesselhoeft, K. M. (2011), "Gendered Secularity: The Feminine Individual in the 2010 Gerin Report," *Journal of Muslim Minority Affairs*, 31 (3): 399–410.

Young, R. (1990), *White Mythologies and the West*, London: Routledge.

Youssef, A. (2019), "I Feel Like a Stranger Here Now," *The Globe and Mail*, December 19. https://www.theglobeandmail.com/canada/article-i-feel-like-a-stranger-here-now-for-six-muslim-w omen-quebecs (accessed April 15, 2020).

Zainiddinov, H. (2013), "What Factors Account for Black–White Differences in Anti-Muslim Sentiment in the Contemporary USA?" *Ethnic and Racial Studies*, 36 (11): 1745–69.

Zarabadi, S. and J. Ringrose (2018), "The Affective Birth of 'Jihadi Bride' as New Risky Sexualized 'Other': Muslim Schoolgirls and Media Panic in an Age of Counterterrorism," in S. Talburt (ed.), *Youth Sexualities: Public Feelings and Contemporary Cultural Politics*, 83–106, Santa Barbara, CA: Abc-Clio.

References

Zebiri, K. (2008), *British Muslim Converts: Choosing Alternative Lives*, London: Oneworld Publications.

Zempi, I. (2019), "Veiled Muslim Women's Views on Law Banning the Wearing of the Niqab (face veil) in Public," *Ethnic and Racial Studies*, Online First, March 13, 1–18.

Zempi, I. and N. Chakraborti (2014), *Islamophobia, Victimisation and the Veil*, Houndmills: Palgrave Macmillan.

Zempi, I. and N. Chakraborti (2015), "'They Make Us Feel Like We're a Virus': The Multiple Impacts of Islamophobic Hostility Towards Veiled Muslim Women," *International Journal for Crime, Justice and Social Democracy*, 4 (3): 44–56.

Zine, J. (2006), "Unveiled Sentiments: Gendered Islamophobia and Experiences of Veiling among Muslim Girls in a Canadian Islamic School," *Equity & Excellence in Education*, 39 (3): 239–52.

Zine, J. (2009), "Unsettling the Nation: Gender, Race and Muslim Cultural Politics in Canada," *Studies in Ethnicity and Nationalism*, 9 (1): 146–63.

Zine, J. (2012), "Stolen Youth: Lost Boys and Imperial Wars," in J. Williamson (ed.), *Omar Khadr, Oh Canada*, 390–449, Montreal: McGill-Queen's Press.

Zopf, B. (2015), "Racializing Muslims: Constructing a Muslim Archetype," *U.S. Studies Online*, July 15. Available online: http://www.baas.ac.uk/usso/racializing-muslims-constructing-a-muslim-archetype/ (accessed September 30, 2019).

de Zúñiga, H., T. Correa, and S. Valenzuela (2012), "Selective Exposure to Cable News and Immigration in the U.S.: The Relationship Between FOX News, CNN, and Attitudes Toward Mexican Immigrants," *Journal of Broadcasting and Electronic Media*, 56 (4): 597–615.

Žižek, S. (2002), *Welcome to the Desert of the Real*, London: Verso.

Žižek, S. (2010), "The Neighbor in Burka," *The Symptom, 11*. Available online: http://www.lacan.com/symptom11/?p=69 (accessed September 30, 2019).

INDEX

Index

God   43, 45, 51, 53, 66–7, 74, 77–8, 81–7, 95, 99–100, 104, 106, 114, 133, 141, 144–5, 149, *see also* Allah

habitus   93
   linguistic   68
Hadith   66, 74, 77, 79, 81–2, 106
hashtags   46–9, 54–6, 63, 82, 141
hijab   4, 18 n.1, 19, 35, 48 n.3, 55, 74, 79, 82–3, 89, 95, 101, 110, 113, 120–4, 127–33, 138, 141
human rights   7
hybridization of identities   2, 51–4

ijtihad   74, 78–9, 82, 106, 145
immigrants   61, 112
intersectionality   13, 71, 119–122, 125, 127, 136–7, 142
Ishaq, Zunera   35, 47, 72
Islam, African American   118, 124 n.1
   as a discursive tradition   75–6, 81, 101
   diversity within   4, 8, 76, 80
   "good *vs.* bad"   7, 13, 17, 39–40
   racialization of   117, 121–2, 143–4
Islamic schools of thought on niqab   8 n.7, 19, 76
Islamic State (ISIS)   27, 57–9
Islamophobia   6, 10, 11, 13, 14, 20, 22, 24, 29, 31, 39–40, 41, 44, 54, 58, 59, 67, 71, 105, 108, 110, 114, 117–18, 120–4, 135–7, 140–4

Jesus   45, 100–1
Jewish   6, 53–4
   Orthodox   101
jihad   11, 23
Johnson, Boris (Prime Minister, 2019-)   60–1, 135, 135 n.3
Judaism   45

Karim, Jamilah   129–30, 143
Ku Klux Klan   24–5

label reappropriation   134–5
language   53, 67–9, 101, 110, 119, 125, 127–8, 132, 134–5, 135 n.3, 143
   of rights and freedoms   45, 91, 114–15, 146–7
   as a tool of racialization   126

Mahmood, Saba   9, 10, 11, 70, 75–6, 80, 83–5, 91, 93, 100, 113
masks   1, 24, 147
   medical   107
May, Theresa (Prime Minister, 2016–2019)   61, 61 n.11, 62, 62 n.12
McGuire, Meredith   12, 84, 88, 142
modesty   77, 82, 84–5
   fashion   2, 131–2

Modood, Tariq   114–15
multiculturalism   7, 41, 61, 68, 109, 114, 140–1

national identity   109–110, 127–8
   9/11   7–8, 22, 25–6, 41 n.1, 43, 55–6, 58, 67, 96 n.4, 140
   American   42, 147
   British   19, 44, 109–10, 123, 147
niqab
   adoption   2, 8, 42–3, 51, 58, 67, 71–2, 76, 78, 81–3, 89, 99, 104–5, 107–8, 111, 118, 120–2, 130–1, 133, 135, 148
   as aiding health and wellbeing   46, 106–9
   vs. burka   1
   causing family tensions   105, 130–1
   as choice   2, 8, 11, 15, 17, 21, 43–4, 46, 55, 69–71, 75, 89, 98–9, 102, 113, 130, 140, 144
   as compulsory   8 n.7, 44, 55, 78, 80
   controversies   2 n.3, 3, 14–16, 20 n.3, 29, 32, 43, 46, 47, 49, 61–2, 65, 92, 132, 147
   cultural translations of   12, 32, 53, 101, 109, 115
   as incompatible with secular culture   16, 17, 39, 109
   as modesty   21, 41 n.1, 45, 50, 52, 54, 66, 74, 77–8, 82, 84–5, 96, 131, 133, 135
   motivations for wearing, *see* niqab adoption
   "niqab for a day"   28–32
   as not compulsory   8 n.7, 77–9
   as not Islamic   5, 8, 8 n.7, 12–3, 18, 65–6, 88
   as patriarchal oppression   10, 16, 22, 39–40, 46, 65, 74, 98, 113, 146
   as protection   54–5, 67, 106–9, 135
   as religious practice   2, 5, 9, 13, 46, 75, 77, 84, 113, 146
   as religious or spiritual practice   2, 5, 9–10, 13, 19, 29, 40, 51, 43, 70, 65–6, 71–2, 74, 76, 81, 83–4, 86–9, 96–7, 105, 109, 145–6, 148
   as security threat   1, 5, 7, 11, 16, 23–4, 27, 31, 39–40, 54, 57, 59, 70, 94, 138–9
   self-representations in photography   49–50
   as separation   3, 146–7
   social outcomes of wearing   71
   as socially deviant   109, 128
   spatial negotiations of   135–143
   as surrender to God   69, 72–3, 114
   taking off   7, 75, 120, 123, 138–9
   visual representations of   32–39
   as a visual trope   57–8

Obama, Barack (President of the United States, 2008–2016)   20
Obama, Michelle   100
objectification of women   103–4, 113, 135, *see also* sexual harassment
online debates   8, 46–51, 54–5, 63

176

Milton Keynes UK
Ingram Content Group UK Ltd.
UKHW022203190224
438088UK00006B/203